An Introduction to Urban Housing Design

AT HOME IN THE CITY

In memory of my mother

Madge

1920–2004

An Introduction to Urban Housing Design

AT HOME IN THE CITY

Graham Towers

ELSEVIER

AMSTERDAM • BOSTON • HEIDELBERG • LONDON • NEW YORK • OXFORD
PARIS • SAN DIEGO • SAN FRANCISCO • SINGAPORE • SYDNEY • TOKYO
Architectural Press is an imprint of Elsevier

Architectural
Press

Architectural Press
An imprint of Elsevier
Linacre House, Jordan Hill, Oxford OX2 8DP
30 Corporate Drive, Burlington, MA 01803

First published 2005

British Library Cataloguing in Publication Data
A catalogue record for this book is available from the British Library

ISBN 0 7506 5902 5

For information on all Architectural Press publications visit
our website at http://books.elsevier.com/architecturalpress

Typeset by Charon Tec Pvt. Ltd, Chennai, India
www.charontec.com
Printed and bound in Great Britain

Working together to grow
libraries in developing countries

www.elsevier.com | www.bookaid.org | www.sabre.org

ELSEVIER   BOOK AID
              International   Sabre Foundation

CONTENTS

PART TWO – CASE STUDIES

Figures 7.10 and 7.11	Photographs copyright PRP Architects
Figures 7.12 and 7.13	By permission of Stedelijke Woningdienst Amsteerdam, Projectmangmentbureau (PMB), dienst Ruimtelijke Ordening (dRO) and the Grondbedrijf city of Amsterdam, Amsterdam, 1999
Figures A1–A7	By permission of Haworth Tomkins Drawings reproduced from *Architecture Today*
Figures B1–B7	By permission of Coolblue PR for George Wimpey City
Figure C1	By permission of Gardner Stewart
Figures D1–D4	Drawings supplied by MBLC Architects + Urbanists
Figures E1–E7	By permission of PCKO Architects
Figures F1–F7	By permission of Alford Hall Mognahan and Morris Photographs by Tim Soar
Figures G1–G3	By permission of Hackland and Dore Isomettric and type plan reproduced from *Architecture Today*
Figures G4–G7	Photographs by John Reiach
Figures H1–H3	By permission of Bill Dunster Architects
Figures I1–I7	By permission of Cartwright Pickard Architects Drawings reproduced from *Architecture Today*
Figures J1, J3, J5 and J7	Copyright PRP Architects
Figure K1	By permission of THOTT Publishing, Bussum Copyright Bob Broddel, Hilversum, The Netherlands
Figures K2, K3 and K4	By permission of 'Projectdocumentatie Woningbouplannen Amsterdam 1994' Stedelijke Woningdienst Amsteerda, bureau P/A – produktonwikkeling, Amsterdam, 1994
Figures K5–K8	Photographs copyright PRP Architects
Figures L1, L2, L3 and L6	By permission of Jan Inke-Hagstróm, Manager – Planning, The Hammarby Sjöstad Project, Stockholm
Figures L4, L6 and L7	Photographs copyright PRP Architects
Figure M1	Copyright Local Government of Ferencváros District number 9, Budapest

All other drawings and photographs are by the author.

FIGURE ACKNOWLEDGEMENTS

Figure 0.2   Photograph copyright Leeds City Council
Figure 1.5   Photograph by Colin Baker
Figure 2.1   Drawing reproduced from *Homes for Today*
                           Tomorrow. London: HMSO, 1961
Figures 2.3 and 2.4   Drawings by Le Corbusier and Walter Gropi
                           reproduced by permission of DACS
Figure 2.5   Drawing by Harley Sherlock
Figures 2.6 and 2.7   Drawings reproduced from *Sustainable Resider*
                           Quality – Exploring the Housing Potential of La
                           Sites (London Planning Advisory Committ
                           2000) by permission of Greater Lond
                           Authority
Figure 3.1   Copyright held by the Duchy of Cornwall
                           Photograph by Provincial Pictures
Figure 3.2   Drawing reproduced by permission of
                           Princes Foundation
Figure 3.3   Drawing reproduced by permission of Tay
                           Woodrow
Figure 4.3   Drawing reproduced from *New Architecture*
                           London (Architectural Association, c 1965)
Figures 5.1 and 5.2   Photographs by Norman Beddington
Figure 6.3   Drawing by Harley Sherlock
Figure 6.7   Photograph reproduced by permission of Tay
                           Woodrow
Figure 6.8   Photograph by Ombretta Romice
Figures 6.9–6.12   Copyright Urban Splash, reproduced
                           permission
Figure 7.3   Photograph by Peter Taylor
Figure 7.4   Reproduced from 'Plan general de la zac' in
                           brochure titled 'Development du plan d'ar
                           nagement de zone de Bercy' by Jean-Pie
                           Buffi & Associes, Paris
Figure 7.5   Drawing reproduced by permission
                           Architeturstudio Herman Hertzberger

FOREWORD

TONY MONK

Housing of course means homes. To most people this is their most treasured possession. It is not just bricks and mortar or a financial investment; it is a vital part of their life. 'You mould the building and the building moulds you' as Winston Churchill is said to have put it. Home is crucial to everybody's daily well-being. As such it is normally treated with pride, and its character and contents are an extension of their personality. The creation of a home is not therefore just an intellectual design exercise detached from the occupant. It should be their design. It is their castle. The user of the home's personal needs and likes should be paramount. You would think this is stating the obvious. Yet it is a strange anomaly that, apart from a few individual houses, the vast majority of dwellings are designed without the tenants or purchasers ever seeing their new home until after it had been built. Almost everybody else, it seems, is involved in the process except the very people who will live in the accommodation. Instead, the developer, the housing association, the volume house builder, the estate agent, the local planning authority, the architect, and the design and build teams all take vital decisions about the content, quality, production and appearance of these properties without any of them actually living in the homes. The future occupants are barely consulted in spite of the decisions having a profound influence on them. The need to involve the users and the existing community in the housing procurement process is indeed obvious.

'The problem of the homeless' has been reducing since the days of Charles Dickens. It is and will always be in the political spot-light and the balance between private ownership and rented accommodation will continually change. Volume house builders are now producing the majority of homes for commercial sales. They are also required with their developments to carrying various direct housing taxes, the largest imposes on them the responsibility of producing 30% or more of the accommodation for a housing association to buy at cost; who then manages and rents out the properties to various types of subsidised tenants or key workers. This novel solution combines the two types of housing, both public and private. It uses private finance while it is viable, but it is only a solution while the market economy permits it. This current method of housing provision relies on a vibrant private housing sector. There is, however, a limit to the type and quantity of housing that this commercial funding and its construction process can produce. It concentrates on reliable repetitive market-driven solutions, usually two bed-roomed flats in viable locations. It therefore tends to neglect the larger family accommodation and smaller units in poorer areas.

The main problem with relying solely on this production route is that insufficient homes are being built in this country in response to local needs, as it only satisfies commercial demands. Only 175 000 homes are being built each year. This is against the projected requirement in the Barker Report of over 200 000 and the minimum target of 189 000 per year until 2021 set by the Office of the Deputy Prime Minister. This volume does not compare at all with the annual production of homes in the years following the Second World War which peaked at nearly 500 000 units. This was a period of housing priority when local authorities were compelled to meet their own housing needs and were directly funded by the Government. Without any expectation of a return to that system, Housing Associations could still expand their activities using more of the security of the equity in their accumulated housing stock. Private Funding initiatives could also be expanded to deliver more of the local requirements if they were controlled and followed housing briefs structured by the local authorities. The lethargic planning could also be improved to avoid inhibiting housing production unnecessarily. Unless there are significant improvements, public housing will continue to languish behind need and at the behest of the fickle market forces.

As an experienced architectural practitioner who was also a founder member of a well-established London Housing Association, it seems to me that the current procurement methods are inadequate to meet these targets. The volume house builders, of course, concentrate on producing developments with a narrow range of house types in viable and affluent areas and understandably neglect the low income first-time buyers or larger family accommodation in less well-off regions. While there are inadequate incentives there will always be gaps in the broad spectrum of housing need. There is insufficient research undertaken on a regular basis to identify the specific regional requirements and local needs vary so much it is always difficult to achieve a balanced urban housing environment. The Urban Task Force Report 1999 is still the most significant document produced, setting out a strategic analysis of housing objectives for urban renewal. There is much still left to be done to implement its recommendations. The improvement of the housing stock is, of course, the key factor to achieving regeneration in the urban areas.

The importance of this new publication 'At Home in the City' makes us re-examine on the issues of providing housing in its wider strategic context.

1 It encourages us to question why so many of the better parts of our historic cities here and in Europe generally, with high-density housing, still retain a charm, character, human scale, open spaces, views and a vibrant community environment that has been lost in most of our modern cities and housing by the ridged application of Planning and Building Regulations and current design.

2 It shows there is a need to look at the provision of the overall supporting community and the social facilities, as well as physical infrastructure, to ensure that there is a balanced neighbourhood in the form of a human scale urban village to integrate these new homes and their inhabitants. There is scope for these laudable ambitions to be incorporated in Special Planning Briefs initiated by the Local authority and the existing residents, by the supporting planning statements and by the expansion of 106 Agreements.

3 Local authorities assisted by the local community could therefore prepare a coordinated structure of social and commercial housing requirements. This could give guidance to housing developers to make sure that they encompass the wider spectrum of local needs.

4 Planning Policy Guidance Note No. 3 is valuable in ensuring higher densities in urban areas, but this is really too low in many central areas and too high in others.

5 Sustainability and energy conservation issues encourage higher densities in urban areas with good communication links that could be consolidated again by positive planning guidelines.

6 The local planning system is a perennial problem. It is often an obstacle, not a positive assistance, in progressing housing schemes. It sometimes takes longer to obtain the planning permission than to build and occupy the development itself. House builders would be prepared to pay extra fees if this would speed up their applications. This funding could be directed towards the production of planning briefs. It is very rewarding to work with proactive local authorities and community groups within a predetermined planning framework that has been initiated by them on appropriate sites.

7 After such pre-application work, the radical idea that planning applications would be approved automatically after, say, 4 months if they were not determined within that time scale, would dramatically improve results and galvanise the process.

There will be lasting benefits gained from Graham Towers' thoughtful housing book that has been written as a result of his own experience in the housing field. The illustrated case studies of live examples of completed housing developments are particularly interesting. These in-use studies are the real test of the success of a housing development. These enable the future residential providers, the clients, the designers or the builders to understand the merits and disadvantages from the analysis of these occupied living communities. This publication has the laudable objective of stimulating the provider to improve the quality of our housing designs, their construction and their occupation, so that the owners can truly feel happy in their homes in the city.

Preface

I have long been an advocate of high-density housing. During my architectural career I have worked on a variety of urban housing types. These have included new-build flats and maisonettes; the conversion and rehabilitation of Victorian terraced houses; and the modernisation and adaptation of multi-storey social housing estates. During much of the past 30 years high-density housing has been held in bad odour. This was largely due to the problems associated with high-rise housing estates which were, wrongly, regarded as the epitome of high density. The degeneration and social stigma associated with urban public housing did much to tarnish the idea of living in flats. So deep was this disaffection that during the 1970s and 1980s there was a general drive to reduce housing densities and a number of prominent and progressive housing specialists advocated the redevelopment of the inner cites with low-density houses with gardens.

That this did not happen was partly due to the alienation that redevelopment had caused during the 1960s when swathes of old urban houses were demolished to make way for unsympathetic and unsuitable new blocks of flats. Community action was the response to this – seeking to promote and protect the interests of those who lived in the inner cities. It was through working with community organisations that I gained an understanding of, and a commitment to, the engagement of building users in the processes of housing design and development. Participation in design remains as relevant as ever as a key to creating buildings that work well, and is an essential component in producing sustainable housing in the coming years. Choice and democracy are critical inputs to create housing that is pleasing to its occupants, meets their needs, and stands the test of time.

Despite my interest in housing my first foray into community politics was in transport – opposition to the building of an elevated urban motorway, the London 'motorway box'. As early as 1972 we argued that new roads would generate new traffic and that, instead, investment should be put into improved public transport. These arguments languished for more than 20 years as new roads proliferated, the railways were run down and traffic congestion increased relentlessly. At long last the traffic engineers' solution has been found wanting. Traffic restraint and the promotion of public transport are now high on the public policy agenda.

For a long time there was no obvious connection between housing and transport; or, more specifically, between the advocacy of high-density housing and opposition to urban motorways. Now, though, these two issues have come together. The two imperatives of urban policy are to meet the growing demand for additional housing and to address climate change by reducing greenhouse gas emission. It is recognised that these cannot be achieved through the continued development of low-density housing sprawl. This not only makes poor use of land – an increasingly scarce resource – it separates people from their work, from social facilities and from personal contacts. They become increasingly depended on the motorcar and increasingly embroiled in congestion. High-density urban housing provides efficient use of land, the delivery of services at low cost, and the development of effective and energy efficient transport systems.

For its occupants it also provides a good quality of life with a wide range of services, entertainment and opportunities for social interaction within easy reach. The increasing popularity of urban living is testament to this. High-density housing, properly planned, can provide good quality homes. But, equally important, it can provide a high-quality public environment. The older cities of Britain and Europe offer abundant examples of such high-quality residential areas. In providing the many new homes which will be needed in the relatively near future we need to draw on the lessons of the past. These need to be combined with new technical and social needs to create successful urban housing for the future.

*　　　*　　　*

A lot of people have helped in the preparation of this book. Special thanks are due to Tony Monk. After a successful career as a principal of a large architectural practice – Hutchison, Locke and Monk – which produced many high-quality housing projects, he became Professor of Architecture at the University of Luton. While there he sponsored and encouraged my research on housing. For this, much appreciation, and many thanks for agreeing to write the Foreword. Thanks are also due to friends and colleagues who have offered advice, information and material for the text – Norman Beddington, John Bussy, Suzy Nelson, Harley Sherlock and Stelios Voutsadakis.

I would also like to thank those who have provided information on the work of their organisations and sources of the material included in the text – Andrew Kliman of the Princes Foundation; Lisa Ashurst of Urban Splash; Barry Munday, Peter Rankin and Brendan Kilpatrick of PRP Architects; Mark Swenarton of *Architecture Today*; Natalie Land of Haworth Tomkins; Kate Harle of Coolblue PR; Jennifer Ross of Tibbalds Planning & Urban Design; Fraser Stewart of Gardner Stewart Architects; George Mills and Ian Beaumont of MBLC Architects and Urbanists; Andrew Ogorzalek of PCKO Architects; Linda McCarney of Alford Hall Mognahan and Morris; Alistair Hackland of Hackland and Dore; Sten Gromark and Michael Eden for information on Swedish housing projects; Judit Székely and Ágnes Cséry for help with the Budapest case study.

Finally, this book has been produced without commercial or institutional sponsorship. While this has had financial disadvantages it has allowed me to reach conclusions unencumbered by external influences.

Graham Towers

WHAT IS URBAN HOUSING?

The design of the house has acquired a prominent place in architectural history. But 'house' and 'housing' areas are not the same thing. While the historians of design lavished attention on the mansions and palaces of the rich they paid little heed to the everyday architecture which surrounded them – the mass of domestic buildings that were home to everyone else and which together constituted housing. Even in more recent times the architect-designed house has attracted a great deal of attention. At their most authoritative, such houses have had a seminal influence on a whole movement. Philip Webb's *Red House* became the lodestone for Arts and Crafts architecture. Frank Lloyd Wright's *Prairie Houses* set the agenda for one branch of Modernism; the early houses of Le Corbusier set it for another.

Ever since, the architect-designed house has remained a distinctive building type. Such houses are, almost exclusively, built for wealthy clients. Being rich they can afford large and often spectacular sites. Some of the most famous houses have exploited such opportunities. Wright's *Falling Water* made much of a woodland stream on a steep hillside. Philip Johnson's *Glass House* enjoyed a site so large that all the walls could be made transparent without risk of overlooking from prying eyes. Being rich, such clients set lavish briefs with large and multiple spaces and expensive materials. These factors make the individual house a challenging design problem. The interaction of many spaces of different functions is a complex problem of spatial geometry and planning. The procurement of rare or expensive materials and components is a time-consuming process. Externally the house has to address all directions, making the most of relationships between indoors and outdoors while at the same time creating a visual impact that reflects the prestige of its owner and the aspirations of its designer. What it does not have to do is to pay much attention to the neighbours.

In the design of housing, on the other hand, neighbourliness is the first principle. All housing schemes involve the design and development of a number of homes together – often a large number. These homes have to relate to each other. As a minimum they will have neighbours on either side often joined on but invariably close by. In multi-storey housing there may be neighbours above and below as well. The homes can only face in two directions and sometimes only in one, giving critical importance to orientation. The homes must be planned to avoid negative interaction such as overlooking and noise nuisance. While housing can be for the rich – the Georgian terrace of the past, the urban penthouse of today – most often it is not. Housing is for everyone. It has to be affordable and, for the most part, that means modest. Spaces are small-scale and limited in number. They are divided into well-understood functions. Materials and components have to be relatively cheap. This means that plans can be standardised and components mass produced.

The critical aspects of housing design lie outside the individual homes. Housing developments must share a common access system. This must be secure and easily maintained. There must be a shared system of service delivery and waste removal. Most importantly, the individual homes will collectively define form and space. The complexity of housing design lies not in the planning of individual houses, flats and maisonettes but in the way they interact. It is this interaction that determines the nature of our towns and cities in terms of their vitality, security, community and, not least, in the quality of the external spaces where we lead the public parts of our lives. Because housing is, by far, the predominant building type it is the quality of its design and the nature of the spaces it creates which defines urbanity in its various forms.

URBS VERSUS SUBURBS

It is often said that Britain is a predominantly urban country. Statements such as 'over 80 per cent of the English population live in towns and cities of over 10 000 people'[1] lend support to this view. But they mask a significant cultural and social divide between the old cities and the suburbs and satellite towns. By the end of the eighteenth century Britain had established a strong urban tradition. These towns and cities are now part of our heritage and are widely admired. What makes them so commendable is not so much the architecture of individual buildings – though some are of key significance. Rather it is the quality of the environment they created.

These old cities were predominantly made up of houses or commercial premises with housing over. The buildings had a harmonious quality. This derived partly from their scale – building height was limited both by

▲ **0.1**   Stamford, Lincolnshire

technology and by the number of stairs that could usefully be climbed; and partly from their design. In the older cities this was determined by vernacular construction methods and the use of local materials; in the later ones by the application of classical principles and the development of the Georgian style, which quickly became an urban tradition. These buildings were joined together partly as a result of the clamour for town centre frontage. The joined-up buildings created coherent spaces – streets, squares, greens and marketplaces. It is these qualities – recognisable and pleasant spaces lined by buildings of consistent visual design – which define what we now regard as traditional urban character.

Even so, only a small population lived in these towns, which had developed incrementally over a long period. In 1801 over 80 per cent of the population of England and Wales lived in the countryside, with only 1.7 million living in towns and cities larger than 5000 people.[2] Urban living, which had been a slowly built tradition, suddenly accelerated out of control. Over little more than a century the population as a whole increased more than fourfold and by 1911 the urban population had reached 28.5 million.[3] This population explosion was fuelled by and, in turn, served to promote the growth of industry, some of which attached to established ports such as London, Liverpool and Glasgow. Most were smokestack industries, which clustered around the coalfields of the North and the Midlands. Rapid population growth meant rapidly built housing. Most of it was poorly constructed and appallingly overcrowded. Worse, it was built cheek by jowl with the noxious factories.

▲ **0.2**   Back-to-back housing in Leeds

By the 1840s, conditions in the industrial cities were a serious cause for concern. To some this was a concern for social welfare[4] but for the most part it was a concern about health.[5] The polluted atmosphere, the damp and overcrowded buildings, were all a breeding ground for disease. A series of reforms were introduced culminating in the 1875 Public Health Act. This legislation set standards for the construction of buildings, for the provision of light and air, and better sanitation. It laid the basis for building regulation to the present day. By the end of the century the problems in the cities had eased. Population growth had slowed. New housing for the wealthier classes had been developed, usually on the south-west of the city centres where the prevailing wind would protect them from the industrial smoke – Kensington and Belgravis in London; Edgbaston and Moseley in Birmingham. New and better housing had also been developed for the less wealthy – the terraces built under the new regulations which have now become the epitome of the Victorian city. A start had been made on clearing the worst of the slums. But most remained and for many the changes were too little too late.

Conditions in the industrial cities were widely regarded as intolerable. This had long since generated a rejection, which affected all classes and all political persuasions. Marx and Engels railed against the oppression of

▲ **0.3**   'By-law' terraces in Birmingham

the enormous capitalist cities.[6] The reformist Chartist movement sought to establish new village settlements in the countryside for urban industrial workers.[7] Philanthropic industrialists created new model settlements away from the grim industrial cities.[8] The Arts and Crafts movement sought a return to a past idyll, extolling the virtues not just of rural life but of pre-industrial architecture and the techniques of craft production. From the middle of the nineteenth century, wealthy individuals sought to escape the cities, building their homes in the pleasant countryside outside. Many of these houses were designed by leading Arts and Crafts architects such as Lethaby, Norman Shaw and Voysey.[9] The growth of the suburbs had begun and was to gather pace.

The philosophy and aspirations of the Arts and Crafts designers spawned the Garden City Movement.[10] This sought to create new settlements where housing would be light, airy and open, surrounded by green spaces. Two such settlements were built – at Letchworth and Welwyn – but the movement's main influence was on the new developments which were to take place in the wake of the First World War. Change was in the air and the government promised 'homes fit for heroes'. The Tudor Walter Report written by the leading Garden City exponent Raymond Unwin set new standards for housing with minimum room sizes, more open cul-de-sac layouts, and much lower densities all in stark contrast to the derided urban housing.[11] These were to set the pattern for a massive programme of new council housing estates in the periphery of large cities. While these

▲ **0.4**   1920s council houses

▲ **0.5**   Early semi-detached houses

estates provided new homes for the less well-off, the middle classes were equally keen to escape the squalor and congestion of the cities. Developers built new estates of semi-detached houses inspired by the standards of the Garden City Movement and the designs of the Arts and Crafts architects.

▲ **0.6** Multi-storey flats of the early 1960s

Great swathes of low-density suburbs were built around all the large cities. During the 1920s and 1930s more than 4 million homes were built – 1 million council houses to relieve the overcrowded urban slums, and 3 million to house the migrating middle classes.

These trends continued after the Second World War. In the public realm the policy of relieving urban congestion by decentralisation continued. It was given new impetus by the programme of new and expanding towns.[12] Private developers continued to build on the outskirts of towns and cities as owner-occupation grew at an accelerating rate. Between 1945 and the end of the century 10.5 million new homes were built in England and Wales and owner-occupation increased from 32 to 70 per cent.[13] Of the 2.35 million homes in Scotland, 64 per cent were owner occupied.[14] Whether public or private this new housing was, almost exclusively, built on the Garden City model – family houses with gardens generously spaced in informal layouts. Meanwhile in the cites a shift of policy took place in the late 1950s. Decentralisation was phased out in favour of a new assault on the slums. Between 1955 and 1976, 1.6 million urban homes were demolished.[15] These were replaced by estates of multi-storey flats to house those displaced by the clearances. In all about 1.7 million flats were built by Britain's local authorities between 1945 and 1975.[16]

By the 1970s the urban divide was complete. The Victorian cities – the old houses now mostly run down and often overcrowded alongside new estates of flats largely unloved and already deteriorating. The suburbs – low-density houses with gardens providing good homes which, to their residents, seemed the perfect antidote to city life. If the nineteenth century was the era of the industrial city, the twentieth was the making of the suburbs. On paper the balance of the rural and urban population had not changed, while in 1911, 80 per cent lived in the industrial cities, by the late twentieth century more than half had moved to the new suburbs and satellite towns. What had been the industrial cities was now home to as little as 30 per cent of the population.

WHO WILL LIVE IN THE CITY?

The divide was marked by a clear distinction between the dense character of the terraces and tall buildings of the cities and the amorphous qualities of the sprawling suburbs. But there was also a clear social division. The suburbs were new housing. Those attracted to them were families with young children who could afford to buy – this meant comparatively well-off families. Most of these new suburbs started off as one class communities – almost all their residents were relatively young and relatively prosperous. They had much in common and social interaction was strong. Their concerns and problems were similar and they could share in the organisation of activities for their growing children. Not least, they could mutually bask in the satisfaction of the increasing asset value of their homes. These are widely regarded as successful communities and all the indices of achievement and social stability are good. But the price for their success was paid for by those they had left behind.

The old cities had become the 'inner cities'. Those who still lived there were mostly those who had no choice – low income denied them the opportunity of owner-occupation and the suburban home: there was a higher than average proportion of the elderly, the sick and the disabled; there was a higher level of unemployment exacerbated by the decline of inner city industry; there was a high proportion of single parents whose poverty was worsened by their inability to work full time. On top of this, there were still high levels of housing stress. Most inner city residents rented their homes. Many, particularly low-income families with young children, were inappropriately housed whether in a multiple-occupied old building or an unsuitable high flat.[17] Partly as a result of this deprivation, there was a higher levels of crime and repeated outbreaks of civil disorder.[18]

The drift of population and the growth of social division seemed relentless. In 1991 most urban areas were still losing population.[19] The trend of the past few years, though, may mark a change of direction. It seems that the inner cities have begun to re-populate. The 2001 census showed that, over a ten-year period, the population of many cities had increased, including London, Birmingham, Leeds, Sheffield and Greater Manchester.[20] More recent figures show a net increase in migration to cities in the north-east – Newcastle and Gateshead – which were previously in decline.[21] In part, this shift may have been fuelled by changes in the suburbs. As they have matured, the social profile of the suburbs has moved closer to the average. There are more elderly, more people affected by sickness and disability, and the impact of rising divorce levels has created more singletons and lone parents. There are fewer young children and as the original offspring of the new settlements have grown up, the character of suburban life has seemed less appropriate for young adults than it was for growing children. There are relatively few local job opportunities, fewer services, and the entertainment and recreation on offer is limited. Frustrations amongst the young lead to increasing incidences of crime and antisocial behaviour, which now seems to be as much a characteristic of the suburb as of the city. Above all, the low-housing density makes almost everyone dependent on the private car for travel. As congestion continues to grow this is increasingly seen as a dubious benefit.

Meanwhile, there have been changes in the inner cities. In the public sector the shortcomings of the multi-storey estate have been recognised. Their construction ceased long since. Many have been modernised and the most problematic ones demolished. New social housing has been limited but most has been designed as groups of terraced houses and low-rise flats in traditional style. At the same time, slum clearance has also ceased. Much of the old housing has been renovated. Partly this has been through the direct intervention of local authorities and housing associations. Partly through the work of new owners who have been prepared to take on run-down and semi-derelict houses and retrieve them by their own efforts, often with the aid of improvement grants. Victorian terraced housing, which might have been demolished a generation ago, has been turned into sound and desirable homes. Encouraged by the investment of the public sector and pioneering individuals, private developers have begun to build new housing on urban sites at densities and in forms, which are a world away from the suburban semi.

▲ **0.7**   New housing association estate of the 1980s

▲ **0.8**   Old terraced housing renovated and converted

Those who live in the city are, in many ways, the same as ever. There are those who work, or have worked, in urban industry and services. Amongst them is a high proposition of low-income households who are mostly tenants of social housing. Young people have always been attracted to the bright lights and, amongst them are students whose

▲ 0.9
Upper Street,
Islington

numbers have been growing at a rapid rate. These established groups have now been joined by growing numbers of younger, wealthier people. Many professional people have recognised that living in the inner city offers the opportunity to live in good-quality homes, close to their places of work; while having the opportunity to enjoy the many recreational and cultural activities that the city has to offer. With them they have brought new spending power, which, in many areas, has generated an increasingly diverse range of shops, restaurants and leisure facilities. At the same time this increased economic activity has generated new employment opportunities.

All this is not to say that the inner city problems are solved. There is still too much dereliction, too much unemployment and under-achievement and too much crime. Some cities such as Liverpool are still in decline and there are many areas, even in prosperous cities, which still suffer from multiple deprivation and dereliction. Some inner city services are still inadequate, particularly secondary education. Further changes are needed to attract more people back into these areas, especially key workers who are indispensable to the functioning of education, health, transport and other essential public services. The recent tentative urban renaissance suggests a start has been made. The inner cities can provide a range of housing which meets the needs of a changing population. The growing numbers of single-person households can be appropriately housed in urban flats. At the same time, family housing with gardens can be effectively developed at high densities in the inner cities. It is the purpose of this book to examine recent changes in urban housing, which may provide the basis for increased urban development as a viable alternative to relentless expansion into the open countryside.

THE STRUCTURE OF THE BOOK

This book does not aim to be a primer on housing design. There is a range of publications, which deal with basic design issues, space planning and domestic construction. Most of these concentrate on the design of low-density houses – these have, after all, been the predominant form of development for almost 100 years. Rather, the aim here is to concentrate on where urban housing differs from the priorities and concerns, which have characterised the design of conventional developments. The focus is on housing issues in Britain, although developments in European countries are also reflected. A review of urban issues is included on a wider sphere. Urban housing is taken to cover a range of user groups and needs, but housing for special purposes such as residential homes and hostels is not included. Throughout the concentration is on practice, drawing mainly on schemes which have been completed rather than on proposed developments or ideas for new forms of housing, which may never come to fruition.

The book is divided into two parts. **Part one** addresses a range of key issues central to contemporary urban housing design.

Chapter 1 sets the context for housing developments in Britain in the early years of the twenty-first century. There are two imperatives. One is the problem of climate change and the need to cut greenhouse gas emissions. The other is population change, which is generating increased demand for homes. Both these issues put a strain on scarce resources and necessitate a new concentration on high-density developments in urban sites. A key issue is to identify a large amount of development land within existing cities.

Chapter 2 addresses standards. Space standards are a key determinant of how living space is divided, yet the established approach does not provide a good framework for the design of urban housing. The measurement of housing density is complex and can be confusing. The concept of high density is often misunderstood and commonly confused with living in tower blocks. Housing forms at different densities are examined. Finally, if high-density housing is to be successful it must improve the quality of life, facilitating access to work and leisure and reducing the need to travel.

Chapter 3 considers the need to build not just housing but a full range of services and facilities. At the same time the idea of neighbourhood is long established both in planning and in community studies. These two concerns come together in the relatively new concept of the 'urban village,' which envisages a socially mixed community supported by services and employment opportunities. The sustainable urban neighbourhood takes this concept further aiming to create development, which is in balance with the environment. Nevertheless, most development does not create whole neighbourhoods from scratch but must integrate with, and foster the development of, existing communities.

Chapter 4 looks at the various forms of urban housing. The traditions of high-density housing in the inner cities is considered. Two forms of successful urban housing are examined – terraced houses of various types; and maisonettes and flats in 'perimeter' blocks of modest scale. The possibility of a new phase of high-rise building is considered. Demographic changes create new needs in urban housing – there are increasing number of elderly people, some of whom will have special needs. There are increasing number of young single people. At the same time more people will be working from home. Finally, the public realm is considered – the way buildings enclose space, the way this is used, and the significance of security and good urban management.

In the construction of new housing the agenda created by climate change must be addressed. This is considered in **Chapter 5**. The need to reduce greenhouse gas emissions not only means that buildings must be more efficient in their use of energy. It also means they must address the implications of renewable sources of energy. The conservation of scarce resources means that use of building materials must be more environmentally conscious and the profligate use of water reduced. The new housing priorities have led to a renewed interest in the use of prefabrication which some see as critical in improving the efficiency of construction.

The reuse of existing buildings is a key facet of conservation. The reclamation of built space is addressed in **Chapter 6**. To combat the effects of climate change there is a clear need to improve the energy efficiency of the existing housing stock. There is a good deal that can be done in occupied homes but there are greater opportunities in housing which is empty, run-down or undesirable. Much older housing and large parts of the stock of the multi-storey estates can be renovated and converted to more manageable forms. The changing economy makes many commercial and industrial buildings redundant. Rather than redeveloping them, many can be converted to provide new homes.

Chapter 7 looks at design quality. In the design of public buildings the ideas of architects have held sway. But in housing, people have more choice and more influence. The field of housing design has been a conflict between architectural concepts and traditional ideas and practices. A key issue is to establish visual order and harmony. This can be done with 'design codes', a set of rules that gives a framework for new residential developments. At the same time, people should be given more influence in the design of their homes – this can be done partly by making housing adaptable to changing needs. They can also be given more choice at the design stage of the appearance and functioning of their new homes, both as individuals and as user groups.

Finally, **Chapter 8** looks at the broader picture. The world has become more urbanised and with a growing population this trend is likely to continue. Cities of the future must work well and provide good conditions for their inhabitants, while striving to be in better balance with the natural environment. Low-density cities of the new world impose too great a burden on resources. Conversely, very high-density housing extract a heavy price in technical and managerial complexity and restrict the lifestyles of their residents. The medium density cities of Europe, despite some problems, offer the best hope for sustainability. They provide high-quality environments which function well and offer diversity and choice in homes, work and recreation.

The chapters are illustrated by drawings and photographs of appropriate schemes. Some projects are covered more fully as 'case examples' drawn from Britain and Europe. These have been selected to provide particularly pertinent lessons supplementing issues covered in the text.

Part two consists of a series of case studies giving more extensive information on selected projects. These are mainly drawn from developments built in British cities over the past few years. They are, therefore, drawn from a common historical, regulatory and fiscal background. For comparison three schemes are included from northern Europe, which has a strong urban history. The case study schemes have been selected not for their dramatic architecture but because each illustrates one or more of the issues which are central to new urban housing. Together the case studies cover a range of these issues:

- *Housing types* include houses, maisonettes, flats and live/work units. These range from terraces of houses to large-scale blocks of flats. At an intermediate scale there are several schemes involving medium rise blocks of flats, maisonettes and mixed uses.
- *Development processes* concentrate on new buildings on brownfield sites ranging from relatively small individual sites to large tracts of redundant land. Schemes are also included which address the problems of run-down urban housing either by redevelopment or renovation.
- *User groups* include families, childless couples and single people of all ages. Schemes are included, which are specifically dedicated for occupation by young people.
- *Forms of tenure* cover not only owner-occupation and social rented but also less common forms such as shared ownership, cost rents, market rents and co-operatives.
- *Construction methods and materials* on many of the schemes meet the new demands of energy conservation and avoidance of waste. Some schemes illustrate the use of prefabrication and off-site construction.

Taken together, the case studies provide a complex picture of urban housing issues. No one scheme provides a perfect blueprint for success. Achieving sustainability in urban housing is a complex process. It requires good environmental design to address global concerns. It also needs good urban design, which can achieve both visual quality and good amenity together with a high level of security. Importantly, it requires strong and stable communities committed to the long-term success of their neighborhoods. Each of these issues is illustrated in one or more of the case study schemes.

PART ONE

ISSUES IN URBAN HOUSING

CONTEXT

THE ENVIRONMENTAL IMPERATIVE

SUMMARY

Two critical trends have combined to bring about a fundamental change in housing development policy in Britain at the beginning of the twenty-first century. One is the increasing evidence of climate change caused by the burning of fossil fuels to generate energy. This has resulted in an accumulation of 'greenhouse' gases causing a rise in world temperatures and changes in weather patterns. Widespread concern over climate change has resulted in agreed targets to reduce the production of carbon dioxide emissions. The other trend is the predicted growth in the number of house-holds primarily caused by a large increase in the numbers of single people. This would require a further 3.8 million homes in the first 20 years of the new century.

These trends threatened to impose an unsustainable burden on scarce resources whether these were land, materials or traditional fuels. The new policy developed to address this threat meant concentrating new housing on previously developed 'brownfield' urban sites. It also meant that new housing needed to be denser in order to reduce both land take and the need for transport, particularly car use. To achieve these ends it was essential to identify land for this new housing in the existing urban areas. On the face of it, these were already fully developed, but subsequent studies have identified significant quantities of unused and under-used land and buildings ripe for renewal.

CLIMATE CHANGE

The opening years of the new century have been marked by dramatic weather patterns. In Britain and northern Europe there has been widespread flooding affecting many towns and cities. In 2002 two of Europe's heritage cities – Prague and Dresden – were inundated and seriously damaged after the entire rainfall of a typical August fell in just 36 hours. At the same time parts of Africa were variously affected by floods and drought. In Australia, prolonged periods without rain resulted in serious bush fires. In 2003 there were record-breaking heat waves in Europe, Asia and north-east America. It seemed incontestable that the world's climate was changing.

Many things can affect the climate including sunspot activity and volcanic eruptions. Cyclical changes take place over a long period. There have been repeated 'ice ages' and there is good evidence that many parts of the world were warmer a few hundred years ago than they are today. Nevertheless there is now a widespread consensus that the recent changes are due, at least in part, to the 'greenhouse' effect. Geological evidence showed that, over millions of years, the proportion of carbon dioxide in the atmosphere never exceeded 250 parts per million. By the end of the twentieth century, though, it had risen to 360 parts per million – an increase of 44 per cent caused by the use of fossil fuels to produce energy.

When hydrocarbons such as petrol, oil and natural gas are burned they produce carbon dioxide and water vapour. The carbon dioxide accumulates in the upper atmosphere, along with other gases such as methane. This layer of 'greenhouse gases' acts as an insulating blanket limiting the amount of heat which can escape from the earth and causing 'global warming'. The actual rise in temperatures seems slight – between 1975 and 2000 mean global temperatures rose by little more than 0.4 degree centigrade. However, small rises can have dramatic effects. The last ice age was caused by a fall of only 5 degree centigrade, a rise of 2 degree centigrade would be enough to make the countries of the Mediterranean uninhabitable, while an increase of only 1 degree centigrade causes a rise in sea levels of up to 12 centimetres through the melting of permanent ice. The main effect of the small rise in temperature over recent years has been the increase in rainfall. This is because evaporation is increased by the warmer climate and, at the same time, the warmer air has the capacity to carry more moisture. Higher rainfall is predicted to continue, characterised by increasingly violent storms.

The Kyoto protocols

Concerns about global warming were first addressed internationally at the world conference held in Rio de Janeiro in 1992. There a generalised target was set to reduce carbon dioxide emissions to 1990 levels by the year 2000. This target was mainly aspirational and had little effect. The issue was tackled again at a follow-up conference in Kyoto in 1997. This time, through tough negotiations, binding targets were agreed. An overall aim was to reduce carbon dioxide emissions, based on 1990 levels, by 5.2 per cent over the period up to 2012. Within this, different targets were agreed for each country. All the participant countries left the summit committed to a specific level of reduction. All, that is, except the USA which is not only the world's biggest economy it is also the biggest producer of carbon dioxide emissions.

The target set for Europe as a whole was 8 per cent but Britain had agreed to a higher target – a reduction of 12.5 per cent by the year 2012. Britain's carbon dioxide emissions come from three main sources:

1 productive industry including power generation;
2 energy inefficiency in housing and industry;
3 transport, especially road vehicles.

To achieve the target, reductions must be made in all spheres. Some early progress was made in reducing emissions from power generation by the switch from coal to natural gas. Further reduction needs to be made by switching to more efficient methods of production such as combined heat and power (CHP) and by increasing power generation by renewable sources. These include wind power, tidal and wave power, solar energy and a number of other new technologies. In 2002 only 2 to 3 per cent of Britain's electricity came from these sources but the aim is to increase this to 10 per cent by 2010 and 20 per cent by 2020.

In the UK, housing accounts for 27 per cent of carbon dioxide emissions. There is a need to reduce both the energy in constructing housing and the energy inefficiency in running homes. The prime target must be improvements in the efficiency of space heating which accounts for half the greenhouse gas produced from housing. Transport accounts for about 26 per cent of emissions. This includes public transport, which generally uses energy efficiently, and air transport which does not. Remarkably, no tax is levied on aeroplane fuel which is one reason for the relentless growth in air travel. However, the main problem is Britain's 25 million cars. These are used more extensively than anywhere else in Europe and are the main source of greenhouse gas emissions from transport.

The need for equilibrium

In the long run the aim must be to reach a balance where energy consumption is in harmony with the capacity of the environment. One definition of sustainability is *economic activity or development which meets the needs of the present without compromising the ability of future generations to meet their own needs*. In terms of the greenhouse effect this means not triggering irreversible environmental change or pollution which damages the health or well-being of our descendants. This is a lofty aspiration and hard to achieve. It is generally considered that to achieve balance the reduction in greenhouse gas emissions is not the 5 per cent targeted at present but 60 per cent. Some consider that the environment is permanently damaged and that the best that can be achieved is to avoid making the situation worse.

While the greenhouse effect is the most pressing environmental issue of the moment it is not the only facet of the search for sustainability. A broader picture can be gained by considering the concept of 'the ecological footprint'. One definition of the ecological footprint of a city is the land area required to provide it with food, supply it with timber products and re-absorb its carbon dioxide emissions by areas covered with growing vegetation. Defined in this way the ecological footprint of London is 125 times greater than its actual surface area. This amounts to 20 million hectares – almost the equivalent of the entire productive land area of Britain. But even this is not the full picture. It does not take account of the land required to produce building materials and manufactured goods or land required to dispose of waste products of all sorts. Adding this in would considerably increase the footprint area.

Ecological footprints can only be calculated on a regional basis, but once compiled they can be broken down to per capita figures. It has been calculated that the ecological footprint per person in India is 0.4 hectares while in the USA it is 5.1 hectares. In equity the citizens of India must be allowed the opportunity to improve their standard of living. But if everyone in the world were to live like the current inhabitants of the USA their ecological footprint would require at least two additional planets like the Earth. Bringing the world into balance requires a dramatic reduction in the ecological footprint of the developed world and sustainable development everywhere else. This does not just mean a reduction in greenhouse gas emissions but a general reduction in consumption and in the production of waste. In broad terms this means reducing the use of scarce resources. Aside from their effects on the atmosphere, fossil fuels are themselves a natural resource in limited supply. So are many minerals and natural products used in manufacturing and building. Demand for scarce resources can be limited by greater efficiency in their use but the recovery and recycling of waste products also plays a critical part.[1]

POPULATION CHANGE

Another scarce resource, particularly in the highly developed parts of northern Europe, is land. The loss of land to housing in the south-east of England had been a concern for some time. Between 1945 and 1990 in the 'home counties' around London, 170 000 hectares were consumed by new development – an area of land bigger than London itself.[2] These concerns were exacerbated by government estimates of the late 1990s which suggested that over a period of 25 years, 3.8 million new homes would be needed to meet rising demand.

These new demands were prompted by changes in the English household structure with fewer families and increasing numbers of people living alone. It was estimated that 80 per cent of these new households would be single people. The biggest increase was among people in their 20s and 30s living on their own. There was also an increase in those divorced, or not in permanent relationships and a growing proportion of elderly people.[3] These projections seemed to be confirmed by the 2001 census which showed that, for the first time, elderly people formed a larger pro-portion of the UK population than children – 21 per cent were aged over 60 years, while only 20 per cent were under 16 years of age.[4]

The Urban Task Force

Concern over these projections led the government to appoint an Urban Task Force led by architect Richard Rogers, to examine how the large quantity of new housing required could be accommodated. The initial assessment of the Task Force was daunting. Pointing to the low density of recent housing development they estimated that if all the new homes required were built at similar densities they would occupy a land area bigger than Greater London. Even if only 45 per cent were built on greenfield land at prevailing densities they would cover an area of coun-tryside larger than Exmoor.

Faced with such enormous losses of open land and the difficulty of ser-vicing such new development, the Task Force defined four key issues which had to be addressed:

1 *The need for increased densities.* Having established the large areas of countryside which would be taken by maintaining existing policies, the Task Force concluded that higher densities would be required in new development with more of it concentrated on recycled urban land. They cited research which showed that the most significant reductions in land used could be achieved by relatively modest increases in density. While modest increases would achieve consider-able land saving, the report points out that relatively high densities have considerable advantages creating better local services and facil-ities, and easier access to them. It, therefore, suggests 'pyramids of intensity' – high-density development around urban foci of services, employment and transport.

2 *The need to reduce car use.* Given the high-energy consumption and the relentless growth in road traffic, there is a clear need to reduce the use of cars. Building at higher densities would reduce dependency on car travel, making better public transport possible. As densities increase so more frequent and efficient public transport systems become viable. With services and facilities closer to homes, far more journeys could be completed by walking or cycling. At the same time, concentrating more development on to urban land would reduce distances between work and home, and reduce transport needs. The report recommends higher investment in public transport and disincentives to car use including lower parking provision and higher charges.

3 *The need to create high-quality environments.* Before the industrial revolution Britain built cities of high quality. Bath, Edinburgh and Oxford provide models of excellence with high-quality buildings and urban spaces (Figure 1.1), while towns such as Brighton are examples of desirable residential locations which exceed current density standards (Figure 1.2). These pre-industrial cities were designed to be accessible by walking, with streets and squares related to the human scale. These urban qualities have been lost in recent development by the fragmentation of urban form and its domination by the needs of motor traffic. The report recommended that government should improve the quality of new housing by developing a national urban design framework, sponsoring demonstration projects and reforming planning and funding guidelines.

▲ **1.1**   Oxford – Britain's pre-industrial cities provide models of excellence

4 ***The need for urban regeneration.*** Many people still reject urban living because of the poor quality of many inner city areas. This ranges from environmental degradation through vandalism, graffiti and anti-social behaviour to run down and derelict buildings and concentrations of unemployment and social problems. Improving the quality of life in these areas is necessary both for the existing residents and to attract people back to them. It depends both on regeneration and better urban management. Both physical and economic regeneration is needed and it requires a more integrated approach. Good urban management of services and the environment is essential to maintain quality of life. Both these objectives should be achieved through the engagement of communities in urban neighbourhoods.

The work of the Urban Task Force demonstrated that accommodating the increased demand created by population change was not simply a

▲ **1.2**   Brighton – a sought after residential location which exceeds current density standards

matter of building more housing, even at high densities. It required a complex interaction of policies aimed at regenerating existing cities and creating more integrated and compact communities.[5]

Variation in demand

Most attention has focused on the overall demand for new housing. It is likely, though, that within this predicted growth there will be variations both between and within regions. Between 1991 and 2001 Scotland's population fell slightly while that of England and Wales grew at a modest rate. Within this there were significant variations. In the north-east and north-west of England there was a fall in population. In the south-west, east and south-east regions there were rises of 10 per cent or more with some popular parts of London recording rises of up to 17 per cent.[6] Differences in demand were reflected in house prices which were stable or falling in northern regions and escalating rapidly in the south-east. These variations were creating some serious problems which are likely to continue into the future.

In the northern regions population change was uneven. Much of the reduction was focused on the inner areas of large cities creating problems of low demand. Some council estates had long been classified as 'hard to let'. But this new phenomenon was characterised by low demand for all social housing with some newly built housing association stock never occupied. At its worst, low demand led to whole areas of inner city housing – both publicly and privately owned – being abandoned. In the most extreme neighbourhoods a majority of the houses were empty, with many demolished or badly damaged, and there was low demand for all types of tenure. These neighbourhoods present a serious challenge to urban regeneration in many northern cities.[7]

The problems of success were different. In London there was a serious shortfall in social housing with 180 000 households on council waiting lists and 26 000 registered homeless.[8] But the shortfall did not just affect low-income families, the normal applicants for social housing. High property prices affected many key workers such as teachers and nurses. In most parts of the country such employees were well able to buy their own homes, but in the areas of high demand they were priced out of good-quality housing. The pressures of high demand created a serious shortfall of affordable housing for households with a fairly wide range of income.

A NEW POLICY FOR HOUSING

The early response of government to the predictions of rapid household growth was to determine that a higher proportion of new housing should be built on previously developed urban land. Initially, this figure was set at 50 per cent but, in 1998, was raised to 60 per cent. Detailed determination of how to do this had to await the deliberations of the Urban Task Force and their consideration by Whitehall. This comprehensive new policy for housing was introduced in March 2000 in the guise of *Planning Policy Guidance Note No. 3: Housing*.[8]

PPG3

Despite its uninspiring title, PPG3 represents a radical departure on what went before. Previous policy towards housing development had been framed by the post-war planning system which sought to address the problems left over from urban industrialisation. The new imperatives of conserving scarce resources and accommodating population change required a fresh approach. PPG3 marked a reversal of some long-standing presumptions and a change of direction in critical policy areas:

- ***Re-use of land and buildings.*** The concentration of new housing development on ex-urban 'greenfield' sites had its origin in the decentralisation policies introduced in the first half of the twentieth century. These were aimed at relieving overcrowding in the inner areas of large cities by allowing people to move to new housing estates built on the urban periphery, or in new and expanded towns. By the 1990s it was clear that this process had run its course with the inner cities depopulating and the loss of countryside casing increasing concern. PPG3 confirms the reversal of this policy and the commitment to concentrate most new housing development within urban areas. This meant not only using previously developed land, 'brownfield' sites, but also creating new housing by the conversion and re-use of existing buildings. Local authorities were required to estimate the amount of new housing required in their areas and plan for its provision. This included calculating the capacity for new housing development.
- ***Higher densities.*** Low densities were an integral component of decentralisation policies. The ideals of the Garden City Movement required new housing to be open and airy as a deliberate counterweight to the overcrowded slums and polluted atmosphere of the industrial cities. The urban plans produced in the 1940s consistently set low densities for new housing development on ex-urban sites.

LEAMINGTON SPA

▲ **1.3**   Regency housing in Lansdown Crescent

At the heart of Leamington is a pre-industrial town of the highest environmental quality. It was mainly developed as a spa town in the early part of the nineteenth century and was beautifully planned. In the south the Old Town based around an old High Street of pre-spa days. In the north the New Town of elegant stuccoed Regency terraces and squares. In between, along the river, a series of public parks were laid out stretching right through the town providing recreation and leisure space. The centre of Leamington is still an attractive place to live. Many of the best Regency buildings – such as Lansdown Crescent (Figure 1.3) – are still used as family houses. These are supplemented by many streets of more modest, but still comfortable

terraced houses. But Leamington's urban heritage is now swamped by more recent developments.

From the early twentieth century industry has developed around the south of the town and by the 1930s a series of ribbon developments stretched out around the historic core. From the 1950s acres of poorly planned low-destiny suburbs were allowed to sprawl to the north and south, consuming many farms and obliterating three small villages. The latest of these is Warwick Gates (Figure 1.4) completed in 2000. This is an extensive development built to the southern outskirts of Leamington on good-quality agricultural land. This new residential area is low density

▲ **1.4**   The new Warwick Gates development

▲ **1.5**   Flooding in central Leamington

and almost entirely lacking in services. Its form, its outlying location and the absence of public transport make its residents dependent on the private car for almost all their needs. As a portent, perhaps, of the unsustainability of such development, central Leamington was visited by serious floods in the summer of 1998 (Figure 1.5).

PPG3 notes that, in the latter years of the twentieth century, new housing in England was being built at an average density of 25 homes per hectare. More than half of it was being built at less than 20 dwellings per hectare on sites taken from open countryside. This required a level of land take which was historically high and unsustainable. The new policy aimed to reverse this trend. A minimum standard for new development was set at 30 dwellings per hectare but local authorities were encouraged to seek higher densities of 30 to 50 dwellings per hectare. In particular, greater intensity of development should be achieved on sites with high accessibility such as city, town and local centres, and around major public transport nodes.

- *Integrated transport.* Housing developments built at low densities could not be serviced efficiently by public transport and few journeys could be made on foot. Their residents, inevitably, became highly dependent on private transport. This meant that new housing had to be provided with high-capacity roads and high levels of parking, up to three car spaces per house. Such dependence coupled with the separations of work and home was the major cause of the continuing growth of road traffic and the intensifying problems of congestion. PPG3 recognised the need to reduce travel by car. This meant ensuring that all new housing was linked by public transport to local centres providing jobs, services and amenities. It also meant that development was planned to facilitate more journeys by walking and cycling. Local authorities were encouraged to seek mixed-use developments which would combine housing with employment and services, reducing the need for travel. Parking standards should be reviewed with a new maximum of 1.5 car spaces per dwelling. Lower parking provision should be made on developments which are highly accessible and in those designed to house groups, such as students or the elderly, whose car ownership levels are low.

- *Mixed communities.* The creation of mixed communities was a key aim of post-war planning. Ideally, people with a wide range of incomes and occupations would live side by side. That this did not happen was largely a result of the process of development. Rented housing was almost exclusively built by local authorities. Owner-occupied housing was built by private developers. In the suburbs this meant large estates of social housing alongside equally large but more numerous estates of private housing. In the cities wholesale redevelopment led to large estates exclusively allocated to low-income families. The result was social segregation and the intensification of problems in urban high-density estates. PPG3 sought to revive mixed communities by ensuring that developments contain a

range of dwelling size and forms of tenure. They should also meet
the needs of specific groups – the elderly, the disabled, students and
young single people – who are likely to form an increasing proportion
of the population. Local authorities were given new powers to ensure
that new developments contain a proportion of affordable housing.

- *Residential quality.* Over several decades the concentration in
  housing quality has been on the individual home. The house and
  garden were usually of good quality and generally appreciated. The
  quality of the residential environment, though, was often poor.
  Suburban developments were commonly monotonous and of poor
  spatial quality dominated by roads and parking. Amenities and open
  space were often minimal. In the inner cities, the average council flat
  was of a high standard internally. Local authority estates, though, were
  characterised by unsafe access systems and public spaces degraded
  by abuse. PPG3 aimed to improve the quality and attractiveness of
  residential areas. Where comprehensive developments of the past
  destroyed urban neighbourhoods, the new policy suggested developments should respect the wider context. They should build on '… the
  local pattern of streets and spaces, building traditions, materials and
  ecology'. New development should be greener, with landscaping and
  open space an integral part. Local authorities should create more
  public green space and protect existing open spaces, particularly
  those that contribute to biodiversity.

Undoubtedly PPG3 marks a radical reversal of many of the priorities
which dominated the planning system for most of the twentieth century.
Given the serious problems created by the profligate use of scarce
resources, though, it is questionable whether the new policy goes far
enough. Higher housing densities may be needed. More needs to be
done to reduce the separation between work and home, and the consequent need for transport. The energy efficiency of new housing is not
addressed and this might be thought to merit the attention of town
planners. Nevertheless, it marks a brave assault on presumptions which
are deeply entrenched – one on which further progress can be made
following the review of its effects in practice.[9]

Implementing the new policy

The great majority of the new housing required will be built by property
developers or by registered social landlords – housing associations and
the like. The key role of local and central government is in facilitating and
monitoring this development. PPG3 charges planning authorities with
assessing housing needs in their areas and estimating housing capacity.

They are then required to identify sites for new housing and ensure their supply. In doing this they are authorised to use compulsory purchase order (CPOs) to assemble suitable sites – the first time these have been used substantially for more than 20 years. In considering applications for planning permission they are allowed to cite a failure to conform to the new policies as a reason for refusal. Local authorities are required to refer large schemes to central government; that is, schemes covering more than 5 hectares or comprising more than 150 homes. The density provisions were later strengthened by requiring the notification of any schemes proposing development at less than 30 dwellings per hectare.

One of the most difficult areas of the new policy is the creation of mixed communities. Owner-occupiers had often been apprehensive about living next to tenants of social housing. Social segregation had become deeply entrenched under the old planning system, though it had begun to break down as the middle classes began to repopulate parts of the inner cities. Recent research on areas of mixed tenure shows that, while there was a low level of social contact, most residents felt that mixing did not cause problems. Owner-occupiers' fears were mollified, while there were positive benefits to many low-income tenants.[10] The new policy aimed to create mixed tenures within new housing developments. One way to achieve this was through partnerships between social and commercial developers. Specific powers were given to planners to ensure that commercial developers included a proportion of affordable housing in new schemes. This would be achieved through binding agreements (Section 106, Agreements).[11] These would prove a valuable planning tool in areas with a shortfall of low-cost housing. In areas of greatest need, such as London, the overall need for affordable housing was high. A target of 50 per cent of all new housing was set in the London Plan though some London Boroughs set lower targets.[12] Some of this would be provided by social landlords, but a significant proportion would be required from private developers through Section 106 Agreements.

In the process of regeneration the state was able to play a more active role. Addressing the most serious concentrations of deprivation had been a continuing concern. Over the years a range of initiatives and funding programmes had been developed. In 1998, research by the government's Social Exclusion Unit identified 44 urban areas which suffered concentrations of deprivation. The *New Deal for Communities* policy selected 17 of these as pathfinder areas where funding would be focused on housing regeneration.[13] This programme was followed in 2001 by the *Housing Market Renewal Initiative*. Nine pathfinder partnerships were set up in inner city areas in the north of England. These were to carry out low key measures, such as crime reduction and selective renewal aimed at regenerating areas of low demand.[14]

WHERE TO BUILD

Targeting the areas in greatest need of regeneration was just a small part of the wider aim to make better use of urban resources by concentrating most development on 'brownfield' sites. The location, over several decades, of most new housing on rural sites had distracted attention from the many opportunities for development in the inner cities. Some of these opportunities have been all too evident. Housing campaigners had, in the past, repeatedly drawn attention to derelict land retained by large public utilities such as British Rail. This land had ceased to have operational use but had been 'hoarded' in case it might be needed in the future. In many parts of Britain there were large industrial buildings which had lost their economic purpose, and stood empty and decaying.

However, these high-profile unused sites are only the tip of an iceberg. In fact, there is a range of opportunities for urban housing development which can be divided into six categories:

1 *Large sites.* These generally result from changes in industrial organisation or market demands. There are some very large sites which might have been railway sidings; dockyards made redundant by changes in freight transport; or gas-processing plants superseded by natural gas. On a more modest scale there are sites made available by changes in demand such as redundant petrol-filling stations or cinemas.
2 *Small site.* Housing can be built almost anywhere. In most urban areas there is a plethora of small sites which might accommodate one or two houses, or a few flats. These might be: a gap in a mews or terrace, a redundant garage block or part of a large garden with road access.
3 *Redundant buildings.* The contraction of the urban manufacturing industry during the 1980s left many buildings empty and unused. In some areas market changes left blocks of offices surplus to requirements. A good proportion of these buildings can be successfully converted into housing.
4 *Unused built space.* In many town and city centres there is considerable unused space over shops and other commercial premises. Bringing this into use not only creates new housing but also intensifies occupation of urban centres and reduces the need for transport.

KINGS CROSS RAILWAY LANDS

▲ **1.6**   Kings Cross Railway Land. Part of the derelict land behind Kings Cross station

Behind Kings Cross Station in London is an enormous area of land previously used for sidings and marshalling yards (Figure 1.6). This operational use ceased more than 30 years ago and there followed a long saga of indecision about the future of the 50 hectares of land. In the meantime it has remained mostly derelict and unused. In the late 1980s the then owners, British Rail, working with a consortium of property developers, produced proposals for a lavish, high-density commercial development, 70 per cent of which would have been offices with token amounts of social housing and community facilities. A consortium of local groups prepared alternative plans with widespread public participation. The community plan proposed a much cheaper solution with the scale of development reduced by more than half, and the bulk of the site devoted to housing, light industry and safe open space.

The arguments raged for some time, with the community plans providing a well worked out focus for socially acceptable development. Meanwhile, economic recession killed off the commercial plan and several of the property companies with it. In the 1990s, government decided to use part of the land for a new terminal for the channel tunnel rail link. When this is complete much of the land will remain available for development. Its location, with excellent transport links to employment and recreation centres, makes it ideal for a significant amount of high-density urban housing. In 2004 developers completed a new plan for 27 hectares of the land. This included a good deal of commercial office space and retailing but it also provided public amenity space and services. Notably 1800 new homes are proposed – 50 per cent of them are 'affordable'. The project is due to commence in 2006 and take 15 years to complete.[15] If it proceeds, it will finally bring into use one of the most high-profile 'brownfield' sites in Britain. The squandering of its potential has created public controversy but it is not atypical of many derelict sites owned by public utilities.

5 *Vacant housing.* There are significant numbers of empty homes which could be brought back into use. There are also large numbers of houses which are under-used or multiple occupied which could be converted to self-contained dwellings.

6 *Unpopular housing.* There are many estates of social housing which are 'hard to let' or suffering serious social or management problems. These include areas of abandonment in parts of northern cities. But unpopular estates can be found in most cities. These present opportunities for redevelopment or adaptation.

While it was possible to identify a range of opportunities for urban housing development, what was not known was the extent of such opportunities. Would they be sufficient to accommodate a majority of new development? The Urban Task Force estimated that there was more than 20 000 hectares of derelict urban land 96 per cent of which would justify reclamation. There was also 16 000 hectares of vacant land which could be re-used without treatment. In addition, there were unused buildings – 4500 hectares of land was occupied by empty buildings. At the same time, a significant proportion of the housing stock was vacant.[16] This was enough to indicate the potential, but more information was needed. PPG3 made it a duty of local authorities to estimate the need for new housing in their areas and the capacity to provide it.

Housing capacity studies

No standard methodology was established for housing capacity studies but guidance was provided. This included a requirement that authorities should include 'windfall' sites in their estimates of the capacity for 'brownfield' development. These are sites that cannot be immediately identified, but which would be expected to become available in the light of past experience of the flow of new sites. While all authorities have carried out housing capacity studies, by far the largest exercise was that carried out for Greater London.

The results of the London study are shown in Table 1.1. Working with the London Boroughs, the study team identified sites available for housing development or conversion. These were divided into several categories which were similar to those set out above, except that, in considering large sites, no distinction was made between derelict land and redundant buildings. Special emphasis was placed on identifying redundant office sites. Small sites and conversions were defined as those accommodating up to 10 dwellings. Assessment of the potential for live/work units was included as a separate category and an assessment was made of the extent of large windfall sites. A calculation was then made of the number of homes which could be created using a density

Table 1.1   London housing capacity study breakdown housing potential of 'brownfield' sites and buildings in Greater London

	Proportion (%)	Housing units
Large identified sites – includes land for development or buildings for conversion	29	115 000
Large windfall sites – as above	30	115 000
Large office identified – sites or buildings available for housing development	4	15 000
Large office windfall – as above	7	26 000
Small sites – suitable for up to 10 new housing units	12	44 000
Small conversions – flats created by dividing large houses, change of use of small offices and retail floorspace	17	63 000
Live/work – assessment of potential sites	1	3 800
Total	100	381 800

matrix. This applied a range of different densities to the identified sites according to their accessibility to public transport and whether they were located in 'central', 'urban' or 'suburban' locations. Finally, an estimate was made of the capacity of windfall sites. The results of these calculations are given in Table 1.1. The calculations were set against London's estimated housing need over a 25-year period. This showed that 97 per cent of the new housing required could be met by building on 'brownfield' sites.[17]

Housing capacity studies by other local authorities are, inevitably, far less complex and they are not publicly available. However, a survey of the whole of England was carried out by the National Land Use Database. This showed that there were 65 500 hectares of derelict land and buildings, 43 per cent of which would be suitable for housing. An estimate was made of the housing capacity of the available land. Even at the minimum density of 30 dwellings per hectare the land could accommodate almost 900 000 new homes and, clearly, densities could be higher in many places. The land was fairly evenly spread between regions and more than 40 per cent of available land was in the regions with highest demand – the east, south-east and London.[18] All the indications are then, that there are more than enough 'brownfield' sites and buildings available to meet the government's targets.

A continuing supply

Given the evident supply of previously developed land within cities it seems surprising that so much new housing in the past was built in agricultural land. This was due:

- partly to the costs of reclaiming urban land: extensive demolitions or decontamination might be involved, ground conditions were uncertain causing higher foundation costs, access for plant and materials might be more difficult;
- partly to availability: there was extensive land hoarding by nationalised industries and local authorities where land banks could be set up for future contingencies without financial penalty; at the same time, large land holdings were often without adequate access or the infrastructure necessary for development.

Much has now changed. The obligations on local authority to identify housing sites, and manage their release should ensure an adequate supply, particularly when they no longer need development land for their own purposes. The direct intervention of government agencies such as English Partnerships in reclaiming urban land also helps this process. Importantly, too, the housing market has changed. Many inner cities now offer desirable locations. New developments are now more profitable, particularly if they are built at high density. Higher profits easily offset the greater costs involved.

While a supply of 'brownfield' sites has been identified for a considerable period ahead there is no guarantee that it will continue indefinitely. However, economic change seems to be an accelerating process. With the cycle of change particular land uses frequently become redundant. In the National Land Use Database survey almost 25 per cent of derelict sites were 'new' and had not been identified in a similar study 4 years earlier. The experience of the past availability of 'windfall' sites suggests that this is a process which will continue in the future. The supply of urban land for development seems assured, particularly if it is used more efficiently than in the past.

KEY POINTS

- ⚷ There is a recognised need to reduce carbon dioxide emissions to limit climate changes caused by global warming. In Britain, housing accounts for 27 per cent of carbon dioxide emissions; transport for 26 per cent. Significant reductions are needed in both sectors.

- In the long term there is a need to reach an equilibrium where energy consumption is in balance with the capacity of the environment. This requires a dramatic reduction of the 'ecological footprint' of the developed world and sustainable development everywhere else.
- Increased demand for housing means that 3.8 million new homes are need in Britain in the first quarter of twenty-first century. Eighty per cent of new households will be single people, many of them young, but with a growing proportion of the elderly.
- Housing demand varies considerably between different areas of Britain. Low demand in the north needs to be countered by regeneration. High demand in the south needs to be tempered by more 'affordable' housing, particularly for key workers.
- To reduce land take, concentrate people in existing cities, and assist their regeneration, a new policy target requires at least 60 per cent of new housing development to be built on previously developed ('brownfield') land.
- To meet both environmental concerns and increased demand, new housing needs to be higher density with its residents less reliant on cars. New communities should be mixed in terms of household size, age groups and social structure, and they should be provided with a high-quality environment.
- Disused industrial sites and buildings provide many opportunities for redevelopment. There are numerous small sites and empty buildings which can be brought into housing use. Studies show there are enough 'brownfield' sites to meet or exceed the 60 per cent target.

2

STANDARDS

DIVIDING THE SPACE

SUMMARY

Environmental and social problems caused by overcrowding in the industrial cities generated reform leading to new standards in housing space and layout. These new standards emerged from a series of official reports and resulted in high internal space standards and increased levels of self-containment. These were, however, designed for individual houses rather than flats. Design standards for multi-storey housing now needed re-assessment. At the same time, there was a concern to drive down densities which resulted in the housing sprawl of the last 80 years. A new emphasis on higher densities needs a better understanding of the implications. The measurement of density causes considerable confusion. Both the units of measurement and the land areas to which they apply vary considerably and need clarification. A number of factors can affect density: levels of occupancy are important, as is child density; intensity of use can have an impact in determining the success of housing schemes. Alongside confusion about the measurement of density there is also misunderstanding of the form which high-density housing takes. Commonly it is associated with tower blocks. This is largely a misconception — many familiar forms of housing can be built at relatively high densities. Finally, high densities have important benefits in generating a wider range of services and facilities, and improving access to them.

THE DRIVE TO RAISE STANDARDS

The concerns about housing and health which arose during the nineteenth century were critical in bringing about the regulation of house construction and planning. But the general aversion to life in the industrial cities was to prove instrumental in shaping urban development for much of the last 100 years. Better construction might have solved the problems caused by dampness and poor ventilation but better building alone did not address the issue of overcrowding. People had flocked to work in the new factories spawned by the industrial revolution at a rate which made it impossible to provide places for them to live in. Existing housing quickly became heavily overpopulated. As new housing was built this, too, rapidly became overcrowded.

This new housing took various forms. In the new industrial cities, which grew rapidly in the Midlands and the North, it was poorly built 'back-to-back' houses. These would be two- or three-storeys high with a single-small room on each floor. Sometimes there would be a cellar room separately entered and occupied. The houses were huddled close together in courts – cramped inside and outside with several families sharing a common toilet. In Scotland it was the tenements. Built as self-contained flats they were let and sub-let, each 'made down' to provide lodgings for several families. In London and some other cities, speculators built generous houses designed for prosperous families with servants. Many of these were never sold but were let in multiple occupation. In each house several families occupied the living space and shared communal facilities.

The masses of people packed together stigmatised the Victorian cities and created housing stress which, in many areas, was to persist well into the second half of the twentieth century. Such conditions were a major stimulus for reform, which then drove up standards on two-related fronts. One was the effort to improve conditions within dwellings by increasing living space and more self-containment to reduce the need to share facilities. The other was to reduce overcrowding by lowering population densities.

Official reports on housing standards

A key concern over conditions in the industrial cities was the low standards endured by many urban dwellers. Whole families would commonly occupy a single room and share inadequate cooking and toilet facilities with many others. Even in the early philanthropic housing, where standards and management were generally good, kitchens and bathrooms were commonly shared. The main focus – and achievement – of housing reform in the twentieth century was to move from this situation to one in which almost every household has a self-contained dwelling designed to good space standards.

The mechanism for progress was a series of influential reports on housing standards. The Tudor Walters Report of 1918[1] was the first official intervention to improve new housing. Generous space standards for new houses were set. Separate living rooms and kitchens were recommended, together with a bath and an integrated toilet for each house. Layout was

Table 2.1   1944 Housing Manual. Minimum room areas

	Minimum room area (square metres)
The kitchen-living room house	
Kitchen-living room	16.7
Sitting room	10.2
Scullery	4.7
The working kitchen house	
Living room separate dining space	16.7
Living room plus dining space	21.0
Working kitchen	8.4
The dining-kitchen house	
Living room	14.9
Dining kitchen	10.2
Bedrooms	
First bedroom	12.5
Other double bedrooms	10.2
Single bedroom	6.5

to be open and spacious allowing the penetration of sunlight and fresh air.[2] These recommendations were for new social housing but they set the pattern for all new housing for the next 20 years.

The Tudor Walters Report established the goal of a generous self-contained house for each family. This was followed by the Dudley Report of 1944 which spawned new Housing Manuals of 1944 and 1949 to give guidance on housing design.[3] The report identified three types of homes which varied according to the use made of the kitchen. In the first, the kitchen was also used as the living room with a separate sitting room – an arrangement which was common at that time. The other two types were homes with a separate dining room or with a dining kitchen. Standards were set for the sizes of rooms in each type of dwelling (see Table 2.1). Though the breakdown of space is out of kilter with modern living patterns, these standards are still a useful guide to appropriate room sizes.

The third, and last, of the official housing studies was the Parker Morris Report of 1961.[4] This addressed changes in living patterns, particularly new expectations in the standard of heating, the greater use of electrical appliances and higher car ownership. In contrast to the earlier reports, it recognised that housing needed to accommodate a variety of living patterns. Rather than set room sizes, Parker Morris established standards

Table 2.2 Parker Morris Report 1961. Minimum dwelling areas

	Minimum dwelling size (square metres)	
	Flats and single-storey houses	**Two-storey houses and maisonettes**
1 person	30.0	
2 person	44.5	
3 person	57.0	
4 person	67.0	72.0
5 person	75.5	82.0
6 person	84.0	92.5
7 person		108.0

In addition, all types are entitled to storage space of 3.0–6.5 square metres.

for the overall size of dwellings for different households. This allowed greater flexibility and choice in the planning of new homes (Table 2.2). These standards were subsequently made mandatory for all new social housing. The report was accompanied by a design bulletin – *Space in the Homes*.[5] This took a terraced town house with integral garage as a model home. Taking each room in turn it established notional patterns for furniture and circulation space. The clear guidance it gave to good internal planning made *Space in the Home* the housing designers' bible. This first bulletin was later supplemented by detailed guides for the layout of kitchens and bathrooms.[6]

Standards for flats

In the main, the official reports were primarily concerned with setting standards for houses rather than multi-storey dwellings. They generally recommended that space and equipment standards in flats should be the same as in houses of an equivalent size. The 1949 Housing Manual does, however, consider flats at some length. Model layouts were given and the planning of blocks discussed, including such issues are access systems, means of escape, refuse provision and sound insulation. The following recommendations were made:

- Lifts are necessary in all blocks of flats or maisonettes where the entrance to the top dwelling is three or more storeys above the ground floor level.
- Each flat should have a deep balcony on the sunny side at least partly recessed and accessible from the living room or kitchen.
- Communal gardens should be provided and made accessible to tenants of upper floor flats and maisonettes.[7]

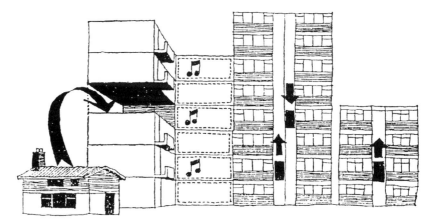

▲ **2.1**   The Parker Morris Report regarded flats as stacked-up houses

While they were not always followed, these recommendations set high standards for the design of flats in the 1950s.

However, the Parker Morris Report was a step backward. Flats were barely mentioned. The planning of blocks and the provision of outdoor space was not discussed. As the illustration shows the report effectively regarded flats as stacked-up houses (Figure 2.1). The new space standards, together with a requirement for a minimum of one car space per dwelling, became mandatory for houses and flats alike. This had some severe consequences for multi-storey flats. The high standards of space and facilities for flat interiors were rigidly enforced, which meant that economies were increasingly sought elsewhere. Communal facilities, essential to good-quality multi-storey housing, were often omitted. The design and quality of the access systems became poorer, with lifts, stairs and walkways being made to serve more and more flats. The lack of control of these public spaces and the large numbers of people using them led to abuse and degradation, which did more than anything to stigmatise multi-storey housing. The mandatory imposition of 100 per cent car parking in inner city areas also had unfortunate consequences. Public transport was good in these areas and car ownership low. The result was the extensive construction of underground and multi-storey car parks which were largely redundant from the start.[8]

In the past, there has been insufficient recognition that flats are not simply stacked-up houses. However, living off the ground has certain advantages and can be successful. If appropriate lessons can be learned from the mistakes of the past and re-applied, more careful consideration of the design of multi-storey blocks can ensure that success.

The decline of standards

Parker Morris standards were a high point in housing quality; at least as far as internal standards were concerned. But they only ever applied to social housing. Space standards of many private developments were often lower. In 1988 the mandatory application of Parker Morris standards to new social housing was abandoned. Under a more stringent funding regime housing associations were often obliged to adopt lower standards for their new developments. A reduction in standards may seem regrettable, and it may impact badly on some households, particularly large families. On its own, though, a modest reduction in space standards may not be of critical importance. The greater problem, perhaps, was the sharing of kitchens and bathrooms and it may be more important to maintain the principle of separate and self-contained dwellings.

A review of standards may well be due in the context of changing lifestyles. Now that there is increased demand for single-person dwellings, new forms are emerging, such as foyers and rented blocks for young singles. So is the concept of the 'micro-flat'. This is a new type of single-room dwelling designed as a starter home for single people. Taking full advantage of the miniaturisation of furniture and equipment, its single space can quickly be adapted for living, eating or sleeping and even provides a small balcony. At 29 square metres it is only slightly below the Parker Morris dimensions but its efficient organisation may make it a useful innovation.[9]

Space standards were particularly influential in eliminating the overcrowding of shared houses of the past. The actual size of self-contained dwellings, though, has limited impact on the quality of housing developments. What can have more influence is the level of ancillary facilities. On the negative side, car parking provision, if set too high, can use up large amounts of ground area or built space. More positively, good standards of outdoor space, both public and private, and high levels of community facilities can greatly improve the quality of urban housing.

CHANGING ATTITUDES TO HOUSING DENSITY

Alongside space standards housing reformers of the twentieth century considered density to be a critical factor. There was a conscious drive to reduce the density of new development as a counterweight to the crowded conditions in the old cities. In the Tudor Walters Report[1] a *maximum* density of 12 houses per acre (30 per hectare) was laid down for building in towns. In the 1940s a series of plans was produced for the development of large cities. These tackled the problem of overcrowding by moving people out into new overspill development and setting density standards for new housing. Patrick Abercrombie's plans for London and Glasgow were particularly influential. These set up New Towns to take people from the inner cities, and a hierarchy of maximum densities for new development. In London these were 200 people per acre at the centre (450 people per hectare); 136 people per acre in the inner areas (340 per hectare); descending through 100 people per acre (250 per hectare) and 75 people per acre (188 per hectare) to 50 people per acre (125 per hectare) at the periphery. This last was the maximum density in suburban areas and is even lower, at about 10 houses per acre (25 houses per hectare) than that set by Tudor Walters.

The aim of these measures was to drive down densities. New development in outer urban areas would be at relatively low densities. The overcrowded and discredited courts, terraces and tenements in the inner cities were redeveloped. But the stigma was not removed. Much of the old housing was replaced by new housing estates built by local authorities. These were built at lower densities than the housing they replaced but they quickly developed social and management problems. The opprobrium which had attached to old high-density urban housing was quickly transferred to the towers and slabs of the new estates. As a result, planning authorities have continued to seek solutions in lower densities, even in urban areas, and set maximum limits on the density of new development. If we are now to move to an era of increasing urban population a better understanding is needed of the implications of housing density.

Defining density

As may already be apparent, one of the key confusions is the way in which housing density is measured. Essentially, density is a measure of the number of people living on a given land area. This may be a large or small area. It can be an entire country, a region, a town or a major part of a city. When applied to an urban area the population is divided by the land area, measured over all land uses, to calculate what is called *Development density* (also known as 'town' or 'district' density). These large-scale measures are used in international or regional comparisons and are factors in determining the distribution of industry or the location of major developments such as airports, shopping centres or sports stadia. At the smaller scale, density may measure the population of a neighbourhood or an individual estate or development. At this level the measurement of housing density becomes important and this determines the demand for services essential to the residential environment.

There are two common measures of housing density – *gross residential density* measures the population of any area which consists predominantly of housing; and *net residential density* measures the population of a site exclusively devoted to housing. A government publication produced in parallel with Planning Policy Guidance Note No. 3 (PPG3) helps to define the difference between these two measures:[10]

1 **Net residential density** includes, as well as the area occupied by the housing itself, any services and facilities for its immediate benefit – private gardens, communal gardens, children's play area and incidental open space. It includes parking spaces, access roads within the site and half the width of surrounding roads. Small-scale facilities such as a few local shops or a community centre may also be included.

2 **Gross residential density** (or neighbourhood density) includes, in addition to the above, open spaces serving a wider area and other landscaped areas: primary schools; local health centres; distributor road and transport networks; and small-scale employment, services and mixed use. It does not normally include large industrial and commercial areas or major roads and transport interchanges.

Net residential density is the key measure used in calculating the housing capacity of a development site and in planning the housing that will be built on it. Gross residential density can become important. In a mixed-use area the gross density may be much lower than the net residential density. This could threaten the viability of a good public transport system or other key communal services such as schools and health centres. Defining the area over which housing density is to be measured is relatively straightforward when considering an individual site. For wider areas there may be considerable variation as to what is included, making cross comparisons difficult. These difficulties are made more complex by the range of different units used in measuring density.

For density measurement the land area is measured on a level plane with no account made of sloping or hilly land. What complicates the measurement is the units used. The traditional unit of land measurement in Britain was the acre and this is still used in some countries. With metrication, the hectare is now the standard unit of measurement which brings Britain into line with Europe. Densities measured in acres must now be translated. Accurate translation at 2.47 acres per hectare can produce some very unwieldy figures so, commonly, an approximate equivalent of 2.5 acres per Hectare is used. The need for translation complicates comparison between old and new density standards and between countries using different units. However, this complication is insignificant when compared with complications in the measurement of people.

While the aim of density measurement is to find the numbers of people living in an area, there are no less than four different measures in use, none of which directly totals the numbers of people. These are:

1 *Dwellings per hectare/acre.* This simply measures the number of houses or flats. It has been the main measure since density standards began. However, dwelling sizes can vary considerably and this is a poor guide to the number of people, particularly in high-density housing.
2 *Bedspaces per hectare/acre.* This is simply measured by totalling single and double bedrooms which can usually be readily identified on design drawings. It was the common measure of density in the 1960s and 1970s. Measuring bedspaces is an accurate guide to the number of people any particular development can house.
3 *Habitable rooms per hectare/acre.* This totals habitable rooms in each dwelling which includes living rooms and bedrooms. It does not include kitchens but does include dining-kitchens and is thus open to misinterpretation. This measure was used in the post-war period and has recently been re-introduced. It is supposed to approximate to people but is, in fact, a fairly inaccurate measure.
4 *Housing floorspace per hectare/acre.* This is a relatively straight-forward and unambiguous measure. It is used in parts of continental Europe but not normally in Britain. It would not be helpful in measuring numbers of people.

It is regrettable that the most useful of these measures – bedspaces – seems to have fallen into disuse. Most publications now give densities in dwelling units and habitable rooms. It is useful to compare these three. Dwellings are a useful measure when considering individual houses. A typical house has five bedspaces and five habitable rooms which makes comparisons simple. However, it is less useful when applied to mixed schemes where dwelling sizes may vary considerably. To cover this diffi-culty it is common to apply a ratio of four bedspaces per dwelling. Even this approximation may be misleading when dealing with high-density hous-ing. A study for the London Housing Federation looked at eight high-density social housing schemes. The number of bedspaces per dwelling in the schemes ranged from just under two to just over 3.5. In the same study the number of bedspaces per habitable room ranged from 0.85 to 1.3.[11] These figures are considerably at odds with the approximations of four bedspaces per dwelling and one bedspace per habitable room.

It is these variations from one type of housing to another which make the measurement of housing density hazardous. Dwelling units per hectare is a useful yardstick, but in applying it to high-density housing it must be supplemented by other measures – most usefully by a count of bedspaces. Knowing the potential population of a housing development is a valuable measure of density. However, the actual number of people living in an area will vary considerably depending in the way housing is designed and used.

Occupancy and use

The levels of occupancy and intensity of use can have a significant impact both on the quality of life in urban housing and the density of population. Density calculations in bedspaces per hectare are a measure of the housing 'capacity' of a given area. But once the housing is built it may be occupied to a higher or lower level. It is commonly assumed that most housing is under-occupied and that most households have one or more spare bedrooms. In translating housing capacity into population an assumption needs to be made about occupancy levels which some studies have taken to be as low as 60 per cent.[12] Generally, the levels of occupancy tend to be higher in new communities. Social housing is usually let, initially, at levels equal to housing capacity. In the private sector, too, financial constraints tend to ensure that newly acquired housing is likely to be fully occupied. As communities mature household structures change and finances ease. The spare bedroom becomes more common.

Levels of occupancy in social housing, however, tend to be higher, particularly in areas of high demand. Housing that is fully used when first let becomes over-occupied as families grow, and the shortage of alternative accommodation makes it difficult to match households to housing capacity. For instance, the levels of overcrowding in local authority housing are high in some parts of London; this is indicated by the large numbers of households on transfer lists, most of whom want larger accommodation. Conversely, overcrowding seems less problematic in housing association stock. Figures for lettings in inner London showed that only 2.3 per cent were overcrowded. While 83.4 per cent matched housing capacity, 14 per cent had spare space.[13]

Levels of occupancy can affect both the quality of life and the provision of services and facilities in an area. Levels of occupation which are too high can cause family strife which can spill out into the public realm. A degree of spare space in each home is a useful safeguard against housing stress and the problems it often causes for urban management. On the other hand, significant under-occupation can cause the population density of an area to fall to a level where some communal services become unsustainable.

The level of child density is now recognised as a key issue in how the intensity of occupation and use can affect the quality of life in a housing development. The association between concentrations of children aged 6–16, and high levels of vandalism was first identified in a seminal study of the 1970s.[14] Since then there have been widespread incidences of gang culture developing on estates with large numbers of teenagers. At the same time statistics show that a high proportion of petty crime is committed by a small proportion of young men. While not all this is necessarily the result of high child densities, there is evidence that this does lead to a pattern of escalating antisocial behaviour.

The *Capital Gains* study of inner London housing estates found that the most successful high-density schemes had low child densities. The report recommended that the proportion of children (aged 0–18) should not rise above the range 35–45 per cent of total population and that '…preferably ratios should not rise beyond 25 per cent'.[15] While it is important to keep numbers of children relatively low it is also important to make sure they are well provided for. Good provision of open spaces, play areas and community buildings for organised activities, are necessary for the well-being of children. But they also help to channel energies and counter misbehaviour.

One final factor affecting housing density is the amount of use people make of their homes. In an area populated largely by professional households without children most people will be out at work all day. They may well be out during the evenings and away at weekends. The area will not feel heavily populated and will not be intensively used. On the other hand, in an area which houses large numbers of children and/or high numbers of people who are not employed, more people will spend a lot of time at home and there will be much more daytime activity. Figures from the National Housing Federation show that in housing association estates almost 65 per cent of households were headed by someone not employed.[16] The same is true of areas where significant numbers of people are employed or working at home. It can be argued that a true measure of housing density should include the numbers of people employed in the area.

A greater intensity of use has both positive and negative aspects. It generates higher use of local shops and communal services such as libraries and sports centres. This, on its own, involves significant levels of social interaction. On the other hand, it puts higher demands on the environment. Common areas will be more heavily used and suffer more wear and tear. Public spaces will be more subject to damage, both accidental and deliberate. There will be more dropped litter and more noise. All these things put higher demands on the management of housing and the urban environment. Therefore, in assessing the quality of a residential area measuring the housing density is only a starting point. The levels of occupancy and activity are important as is the intensity with which the area is used.

DENSITY AND HOUSING FORM

A key area of confusion is the common association of 'high density' with 'high rise'. This is partly an elementary word association. But it is also due to the continuing poor reputation of the multi-storey estates built in Britain's inner cites in the 1960s and 1970s. Many of these comprised high-rise tower and slab blocks. Many of the later ones were not so high but composed of warrens of blocks linked by labyrinthine access systems. The social problems evident on many estates, coupled with their run down and abused common areas and the poor surrounding environment, made these forms of high-rise housing understandably repellent. It is a mistake, though to confuse them with high density.

Many of the multi-storey estates were built at relatively low densities. Most of the multi-storey estates in inner London were built at the standard zoned density of 136 people per acre (340 per hectare). The tower blocks in Glasgow, which are numerous, were built at a density of 100 people per acre (250 per hectare). Such densities were the same or lower than the Georgian terraces of London or the prosperous middle-class tenements of Glasgow. The difference lies in the way these different building forms related to the space they were built upon.

Basic forms of urban development

In 1972 Leslie Martin and Lionel March published a cogent analysis of the key forms of urban development. They postulated that on any given site development can take three basic forms which they called 'pavilion', 'street' and 'patio'.[17] These forms cover different proportions of the ground area. If developed with buildings of the same height and depth the pavilion form would provide the lowest density and the patio form the highest. On the other hand, constructing a given amount of floorspace would need buildings of different height depending on which form they took. Figure 2.2 illustrates this principle. It shows that the same amount of floorspace could be built on the same site as a fifteen-storey tower block, five-storey linear blocks or a three-storey perimeter block.

These basic forms correspond to traditional types of housing. The pavilion corresponds to the detached house set in generous grounds; the linear form to the traditional street; while the perimeter block takes the form of urban blocks in continental cities and in Scotland; these higher-density

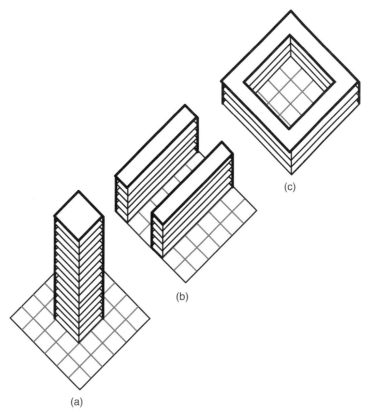

(c)

(b)

(a)

▲ **2.2** Basic forms of urban development. The same amount of floor-space built as 'pavilion', 'street' and 'patio' forms

traditional forms were objectionable to reformers because of the high proportion of land they covered. In Britain, the Garden City pioneers regarded terraced housing as cramped and dark. They preferred small blocks of houses more generously spaced – a version of the pavilion type of development.

The Modern Movement similarly objected to the layout of the continental urban blocks with their deep plans and dark internal courts. They consciously sought housing types which would provide more light and air and which would release more of the ground as open space. Le Corbusier worked up several ideas for cities composed of huge tower blocks set in parkland, including *La Ville Radieuse* and a plan for the redevelopment of a large area of central Paris (Figure 2.3). Walter Gropies investigated linear blocks (Figure 2.4). He calculated that eight-storey slab blocks provided optimum conditions of fresh air, sun, views and distance from neighbours. These blocks would best be orientated east/west in parallel rows – a formation known zielenbau.

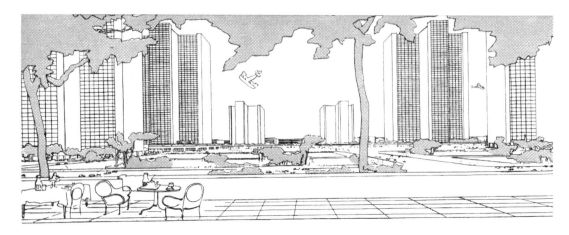

▲ **2.3**   La Ville Contemporaine – Le Corbusier's vision for a city of towers

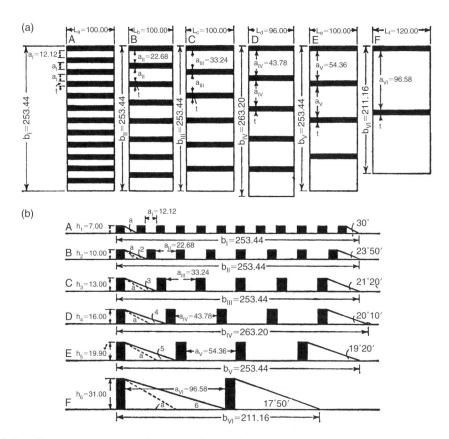

▲ **2.4**   Walter Gropius' analysis of slab block layout to maximise sunlight and daylight

These concepts were highly influential and formed the basis for the design of many of the multi-storey housing estates built in the latter part of the twentieth century. Estate composed of tower and slab blocks did free up more open space, though most of it was ineffectively used. The tall buildings did not provide successful housing particularly for families with children. The plethora of problems associated with them gave high rise a bad reputation. But they were, essentially, a large-scale re-interpretation of the 'pavilion' form. The twentieth century search for openness, light and air ended; on the one hand in the suburban house and on the other in the tower block estate. The search for successful urban housing must look to the basic forms which are inherently high density.

Higher densities with modest forms

Most multi-storey estates were built at a density of 340 persons per hectare or less and yet they did not succeed in providing satisfactory forms of housing. Harley Sherlock, an architect with long experience of urban housing design, turned to the traditional street for comparison:

> ...let us look at the Victorian street pattern typical of inner London. We find that it is made up of houses three storeys in height, with two-storey back additions and back gardens on plots about 25 metres deep and 5 metres wide. Goodness knows how many people such buildings might have housed in the past, in overcrowded and unsanitary conditions but, rehabilitated, each building could comfortably accommodate a four-person dwelling on the lower two floors (using the basement entrance) and a two-person dwelling on the top floor (using the original front door). The existing back addition would provide a kitchen and bathroom for each dwelling and the road could be adapted on a pedestrian priority basis to provide one car parking space for every two dwellings.[18]

Sherlock calculated the density of such housing which works out at 385 bedspaces per hectare (129 dwellings per hectare). So the modest three-storey Victorian terraced house is capable of providing densities which are substantially above those of multi-storey estates and more than twice as high as the new density recommendations of PPG3. Many such houses in the inner cities have been modernised and converted in this manner and now provide successful and valued homes both for tenants and owner-occupiers.

Based on his studies of older terraces, Harley Sherlock devised a notional form for new housing. This is shown in Figure 2.5. It is based on four-storey buildings spaced slightly further apart than the three-storey terraces described above. This allows more open space and wider streets

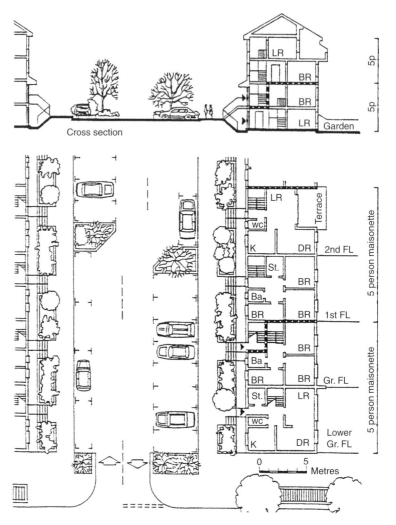

▲ **2.5**   Harley Sherlock's model for high-density housing at modest scale

which can provide one parking space per dwelling. The model provides
two family maisonettes, each entered separately. The lower maisonette
has a private garden and the upper one a generous terrace. It could
equally well be planned as a maisonette topped by two flats which might
better suit the pattern of demand expected in the future. The density of
such housing would be approximately 400 bedspaces per hectare – equivalent to 90–135 dwellings per hectare depending on the size mix. At this
level it would exceed the maximum density standards in force until recently,
and would not have previously been permitted. In the changing climate it
provides a model for the future based on proven success.

A range of options

A major study was carried out by consultants Llewelyn Davies on types of housing suitable for redevelopment sites in London.[19] This gives a good indication of the densities which different forms of housing can achieve. The housing forms fell into three basic types:

1 **Detached and semi-detached houses.** These are the predominant types of housing in most developments of the recent past. The densities of this form of housing generally fell in the range 10–20 dwellings per hectare though tightly planned semi-detached houses could reach 30 per hectare – the threshold of PPG3 standards.
2 **Terraced houses.** These are capable of significantly higher densities, Even generous terraced houses with a wide frontage of 8 metres and large gardens could achieve a density of 44 dwellings per hectare. More commonly, terraced houses have a frontage of about 5 metres. Even with integral car parking, two-storey terraced housing of this type can achieve densities of well over 50 units per hectare (see Figure 2.6).
3 **Flats.** Flats can be built at much higher densities. Modest blocks of four-storey flats set in their own grounds can be built at 67 units per hectare. Four-storey flats in perimeter block form, with on-street

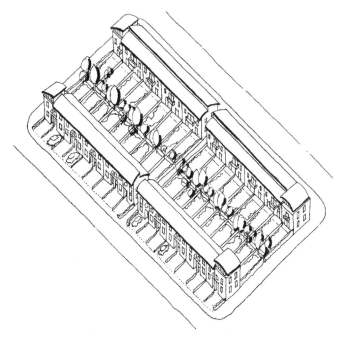

▲ **2.6**   Two-storey terraced houses at a density of 53 units per hectare

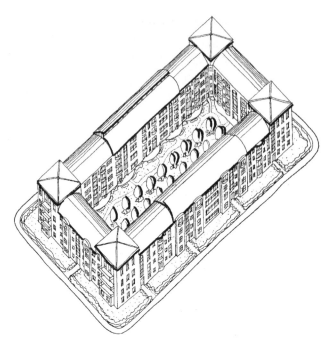

▲ **2.7**   Four-storey flats in perimeter block layout at a density of 155 units per hectare

car parking, can achieve densities of 155 dwellings per hectare (see Figure 2.7). Flats in this form can be built up to eight or nine storeys and at very high densities of over 400 units per hectare.

The study looked at a range of urban and suburban locations with variable access to public transport. It suggested suitable densities for each starting with 30–50 units per hectare for the more remote sites. This could be achieved with a mix of house types with some small blocks of flats. Urban sites with good public transport could be developed at densities from 50 to over 200 units per hectare. This would mean a mixture of terraced houses and flats – the housing forms which characterise many inner city areas. Sites in central areas, on waterfronts or surrounding open spaces were considered suitable for large blocks of flats at densities from 240 to 435 units per hectare (refer to Case Studies A and B for examples of high-density social housing, and high-density commercial housing).

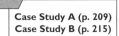

Case Study A (p. 209)
Case Study B (p. 215)

THE ADVANTAGES OF HIGH DENSITY

The key concern which lay behind the setting up of the Urban Task Force and subsequent policy changes was the large amount of land which would be taken by the new housing required to meet greatly increased household formation. Reducing land take became the main motivation for seeking higher densities and this is an objective which is relatively easy to achieve. As land take diminishes progressively as densities rise, the greatest savings can be achieved with relatively modest increases. It has been estimated that an increase in density from 24 to 40 dwellings per hectare saves ten times as much land as an increase from 160 to 220.[20] While the land saving threshold can be crossed with relatively modest increases in density, there are advantages to be gained by building to considerably higher densities. Many of these are central to the other key policy objective – reducing carbon dioxide emissions.

The advantages of high-densities fall broadly into three areas:

1 *Economic.* Essentially, high-density areas are easier to service. The cost of providing infrastructure services such as gas, electricity, water and sewage disposal progressively reduces as more and more homes can be served by each kilometre of pipeline. The same applies to the distribution of food and other goods. These can more easily be distributed to large concentrations of population. Perhaps the most significant economic benefit is the more efficient transport systems which can be developed in high-density areas.

2 *Environmental.* Greater economic efficiencies have environmental benefits. More efficient transport and distribution uses less energy. High-density housing is inherently more energy efficient. In terraced houses and multi-storey blocks dwellings are joined together and provide mutual insulation which means that less energy is used in heating. This reduction in energy consumption causes less pollution. This not only means lower carbon dioxide emissions, it also produces improved air quality.

3 *Social.* Larger concentrations of people create greater demand for communal facilities. A larger number of customers makes more services viable and means that a more diverse range of minority requirements can be met. High-density areas often have a wide range of shops serving both general and specialised needs and a good choice of leisure facilities from cinemas and restaurants to sports clubs and swimming pools. They also have large numbers of social and community organisations through which people can become involved in child centred activities, services for the elderly, or political and environmental campaigns.

Of course there are disadvantages, too, not least the higher cost of urban management necessary to make high-density urban areas function well. But this is a price which must be paid to gain the considerable economic and environmental advantages. The greatest of these is, perhaps, the possibility of more efficient transport systems.

More efficient transport

People living in high-density urban areas travel less that those in smaller settlements – estimated at between 30 per cent and 50 per cent fewer miles each week. This is important in the context of an overall increase in travel of 33 per cent between the 1970s and the 1990s and the need to reduce greenhouse gas emissions.[21] Equally important is that high densities make more efficient transport possible. People in low-density areas are highly dependent on the motor car for transport. Hardly anything is within walking distance and bus services are few and far between. As densities increase more effective public transport becomes viable.

The Local Government Management Board estimates that a density of 100 people per hectare is necessary to support a viable bus service – that is one which is frequent, reliable and low cost. This is a gross figure and would translate into a net density of 200–330 people per hectare or 50–100 dwellings per hectare depending on size and occupancy. This is at the margin of the higher densities recommended by PPG3. Even higher densities would be needed to support a tram system – 240 people per hectare gross, 480–550 net or 120–250 dwellings per hectare.[22] The existence of good public transport means greater efficiently in fuel use and significant reductions in the use of cars. But the transport advantages of higher densities do not end there.

It is estimated that people will walk up to one and a quarter miles reasonably happily, although half a mile – a 10 minute walk – is a more comfortable distance.[23] In high-density areas many more preferred destinations are within reasonable walking distance. Cycling also becomes more viable. Many people will happily cycle a distance of 3–5 miles and this puts a great many more destinations within reach. Travelling smaller distances does not, then, mean visiting fewer people or places – and many more of these journeys can be completed with little or no consumption of fossil fuels.

A cultural divide

The move to higher housing densities is necessary to both reduce land take and preserve more of the open countryside, and to meet international agreements on the reduction of harmful gas emissions. Higher densities do have clear advantages in meeting these objectives and they also generate economic savings and efficiencies. But between one form of living and the other there is a clear cultural divide.

Someone living in a low-density development typical of most built during the past 40 years will probably live in a detached or semi-detached house with a reasonably large garden. They will probably work a long way away, often 30 miles or more. This will entail a long drive on increasingly congested roads, or a long-time standing in a crowded train. Evening and weekend leisure and shopping trips will also involve driving, though not so far, and there is the compensation that countryside walks and amenities are within relatively easy travel distance.

The urban dweller will live in a terraced house or a flat. He or she may have a small garden or a balcony but will probably have a small park within a short walk and a substantial one a little further away. The workplace will probably be reasonably close, usually less than 4 or 5 miles away. The journey will involve a walk or cycle ride or walking to a bus stop or train station. The train may well be crowded, but the journey will be mercifully short. At evenings and weekends there is a good choice of shops and other facilities within a short walk, and restaurants, clubs and theatres a short ride away. If high-density development is to succeed more people will have to choose this side of the divide.

KEY POINTS

- The development of improved housing standards through a series of official reports during the twentieth century resulted in most people being housed in self-contained accommodation with high standards of space and facilities.
- The misapplication of standards designed for houses to multi-storey flats was the root of many of the problems which led to deterioration and stigmatisation of multi-storey estates. Standards for flats need to be reviewed in the light of new demand from small households.
- For much of the twentieth century it was an aim of public policy to reduce housing densities. Now that aim has been reversed. The measurement of density is complicated and has been much misunderstood. Clearer definitions and a common method of measurement are needed.
- Density calculations can establish the notional housing capacity of a site. The impact of new development will also be affected by levels of occupancy and the intensity with which it is used, including the number of people employed. Child density can also be a significant factor.
- 'High density' is not the same as 'high rise'. Multi-storey housing forms were developed by the Modern Movement primarily to improve

standards of light, air and communal open space. As built they are often lower density than traditional urban streets.

- Housing of similar densities can be built in different forms. Individual houses with gardens can be built to quite high densities, while the highest desirable densities can be achieved with flats of relatively modest scale in 'perimeter block' form.

- High-density residential areas have clear advantages. They are more economic to service; they have a lower impact on the environment; and they provide a wide choice of facilities within easy reach. Above all they make transport systems of high energy efficiency possible.

3

INFRASTRUCTURE

THE URBAN NEIGHBOURHOOD

SUMMARY

It is widely recognised that housing is not just an aggregation of homes. It must include all the services and facilities necessary for domestic life and good access to the wider community. Successful housing must be integrated with its essential infrastructure and in cities this relationship forms a clear pattern. The idea of neighbourhoods has an extensive history and has long been recognised as a basic concept in planning new urban developments. Existing cities, too, commonly have distinctive social and physical subdivisions. At the end of the twentieth century this established pattern gave rise to the concept of the 'urban village'. This provided a model for development and regeneration based on the successful urban neighbourhoods of the past. Government policy progressed the idea further with the establishment of major new settlements – the 'millennium villages'. With the new recognition of the impact of climate change, there is growing realisation of the need to integrate housing with workplaces and support services to make sustainable urban neighbourhoods which would aim to be neutral in their environmental impact. At the same time, most new developments will be in existing built-up areas. New housing needs to be integrated into the older urban fabric in a manner which makes it more suited to the needs of its residents and less wasteful in the consumption of resources.

COMMUNITY FACILITIES

It is an essential concomitant of any housing development that its residents have easy access to a range of community facilities. These include open spaces and meeting places, education and health services, and shops providing goods and services. In many of the low-density developments of the past scant attention was given to such considerations. The provision of facilities was left to others – the local authority or the private market. In new estates which consisted of houses with their own gardens, where every family was expected to own at least one car, perhaps it was enough just to link up to the local road network. Individuals would make the necessary connections under their own steam. In urban housing both the needs and the opportunities are different. In high-density housing, private outdoor space is limited. Many households will have only a balcony or small garden at best. Some will have nothing at all. Good-quality communal and public open space is essential for success. At the same time, the denser population makes possible a wider range of services and facilities within easy reach.

The government's new approach to housing development recognises the need to plan for communal facilities. The companion guide to PPG3 – *Better Places to Live* – draws attention to the importance of 'contextual analysis':

> ...*greater emphasis now needs to be given to the linkage between new housing and:*
>
> - *local facilities and community infrastructure*
> - *the public transport network*
> - *established walking and cycling routes.*
>
> *Making these linkages is fundamental to achieving more sustainable patterns of movement and reducing people's reliance on the car.*[1]

Contextual analysis of a development site identifies the location of existing facilities and networks. This helps to determine the suitability of the site for housing and indicates what types of housing might be most appropriate. It can identify a shortfall in facilities which might be made good within the development itself or provided nearby through the planning system. Finally, it can help to ensure that the site is planned in such a way as to link into local networks, providing good accessibility to nearby destinations and the wider community.

The service hierarchy

The provision and use of facilities and services has a hierarchical structure. The smaller-scale and most frequently used facilities need to be closest to the home. The most large-scale or specialist services are, of necessity, furthest away. This hierarchy can be illustrated by the pattern of provision for children's play. A very young child needs constant attention and supervision. As it grows it needs decreasing supervision, and increasing complexity and scale of provision (Table 3.1).

The pattern of the hierarchy depends partly on need and partly on the catchment population required to support a large-scale or specialised service. People need services such as a doctor's surgery or a primary

Table 3.1 Provision for children's play

Age	Provision
0–3	Toys in private garden or balcony
2–6	Small-scale equipment in local open space or communal garden
5–12	Robust and complex equipment in small urban park or adventure playground
8+	Outdoor games in major urban park specialist activity centre/theme parks

Table 3.2 Examples of hierarchy of facilities which can be reached at different distances in a relatively high-density urban area

	5-minute walk	10-minute walk	20-minute walk, short journey	40-minute journey
Open space	Communal garden	Local open space	Small urban park	Major urban park, country park
Education	Nursery, child minder	Primary school	Secondary school	Further and higher education
Health		Doctor's surgery dentist	General hospital	Specialist hospital
Shops		Daily needs	Weekly needs	Occasional needs
Communal activities	Meeting room	Community centre, library	Sports centre swimming pool	Sports club
Entertainment	Pub/café	Restaurant	Cinema	Theatre

school near to their homes. At the other end of the scale, a further education college or a teaching hospital has to draw on a large area to justify its size and range of specialisms. In an urban area of relatively high density a good range of services can be expected within easy reach of most homes. Table 3.2 gives examples of services which might be provided within a 5-, 10-, 20-minute walk or a short bus journey; and a 40-minute journey by car or public transport.

Transport links

A hierarchical pattern of movement characterises key aspects of many people's activities whether they be child care, shopping or visiting friends and relatives. It does not, at present, characterise the most common movement – the journey to work – and if more sustainable living patterns are to be developed the distances between work and home need to be reduced. Nevertheless any new housing development has to provide for a hierarchical pattern of travel – a large number of short journeys with frequency decreasing as distance increases. In the past this was done entirely through the road system – a network of primary, secondary and local distributor roads. In the layout of housing estates priority was given to cars with road widths and junctions easing and speeding their paths. The needs of pedestrians were little considered. Few destinations could be easily reached on foot and those journeys inevitably meant following the road layout. This often meant a long diversion from the most direct route. In new urban housing developments vehicles will need to be catered for – many people will still own cars, and goods and services will still be brought to the home by road. But if car dependency is to be reduced then the priorities will need to be reversed.

Greater use of public transport, and more walking and cycling means planning for that from the start. In contextual analysis, alongside the location of community facilities, the transport infrastructure needs to be mapped out. The routes and destination of buses needs to be established. Bus stops and railway stations need to be identified. Priority then, needs to be given to direct and easy pedestrian and cycle routes, both to local destinations and to join the public transport network. This means pedestrian desire lines need to be identified and routes worked out which take people along them easily and safely. Pedestrians should not be forced to take major diversions to get around buildings or to cross major roads.

In many older urban areas the traditional street pattern provides reasonably well for pedestrian movement. Pedestrians and vehicles can be successfully combined, as *Better Places to Live* puts it:

> *Pedestrians and cyclists need routes which are positive, safe, direct, accessible and free from barriers. Generally streets which are designed for low traffic speeds are safe for walking and cycling (ideally 20 mph or less), especially when the detailed layout design (of junctions crossings and surfacing) has their needs in mind. People feel safer on streets where there is activity, where they can be seen by drivers, residents and other users.*[2]

If priority is to be given to pedestrians and cyclists, proper provision must be made for safe routes with better signing and identification. If the needs of pedestrians are to be supported the needs of drivers must be secondary. They must be forced to travel more slowly and take the more circuitous routes. Given this new priority people will be encouraged to walk more. Many of the most frequent journeys – taking young children to school, going to the local shops – are to nearby destinations. In low-density areas these journeys are frequently made by car. In denser urban housing with pedestrian priority these journeys could more easily be made on foot.

THE IDEA OF NEIGHBOURHOOD

In small towns and villages the distribution of housing, community facilities and the networks between them form a distinct pattern. Shops and public buildings are clustered in the centre often around a public space used for street markets. Roads and footpaths radiate out to the houses around the centre. Traditionally, such communities often housed several generations of the same family. But whether related or not, residents would come to know each other through regular and frequent contact. This ideal of community lay at the heart of many of the model settlements of the nineteenth century and was the basis of the early Garden City developments such as Hampstead Garden Suburb and Letchworth.

The idea of neighbourhood became embedded in the post-war planning system by its inclusion in the Abercrombie plan for London (1943) and the Dudley report on housing standards (1944). These reports envisaged that new neighbourhoods would house 6000–10 000 people; they should have their own centre with a school, shops and public buildings; they should be defined by perimeter roads or open spaces; and they should be highly pedestrianised with key facilities within walking distance of every home.[3] As a result, the 'neighbourhood unit' became the basis of planning for the fourteen New Towns designated in the 1940s. Each neighbourhood had 2000–4000 homes housing 5000–10 000 people and each was focused on a primary school which lay at its centre.[4]

The neighbourhood unit was modelled on an idealised traditional rural community. Despite its prominence in the planning of new urban development there was no recognition of its relevance to existing cities. These were considered to be largely undifferentiated socially and physically. Given the high levels of overcrowding it is not surprising that the key urban issues were seen to be housing stress and deprivation. It was in the process of clearing the slums that new evidence of urban social interaction came to light. During 1953–1955 Michael Young and Peter Wilmot studied life in Bethnal Green where residents were being relocated to a new estate 20 miles away on the fringes of East London. The research revealed the importance of kinship networks in an established urban community. Life in Bethnal Green revolved around a complex pattern of connections with relatives, friends and acquaintances established over years of living in close proximity.[5] This research was supported by a government study, in the early 1960s, of an area of old terraced housing near the centre of Oldham. The St. Mary's district was condemned and scheduled for demolition. The study found a vibrant community life. There was a high degree of social recognition and many small shopkeepers and residents had an intimate knowledge of the daily movements of people living in the same street. Many families living in the area were related, partly because young people leaving home were easily able to find housing nearby. Relatives lived close together and visited each other frequently. They gave each other vital support at times of sickness or misfortune.[6]

Following on from his work in East London, Michael Young was engaged to carry out a new study by the Royal Commission examining local government reform in the late 1960s. His task was to carry out a 'community attitudes' survey. The survey found that even in urban areas people did identify with a 'home area' and could define it relatively accurately on a map.[7] These findings were confirmed by similar work in Sheffield by William Hampton and Jeffrey Chapman. The home areas were relatively small in terms of population and, though there was considerable variation, most fell within the range of 6000–10 000 people.[8] Their geography might be defined by barriers – railways were the strongest, though major roads or waterways might prove similar barriers. Or it might surround a focus – a shopping centre, a station or a local park.

Neighbourhoods in existing cities do not conform with the traditional ideal to which the planners of garden cities aspired. They are not so clearly differentiated though major transport routes do form effective barriers. Nor do they very often have clearly defined centres of concentrated facilities. Their residents have a network of activities which range across a wide urban area. But most people do identify with a relatively small area around their home. Urban neighbourhoods have commonly been defined for the smallest units in a hierarchy of local government and administration. Many local authorities have set up neighbourhood offices to deliver some of their services, while the Police have established 'Neighbourhood Watch' and 'Home Beat' policing.

URBAN VILLAGES

The Urban Villages Forum was formed in 1989 on the initiative of the Prince of Wales whose concern over the quality of urban development had long been evident. In May 1984 the Royal Institute of British Architects organised a banquet at Hampton Court Palace to celebrate its 150th anniversary. Prince Charles was known to be interested in architecture and was invited to give a keynote speech. As the luminaries of the architectural establishment digested their dinner, the Prince launched into a wide-ranging attack on Modern Architecture. His speech is best known for its dismissal of the proposed extension to the National Gallery as

'…a monstrous carbuncle on the face of a much loved and elegant friend' and much of it was devoted to criticism of the design of major public buildings. But he also criticised the way architects and planners had '…ignored the feelings and wishes of the mass of ordinary people…' and destroyed extended family patterns and community life by insensitive housing redevelopment.[9]

Prince Charles' ideas on architecture were further developed in his book *A Vision of Britain*.[10] In this he elaborated on the shortcomings of Modernism. The ideas of Le Corbusier and other pioneers, he considered, had taken a grip on the architectural elite. Through their control of architectural practice, education and the professional press, Modernists had ensured the destruction of familiar urban environments and their replacement with unsympathetic high-rise housing estates. Instead, the Prince extolled the virtues of traditional building design and he praised the quality of older towns and cities which worked well and had stood the test of time. He set out ten principles for good urban design combining respect for existing environments, local heritage and materials; the harmonious inter-relationship of buildings and the scale of spaces they form; and high quality of visual design and decoration. This appreciation of traditional values, together with concern over the destruction of urban communities, formed the bedrock for the Urban Villages Forum.

Their first report was published in 1992. It was a combination of the Prince of Wales' urban design ideas and the neighbourhood concept. At the same time, it prefigured the coming debate on demographic change and sustainability which had then hardly begun. The concept drew heavily on the qualities of small heritage cities such as Bath, York and Edinburgh New Town in the UK; San Sebastian in Spain; San Gimignano in Italy and Bern in Switzerland. These urban environments were admired for the spatial and visual qualities of their streets and squares, the interest and variety of the skylines, and for the softening offered by urban parks and green spaces. The neighbourhood concept evoked was a traditional one of the self-contained community clustered around a town centre providing employment and services.

The report identified six essential qualities for a successful urban village:

1 It should be small enough for any place to be within easy walking distance of any other, but large enough to support a wide range of activities and facilities. The forum envisaged a combined resident and working population of 3000–5000 people and a notional area of 100 acres (40 hectares).

2   There should be mixed use providing both homes and workspaces aiming to achieve a 1:1 ratio between jobs and residents available for work. This would reduce, but not eliminate, the need for commuting as a degree of inward and outward travel to work would be expected.

3   Tenures should be mixed both for residential development and employment uses. This would allow flexibility to accommodate demographic change, particularly the increasing number of elderly, and changes in work patterns, including increasing numbers working from home.

4   It should provide an admirable environment. There should be a mixture of different types and sized of buildings with a more densely built-up central area. Main streets should have a mixture of uses within buildings, with precedence given on ground floors to shops, restaurants, pubs and other public uses.

5   There should be a pedestrian-friendly environment which caters for the car without encouraging its use. A wide range of traffic calming measures and devices are available which civilise driving and enhance pedestrian priority.

6   There should be a mixture of different types and sizes of buildings and, in the more built-up central area, a mix of uses within buildings. On main streets the ground floors should be given over to public facilities and services which bring life to urban spaces.

In view of the way urban communities had been destroyed by redevelopment in the past, the creation of urban villages should be achieved through a high level of public involvement. This should not be confined to consulting public bodies and elected representatives. It should engage a wide range of processes and techniques to embrace the views of those who live and work in a new urban village. This would include both people already in a designated development area, and potential new residents and building users.[11]

The concept applied

The idea of the urban village is highly appealing. It is based on the model of the small pre-industrial town which everyone admires and few now live in. Its density is relatively low, barely reaching PPG3 levels, causing no qualms in developers or homebuyers. A short journey to work is the commonly held ideal. Although the idea of more walking seems a less than universal aspiration, even the most ardent motorists accept that they have to walk around shops and entertainment venues.

Above all, the concept *is* ambiguous, even in its title. Is it an urban development with village-like community services and networks? Or is it a development in the countryside with urban townscape and spatial qualities?

It was perhaps this very ambiguity, coupled with the spur of Royal patronage, which created such widespread interest.

A survey of all local authorities in Britain, completed in 2002, revealed no less than 55 developments described as 'urban villages'. Most of these were in inner urban areas where regeneration and development of 'brown-field' land were the key considerations. The size and density of the 'villages' varied considerably. Populations ranged from 160 to 15 000 on-site areas from 1 hectare to nearly 300. Most, though, seemed to be in the range 2000–6000 people on land covering 40–150 hectares. The overall density of these new settlements was mostly in the range of 30–50 dwellings per hectare – very similar to that originally envisaged. Most of the villages included small shops selling a general range of goods, play facilities and a community hall. Most had some form of employment, though it was often minimal, and in only two there were a significant number of jobs. Partly this was because most new urban villages were located in existing cities close to large employment centres.[12]

Most of these newly designated settlements seem to conform to the 'village in the city' interpretation. The best-known example, however, is more 'the urban countryside'. To promote the urban village concept the Prince of Wales himself organised a demonstration project. Poundbury in Dorset is a development by the Prince's Duchy of Cornwall. The development is being built in a greenfield site on the edge of the town of Dorchester (Figure 3.1). Eventually it will comprise 2000 new homes on an area of

▲ 3.1   Poundbury – the Duchy of Cornwall's new 'urban village' in Dorset

160 hectares. The density of the development is low – net densities barely rise above 30 homes per hectare – and though it does include some employment and social housing these are on a small scale. Its chief significance is that it does realise the urban design ideals of the urban village concept. Most of the houses are terraced without garages and front directly on to the back of pavement. Parking is on the street and traffic calming is achieved by creating narrow winding carriageways. This combination produces continuous streets which have a good sense of enclosure and recreate the informality of the traditional village.[13]

Built, as it is, on grade I agricultural land, Poundbury does not offer a good model for the new agenda in which most housing will be built on urban 'brownfield' sites. Two new urban villages do offer more widely applicable models for high-density urban housing. Both the Crown Street Regeneration Project in the Glasgow's Gorbals and West Silverstown Urban Village in London Docklands comprise comprehensive redevelopment of large inner city areas. But while the Gorbals is a long-established residential neighbourhood, West Silverstown is built in a former industrial area.

In the 1860s the streets of the Gorbals still had a village quality – an irregular hotchpotch of two- and three-storey buildings. Over the following few years these were swept away and replaced with wide streets lined with substantial four-storey tenements designed for middle-class occupation. But gradually the generous self-contained flats were divided up and each came to house several families. By the 1930s, the Gorbals had the most densely crowded housing in Britain. In the post-war period grossly overcrowded housing was seen as unhealthy and routinely condemned. Despite their substantial construction, the Gorbals tenements were torn down in the early 1960s to make way for tower and slab blocks. In the process a colourful community of great vitality was destroyed.[14] In the early 1990s many of the multi-storey sixties blocks – physically degenerate and socially stigmatised in their turn – were demolished. Community networks were again shattered as their tenants were dispersed. By 1993 much of the Gorbals was a rubble-strewn urban desert. The new urban village being developed on this cleared site will eventually provide 2000 homes – 600 for sale, 200 for students and the remainder social rented. There will be new shops, a supermarket and a refurbished industrial mill providing 340 jobs. The area is planned as a series of perimeter blocks fronting on to streets and public spaces and each enclosing a communal garden. The buildings are mainly four-storey walk-up flats – very similar in form to the original tenements. In little more than 100 years the physical form of the Gorbals has come full circle.[15]

London's Royal Victoria Dock was part of a large network of warehousing and industry which, by the 1970s, had been made redundant by changes in the way goods are handled and transported. Much of the area was developed commercially under the guidance of the London Docklands Development Corporation. In 1992 the Corporation promoted the development of a new urban village on the south side of Victoria Dock. The new community was developed as a partnership between a commercial housing developer, two social landlords and the local authority. The 50-hectare site accommodates more than 1000 homes, two-thirds of them for sale with the remainder social rented. At the heart of the scheme is a new primary school, a community centre and a public open space. On the dock front the 'crescent building' provides ground floor shopping with social housing above[16] (refer to Case Study C).

Case Study C (p. 221)

Millennium villages

Following its election in May 1997, the new Labour Government was keen to express its commitment to the new agenda generated by climate change. To do this it chose a variant of the urban village concept which, by then, had gained considerable currency. The government had reviewed and eventually supported the proposals for an exhibition to mark the turn of the century – the 'millennium dome' to be built on derelict land at Greenwich in, East London. Adjacent to the dome was a 13 hectare derelict site. This had been used for the production of 'town gas' and had been made redundant by the use of natural gas. In July 1997 this was designated as the site of a new millennium village. 'This new benchmark community will be a tangible, living exemplar of sustainable development – providing a new environmentally friendly way of twenty-first century living' said Deputy Prime Minister John Prescott. He promised that several similar high-quality energy-efficient and adaptable housing schemes would be developed on 'brownfield' sites in other parts of the country.[17]

A second millennium village was designated in 1999 at Allerton Bywater near Leeds on the site of a disused coalfield. A third was announced in 2002 to regenerate a run-down social housing estate in Manchester. Though it was low density, the Cardroom estate was beset with problems of crime, low attainment and unpopularity. To assist its rejuvenation it was renamed New Islington.[18] Of the three, it is the Greenwich Millennium Village which has attracted most attention. This is not just because it is the only one where work is significantly advanced. It also expected to reach high standards. The scheme was distinguished by a master plan by the veteran Swedish-based British architect Ralph Erskine. Erskine was the architect for the Byker estate in Newcastle. Built in the 1970s Byker is still widely considered the most successful social housing estate in Britain both for its neo-vernacular design and its pioneering of resident participation (see also Chapter 7 and Figure 7.14 for more insight on the Byker Estate).

Erskine's ideas promised a high quality of design. The new millennium village was also intended to demonstrate significant improvements in construction speed and efficiency. It was to create a mixed community in which residents were given a high degree of choice in the design and adaptation of their homes. When complete, it was to address the new environmental agenda with a major reduction in energy consumption. The results have fallen some way short of these ideals. Many of the non-traditional approaches to construction have been abandoned and development has fallen well behind programme. The 'mixed community' concept was watered down and there is little evidence of the expected energy efficiency or adaptability. Most disappointingly, and despite some good-quality high-density housing designed by Erskine himself, the urban design quality of the new village is poor. There is a lack of space formation and enclosure and far to much open space – wide roads edged by extensive green verges; swathes of tree planting of little value, The whole scheme is far too open, much too dominated by vehicles to make it a model for the new urbanity.

SUSTAINABLE COMMUNITIES

The urban village idea evoked communities of the past to promote high-quality housing in new urban neighbourhoods. But is also introduced the concept of sustainability. In environmental terms the sustainable community should aim for ecological balance, not necessarily within each neighbourhood but certainly within the urban region as a whole. However, sustainable communities need to achieve more than that. They should endure in the long term and that means they need to have high-quality physical environments, social stability and economic viability.

In 2000, government research was published on the achievement of sustainable communities in the context of the Millennium Village programme.[21] The project set out seven tests of sustainability which can be interpreted as follows:

I   *Minimising resource consumption.* This means using high-density forms which consume less land and make more efficient use of other resources. It means reducing the energy used in the construction of buildings by the increased use of local materials, more recycled products and more efficient methods. Greater energy efficiency is required in the

GREENWICH MILLENNIUM VILLAGE

The first Millennium village at Greenwich was the subject of an international project in 1997. Ralph Erskine, probably Europe's leading housing designer, was appointed master planner for the project which was to have 1377 homes, a commercial centre, a school and health centre together with an ecology park. At the outset the scheme was not just to be a model for high-density urban living, but a demonstration project for many of the key concerns of the time. It was to be environmentally friendly using 80 per cent less energy than conventional housing. It was to be constructed speedily and efficiently with off-site construction leading to 30 per cent reduction in cost, 50 per cent reduction embodied energy and the elimination of defects. It was to be a mixed community

▲ **3.2** Phase 1 housing

Case Example Continues . . .

with low-income households living cheek by jowl with wealthy neighbours. There was to be a high level of user participation with customisation before occupation and a high degree of adaptability to allow future changes.[19]

Within 18 months the project suffered a major setback when the lead British architects Hunt Thompson resigned claiming that the key prefabrication system had been abandoned and the social objectives had been watered down. Low-income households, it was said, were to be segregated in separate housing zones.[20] These claims were denied but the project clearly lost momentum. The target of completing 500 homes by 2000 was not met. Indeed, significant progress was not

made until 2003 with phases 1 and 2 nearing completion and a school/health centre and a cinema finally in use. The use of some prefabrication was retained but, clearly the project failed to meet its efficiency targets. The most disappointing aspect of the development, though, is the character of its urban design.

The housing in phase 1, designed by Ralph Erskine, and phase 2 by Proctor Matthews did achieve some quality and demonstrates effective design for high density. The trouble is that these developments sit as isolated clusters separated by swathes of open space. While green space is essential for urban quality, here it is so excessive as to dilute the density of the overall project. Worse, there is no attempt to recapture the quality of the urban street.

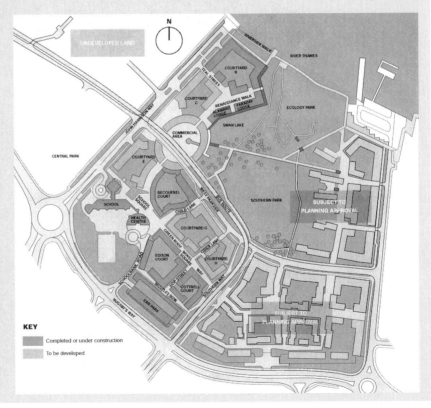

KEY

■ Completed or under construction
□ To be developed

▲ **3.3**
Development plan
for early phases

Pedestrians are catered for but only on a network of segregated and probably insecure paths. The project is dominated by dual carriageway roads which, in places, are duplicated by separate roads for buses. Overall the scheme is relatively low density and heavily car-dependent – the antitheses of sustainable urban development.

▲ **3.4** Phase 2 housing

▲ **3.5** Typical distributor road

use of buildings through better insulation and conservation, through more efficient energy generation, and the use of renewable sources. Reduced water consumption is needed. Not least it means reducing greenhouse gas emissions from daily travel by increased use of public transport and low-energy personal transport – and by reducing over-all transport levels altogether.

2 *Protecting and enhancing environmental capital.* This means that environmental value should be enhanced by development. On a green-field site it is questionable whether the value if new housing offsets the loss of amenity and agricultural productivity. In the development of a derelict 'brownfield' site the gain in environmental capital is more obvi-ous though on the negative side reclamation may be costly and diverse wildlife habitats may be lost. Efforts should be made to preserve valu-able features of the existing environment.

3 *Urban design quality.* A good quality environment formed by build-ings which are well-designed and well-built will be highly valued and more likely to stand the test of time. This applies not just to pre-industrial towns but to many of the Victorian areas of large cities. There should be a coherent pattern of streets and public spaces which is permeable to pedestrians and provides access to facilities and amenities. It should aim to accommodate personalisation and respect privacy. At the same time safety and security should be a high priority.

4 *High quality of life.* There should be a full range of public services, local amenities and public transport and these should be provided before the new residents move in. However, large facilities, such as a super-store, can impose quality of life costs such as congestion and visual intrusion. Urban management is important with measures taken to ensure law enforcement and maintenance systems to counter envir-onmental degradation. Residents should have access to employment opportunities and training. The development of local employment improves quality of life and also reduces the extent of daily travel.

5 *Increased social inclusion.* The development of mixed communities depends on accommodating a range of incomes, social status and house-hold structure. This means providing a range of different housing types and sizes. It also means a range of different forms of tenure. Ideally, these should be 'pepper-potted' so that tenure is not discernible by built form and the social segregation of many developments of the past is avoided.

6 *Broad participation in governance.* Residents should be involved in decisions about design, planning, construction and management. A wide range of techniques and processes is available through which this can be carried out. Critical choices should involve consideration of a range of options. Experience has shown that effective participation

produces better solutions. It also ensures that residents are more committed to the environment and more protective of it.

7 **Commercial viability.** This is not to say that public funding is unnecessary. Government investment is commonly needed to kick-start major developments. Public subsidy is also necessary to realise social housing which is an integral part of a balanced community. But to be sustainable, a neighbourhood must attract people to live there and employers and service providers to locate there. The interaction of all the aspects of sustainability must ensure that, in the long run, housing, employment and services are commercially viable.

The researchers considered that a sustainable community should perform well on all seven tests. The tests were used to evaluate five partially completed projects – the Greenwich, Allerton Bywater Millennium Villages, Poundbury, West Silvertown Urban Villages and Waltham Forest Housing Action Trust. The result was a mixed picture. Some aspects of the schemes were considered exemplary – Greenwich provided a major gain in environmental capital by its reclamation of a derelict site; Waltham Forest was outstanding on social inclusion and public participation; while Poundbury reached a high standard of urban design. On the other hand, none of the schemes were rated highly on resource consumption with insufficient energy-conscious building design and a weak transport system leaving residents too reliant on private cars. Overall, none of the schemes provided a model of sustainability on the basis of the seven tests. And it can be argued that the tests themselves need to be sterner in order to achieve true sustainability, particularly in the provision of local employment and the reduction of commuting.

A model neighbourhood

The regeneration of the Hulme area in Manchester involved the demolition of a huge area of troubled multi-storey housing – a legacy of the 1960s. The aim was to redevelop the entire area. Many new housing schemes and other developments were completed, but at the end of the process, large tracts of land remained empty and derelict. For one of these complex sites the urban design consultancy URBED, based in the area, prepared a detailed scheme which aimed to provide a model for sustainable urban development.

The proposed new neighbourhood would cover 45 hectares (112 acres) and accommodate 4000–5000 people. It would include 2500 homes and 45 000 square metres of commercial space. Its built form would provide a prototype for a city of high densities:

> The aim has been to create a high-quality urban environment with well-pro-
> portioned buildings and attractive streets, squares and parks. The public realm
> is human in scale but urban in nature and designed to promote interaction and
> to accommodate the diversity of urban life. The plan is based on a clear frame-
> work of streets designed to serve both as routes and as public spaces supervised
> by the occupants of the surrounding buildings. The street framework contains
> a density of different uses, buildings and tenures to create a balanced commu-
> nity, to reduce car travel, to animate streets and public places, to sustain shops
> and other public facilities and to foster activity and security throughout the day.[22]

Such a vision might well find favour with proponents of the urban village.
But the URBED concept has a number of key features which push the
boundaries of sustainability towards a high degree of self-sufficiency. There
would be a high level of employment so that a balance was reached
between jobs and the available workforce. Some of this could provide a
basis for 'green' industries such a recycling. The neighbourhood would also
be expected to have good public transport links. The need for car use
would therefore be reduced and so would the need for car parking. The
saving of land by reducing car parking would allow much more to be given
over to green space. A small local park would be included, as well as
courtyards within each block and a variety of planted terraces and roof
gardens at different levels. The most radical aspect of the scheme was that
it would aim to achieve a net balance of carbon dioxide envisions. This
would be realised through a composite system of energy conservation,
garnering energy through renewable sources and combined heat and
power (CHP) generation using the neighbourhood waste products as
fuel. The neighbourhood would also have a closed water system which
relies on collection of rainwater and local processing of waste.

This was a paper exercise rather than a practical proposition. However,
it did incorporate the *Homes for Change* project completed in 1999. This
is a high-density mixed-use building complex containing flats and
maisonettes on the upper floors. The lower levels have a mixture of
offices, workshops and training spaces, together with recreation facilities such as a theatre and exhibition space. Homes for Change is an
innovative concept which provides a model for more sustainable forms
of urban development (see Case Study D).

Case Study D (p. 227)

FITTING IN WITH URBAN FORM

All the models of neighbourhood renewal cited so far have involved comprehensive new developments. But the lessons of history warn against

such an approach. The large-scale clearances of the 1960s and 1970s broke up established communities and destroyed familiar urban environments. The more recent redevelopment of places like the Gorbals in Glasgow and Hukme in Manchester repeated this process on a lesser scale. The process of redeveloping these areas has been long and slow and it is still in question as to where it will end in successful regeneration.

There is growing recognition that a more sensitive and piecemeal approach to urban regeneration may be more successful. The government publication *Better Places to Live* emphasises the importance of understanding the context of any new housing development. It stresses the need to support existing communities by providing new facilities and services and improving access to existing ones.[23] An appropriate approach to urban renewal involves keeping what is good, renovating and adapting what can be retained and improved, and replacing only those buildings and land uses which are completely outmoded. This means more selective renewal than comprehensive redevelopment. It also means building more housing on small infill sites which are surprisingly numerous even in inner urban areas.

A more low key incremental approach to regeneration is likely to produce successful and sustainable results more quickly than extensive redevelopment. It is also the key to addressing some of the problems left over in urban developments of the past. The new agenda of addressing climate change and demographic trends can only very partially be addressed by adopting different policies and standards for new developments. There remains the legacy of the large quantity of housing developed during the latter part of the twentieth century. Most of this is very far from meeting the new agenda and is a particular burden in terms of the vehicle traffic it generates and the consequent high-energy consumption and congestion.

Research completed in 1998 examined the potential renewal of suburban areas to make them more sustainable.[24] It concluded that, apart from the separation of work and home, and the long commuting distances involved, the suburbs have, in many respects, become outmoded. This was partly to do with population changes in suburban areas. There were more elderly, single people and small families than when the suburbs were built. This changed population needed different forms of housing, new facilities and better services, including improved public transport. All the same, large-scale redevelopment of suburban areas was considered impractical. What was needed was an increase of mixed uses to develop services and employment; reinforcement of suburban centres by focusing new development; building on 'brownfield' and void sites; the selective 'densification' of housing; and the development of sustainable transport.

Right: 80-acre (33-hectare) area of a typical suburb devoid of all but residential accommodation.

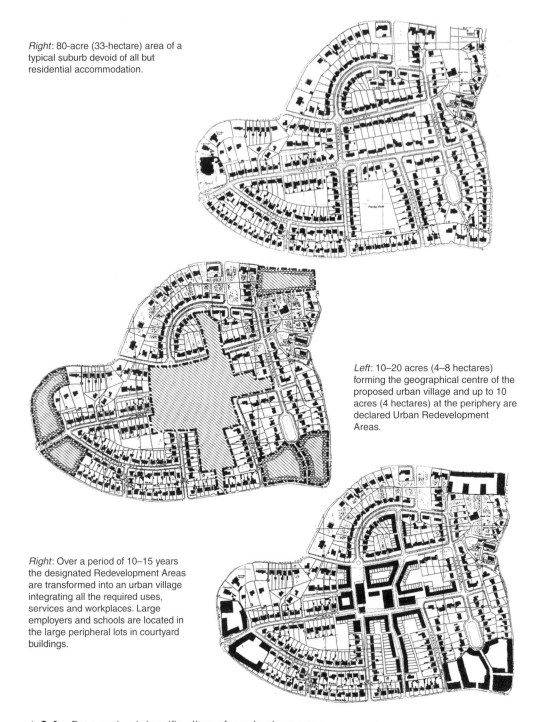

Left: 10–20 acres (4–8 hectares) forming the geographical centre of the proposed urban village and up to 10 acres (4 hectares) at the periphery are declared Urban Redevelopment Areas.

Right: Over a period of 10–15 years the designated Redevelopment Areas are transformed into an urban village integrating all the required uses, services and workplaces. Large employers and schools are located in the large peripheral lots in courtyard buildings.

▲ **3.6**   Progressive intensification of a suburban area

The Urban Villages Forum has shown how this could be done.[25] A 35-hectare suburban area containing just housing could be selected. Sites for improvement could be defined and developed over a 10–15-year period. Four to eight hectares of land at the centre of the area could be transformed into a new urban centre. This would contain shops services and new high-density housing. It would also act as a transport node. Around the periphery, sites could be developed to accommodate large employers and schools. In the course of remodelling, some housing would be lost but under-used land would also be developed. The whole process would not only make the area better suited to the needs of its residents, but also become more self-sufficient (Figure 3.6).

The urban neighbourhood is a concept which grew out of the way existing cities function. It is a useful model for designing major new developments. But it can also be helpful in assessing how new developments can fit in with urban forms ensuring that services and infrastructure are focused and located to meet the needs of a community. Neighbourhood principles can be applied both to the regeneration of the more densely developed inner cities or the intensification of the low density suburbs.

KEY POINTS

- In any housing development it is essential that residents have access to a range of community facilities. These include health and welfare centres, education opportunities, and outlets for commercial goods and services. Access to open space and recreational opportunities is particularly important.
- Service provision has a hierarchical structure. The most frequently used facilities need to be closest to home while those used rarely can be further away. This hierarchy is marked by similar patterns of travel needs, with a large number of short journeys and a smaller number of longer ones.
- The neighbourhood unit was a key element of post-war planning. Existing urban areas have also been recognised as having identifiable neighbourhoods defined by geographical barriers, local foci and social networks.
- The 'urban village' concept is based on a combination of urban design qualities from traditional towns and the neighbourhood idea to create a model of communities which are socially and economically mixed, and of high environmental quality.

- ⊶ The 'urban village' idea is ambiguous and has been used to create new low-density communities on 'greenfield' sites. Its more appropriate application is in the regeneration of urban 'brownfield' areas to provide coherent integrated communities.
- ⊶ The aim now should be to create sustainable communities which should be in ecological balance. These would be high density and have low-energy transport systems, be efficient both in energy use and the consumption of scarce resources, and be socially and economically mixed.
- ⊶ Much regeneration is likely to include a range of incremental improvements rather than comprehensive redevelopment. This should address urban and suburban areas sensitively to intensify land use and meet social, environmental and economic needs.

4

HOUSING FORMS

THE DESIGN OF URBAN SPACE

SUMMARY

The development of new urban housing, predominantly on 'brownfield' sites, is inevitably set within the context of the existing urban fabric. Cities have been developed and renewed in a variety of ways and this process has encompassed a range of housing types. Some of these have failed and been swept away. The last 50 years have seen a lot of experimental housing designs, much of which had serious shortcomings. Two forms of urban housing have endured over more than 100 years and have proved adaptable and successful. These are the terraced house and multi-storey flats in 'perimeter block' form. The success of these forms requires the achievement of good standards in their planning and layout. In multi-storey forms the inter-relationship between dwellings and, in particular, the design of their access systems, is critical. The demographic changes of recent years create the need for new forms of housing. The elderly, on the one hand, and young single households on the other, may not be best accommodated in traditional forms. Apart from their common need for small dwellings these groups have a range of needs in support services and security. New forms, too, are needed to facilitate the increasing need to integrate work and home. A key significance of the enduring forms was their success in defining coherent urban space. The design of the public environment both in spatial and functional terms is critical to the creation of urban housing which is both attractive and works well.

THE URBAN LEGACY

Most towns and cities have their origins in small settlements which grew up around a river crossing or a local market. Roads radiated from a central point and buildings developed along them. Over time new streets were built to connect the main roads, forming a pattern in the shape of a

▲ 4.1   Radial-concentric form

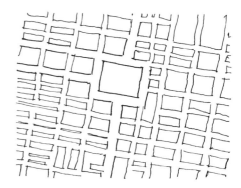

▲ 4.2   Grid-iron form

spider's web. While most British settlements had this 'radial-concentric' form a few were planned. A number of medieval towns were developed as military forts. These were based on the 'Bastides' – walled towns developed by French kings in the thirteenth century. The layout of the Bastides was derived from the layout of Roman military camps and introduced the 'grid-iron' form as the basis of planned towns (Figures 4.1 and 4.2).[1]

The most significant step forward in the planning of cities came during the European Renaissance when major new developments were planned as large-scale architectural forms. Grand public spaces were created linked by broad avenues radiating from focal points. Such large-scale planning concepts first began to contribute to the development of British cities in the eighteenth century with the growth of spa towns. The expansion of Bath, from 1750, was particularly significant with the introduction of the square, circus and crescent forms – terraces of large houses enclosing communal green space. The Bloomsbury squares in London and the 'New Town' in Edinburgh were also developed during this period. A similar landmark of a slightly later period was the planning of Regents Park by John

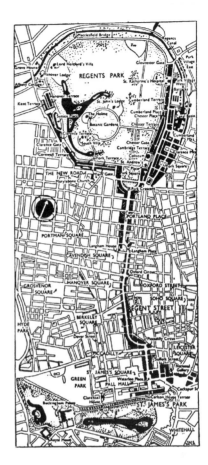

▲ **4.3** Nash's West London development

Nash in 1811. The development of the grand terraces around it and their connection to central London via Portland Place and Regents Street were a major achievement in urban design (Figure 4.3).

The developments by landed estates set the pattern for urban expansion. Land would be acquired on the periphery of existing development. This might have been in agricultural or other rural use, and would be in parcels of different ownerships. Each land parcel might be acquired and built on by a different developer and the boundaries between them are still visible in the urban fabric. Each of these large developments was laid out using the principles of town planning already established. Many were based on the grid-iron pattern, or a regular and repetitive layout of rectilinear street blocks. The most imaginative and successful drew on the forms of the Renaissance. These might include broad avenues focused on a key landmark, well-proportioned squares around communal green space, and elegant curving crescents of terraced housing.

Slums and their remediation

These grand developments were of relatively large houses often intended for families with servants. They were not designed to house the hundreds of thousands of manual workers and their families who flocked to the cities in the industrialisation of the nineteenth century. Though, eventually, many of the large terraced houses were subdivided into crowded multiple occupation, the new urban working classes initially found homes in two types of housing.

In the older cities, such as Glasgow and London, there were many areas of old buildings. These were often developed piecemeal along narrow streets and around tiny airless courts and alleys. The dense occupancy of these insanitary and damp buildings made them a breeding ground for disease. At the same time, areas of new housing were purpose built for the new urban workers. This was particularly characteristic of the new industrial cities where concentrations of poorly build back-to-back housing clustered round the factories. Even in older cities new workers housing was built close to industry – not back-to-backs but mean terraced housing of equally poor quality. These two types of slum housing were the focus of growing concern and the action taken to remedy these problems gave rise to two new forms of urban housing:

1 **By-law housing.** From the 1870s the standards of new housing were regulated by building by-laws. These ensured better standards of construction in general but, in particular, they regulated the space around houses. Under this regulatory regime, streets of terraced houses were constructed on a large scale. The houses faced each other across a street wide enough to ensure light and air, and respect privacy. The backs of the houses faced each other from a similar distance – each overlooking a small garden or yard. In the middle was a narrow access lane or alley for the removal of refuse and sewage. These terraced streets were often constructed in long, straight, repetitive rows and their arrangement became known as 'tunnel backs'. The by-law terraces became the predominant form of urban housing until the First World War.[2]

2 **Tenements.** In Scotland, by the late nineteenth century, blocks of four-storey flats built around courts had become a significant form of urban housing, for all classes. At the same time, 'mansion blocks' of flats were being developed in London for the wealthier classes. Prototype blocks of flats for workers had been developed from 1850 by philanthropic societies. From the 1870s onwards efforts began in London and other English cities to clear the worst of the slums and

replace them with tenement blocks. Initially, these developments were very dense with six-storey blocks packed tightly onto each site. The excessive density requirements soon eased and a form of tenement estate emerged which was widely replicated – blocks of four- or five-storey flats arranged around communal courts or open space. These estates remained the predominant form of urban slum clearance housing until the middle of the twentieth century.[3]

By then, however, relatively little impact had been made on poor quality urban housing. In the 1950s and 1960s new forms of urban housing emerged under the influence of the Modern Movement.

The post-war estates

In the 1940s and early 1950s a number of influential housing estates were built, based on Modern Movement ideas such as zeilnbau and radian city. These introduced new forms of housing based on the 'pavilion' form – the detached building set in its own grounds:

- **Slab blocks.** The tenement estates were made up of blocks which addressed the street frontage and turned corners to enclose and create space. Slab blocks estates ignored the surrounding streets. They were generally made up of single straight blocks up to eight-storey high. Each was orientated to maximise sunlight and was set in open space which was intended to provide amenity and recreation. The most influential of these were the work of Bethold Lubetkin such as Spa Green (1943) and Churchill Gardens, Pimlico by Powell and Moya (1946) (Figure 4.4).

▲ **4.4**   Churchill Gardens Pimlico

- *Tower blocks.* Like the slab block the tower block stands in its own ground surrounded by open space. Some prototypes had been developed in Sweden and in France in the 1930s, but the first tower block estates in Britain were developed in the early 1950s. These early blocks were only 11-storey high and for some time technical requirements restricted towers to a similar height. These problems were soon overcome and, stimulated by favourable subsidy, by the early 1960s tower blocks were a common form of housing throughout Britain. Blocks as high as 30 storeys were constructed at Red Road, Glasgow (1968) and up to 40 storeys in the Barbican in the City of London (1973) (Figure 4.5).

▲ **4.5**   Red Road
Glasgow

These forms were compared unfavourably with the traditional urban street, where people usually lived in houses with a small yard or garden. Their doors and windows opened onto a thoroughfare where they could meet and observe neighbours and keep an eye on children playing outside. By contrast, people were isolated in the new blocks, they could not easily meet and chat to neighbours, and if there was an outdoor play space for children, it was several floors away and well out of sight of their homes. The response was to try to recreate the traditional virtues at high levels by building 'streets in the sky':

- **Deck access estates.** These avoided the constrictions of tower and slab blocks where flats were reached by narrow corridors or walkways. These were replaced with wide pedestrian decks which linked several blocks together. The decks were supposed to provide an opportunity for social interaction and an easy means of access for deliveries. This form had some advantages over tower and slab estates. The need to concentrate movement at a few levels meant that buildings were of modest height – usually six storeys or less. The fact that blocks were joined together meant they could be designed to enclose coherent amenity spaces which were relatively easily reached and managed. The first scheme to apply the 'streets in the sky' concept was at Park Hill in Sheffield (1961) but it gained wide influence, and many deck access estates were completed on this model during the late 1960s and early 1970s (Figure 4.6).

▲ **4.6**
North
Peckham
Estate

Another response to the restrictions and uniformity imposed by Modernist estates was the design of innovative housing schemes which provided an enhanced quality of life in high-density multi-storey housing:

- **Innovative housing.** A number of projects were developed in the 1970s which broke new ground in housing quality. Their main objective was to provide designs which offered variety and environmental quality and, above all, seriously addressed the provision of good-quality outdoor space for the inhabitants of multi-storey blocks. Among these were three central London schemes:

– *Lillington Gardens, Westminster* (1972): This scheme was principally noteworthy for the provision of generous sheltered projecting balconies to each flat – a contrast with most multi-storey estates where, if balconies were provided at all, they were tiny and windswept. The project was also notable for its use of traditional materials, its high-quality landscaping, and for its respect for the context of surrounding buildings (Figure 4.7).

▲ **4.7**   Lillington Gardens

- *Bruinswick Square, Bloomsbury* (1973): This scheme was based on the A-frame or 'ziggurat' principle where each floor steps backwards. This form creates a built space for services in the centre of the building. More importantly it allows each flat to be provided with a wide terrace on the roof of the dwelling below. The principle was used elsewhere, notably in Camden Council's Alexandra Road (1979) and the Highgate New Town (1981) schemes (Figure 4.8).
- *Odhams Walk, Covent Garden* (1979): This scheme was developed by the Greater London Council in the heart of Covent Garden and includes 102 dwellings built above commercial premises on the street frontage. The flats are arranged in an informal manner around a series of pedestrian courts. The floor plans are stepped and staggered so that each home is provided with a large balcony or terrace[4] (Figure 4.9).

▲ **4.8** Bruinswick Square

▲ **4.9**   Odhams Walk

These were among a number of projects which attracted widespread attention and admiration. But they were completed at a juncture when the extent of the failure of the post-war estates was becoming fully evident. It was not just the isolation and lack of amenities. These were compounded by technical shortcomings and cheap construction – the frequent break-down of lifts, electricity and water services; the leaking joints and roofs; the condensation caused by poor insulation. The access systems were subject to widespread vandalism and abuse. Ironically, this was worst in the deck access estates which were supposed to solve key problems. The 'streets in the sky', which were meant to improve access and social interaction, became the haunt of teenage gangs and drug dealers and provided the opportunity for 'joy-riding' on motorbikes. Within and without the estates these shortcomings were often exacerbated by a lack of communal facilities and services.[5]

All this was not entirely the fault of the designs. Partly it was due to the key decision to allocate multi-storey flats to low-income families with children – the social group which was probably least suited to living in this form of housing. Nevertheless, it gave large-scale high-density housing an insuperable stigma. There was a hiatus on the development of this form of housing which lasted the best part of two decades. The new urban housing was safe – small scale, relatively low density and architecturally conservative.

THE ENDURING FORMS OF URBAN HOUSING

If there is now to be a revival in urban housing it is essential to gain an understanding of the forms which are likely to succeed – in contemporary jargon – 'what matters is what works'. Twenty or thirty years ago Britain's inner cities were a bleak scene. The post-war estates were failing, much of the Victorian-terraced housing was overcrowded and run down, many of the tenement blocks had become outmoded and degenerated into slums. The only bright areas were the affluent districts of old housing and the relatively small number of blocks of flats purpose built for middle-class occupation.

Since then, most of the terraced housing has been repaired and improved. Provided with bathrooms and new kitchens, equipped with modern services, this form of housing has been shown to succeed and is particularly suitable for families with children. Tenement blocks were usually well constructed but often had poor space standards and outmoded services. These, too, have been successfully improved and compare well with similar blocks developed by the private sector. Some of the post-war estates too have been improved and prove suitable for certain user groups. What is now clear is that terraced housing does work, that small blocks of flats in the 'perimeter block' form, integrated into the street pattern, are also successful. A question mark, though, still hangs over the high-rise forms so beloved of post-war housing designers.

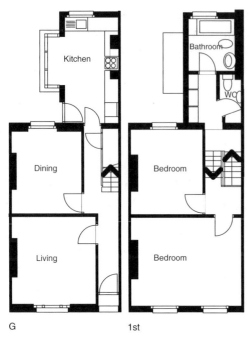

▲ **4.10**   Plans of typical Victorian-terraced house

▲ **4.11**   Plans of typical 1960s semi-detached house

Terraced housing

A wide range of terraced houses were constructed during the nine-teenth century. At the lower end of the range were 'two-up, two-down' cottages with a living room entered from the street, a kitchen at the back, a staircase in the middle and two bedrooms above. At the other end were the grand houses built for wealthy families – five or even six storeys with servants quarters top and bottom. The former have mostly been demolished; the latter have largely been converted into flats. In between were the great masses of terraced houses two- or three-storey high. Mostly these were well built and have been adapted to provide successful family housing.

Attempts have been made to analyse and categorise the plan forms of houses though these seem to have provided no startling revelations.[6] Essentially, the plan form of most surviving terraced houses is the same – an entrance hall leading to living and dining room and kitchen at the back; a staircase at the side leading to bedrooms (Figure 4.10). Rear extensions, which were common in Victorian terraced houses, were gen-erally omitted during the twentieth century to reduce overshadowing.

From the 1930s onwards the terraced house gave way to the semi-detached which has become the predominant house type over the last 50 to 60 years. Apart from the rear extension, however, the floor plan of the typical semi-detached house is remarkably similar to terraced houses (Figure 4.11).

TERRACED HOUSING – COMPARISON WITH SEMI-DETACHED

The two house types are much the same size and in the range and function of spaces they are similar. Given the similarity in standard of accommodation and internal layout, it is instructive to compare the two:

- *Density.* Terraced houses can be built at densities from 45 dwellings per hectare upwards. Many Victorian-terraced streets were built at a density of 125 houses per hectare.[7] By contrast, most semi-detached houses were built at densities ranging from 16 to 30 dwellings per hectare. With housing standards comparable, the main difference lay in the inefficient use of land with overlarge gardens and much space wasted between and in front of houses.
- *Cost.* Terraced houses are inherently cheaper because they are all joined together. This means more party walls and fewer expensive external walls which reduces both construction and maintenance costs. It also means there is less heat loss and lower energy costs. Infrastructure costs are reduced because houses are closer together.
- *Noises transference.* It is commonly assumed that there is less risk of noise nuisance in semi-detached houses but both forms are normally constructed in 'handed' or 'mirrored' plan layout. Most semis were, for cheapness, built with the chimneys back-to-back so that main living rooms and bedrooms in adjoining houses abutted. In terraced houses the halls and staircases and kitchens also abutted together with one or two bedrooms. Noise transference along most of this juncture would be of limited significance. While terraced houses are slightly more prone to noise nuisance, this can largely be counteracted by sound reduction construction.
- *Rear access.* Terraced housing undoubtedly has more limited access from the front to the rear garden. This presents some inconvenience in gardening, rubbish disposal and maintenance, but terraced housing can generally be provided with common paths or alleys to provide access to the rear.
- *Car parking.* Semi-detached housing often has space for parking two, three or more cars, but this is a concomitant of low-density development. Residents have to travel further to all destinations and are more dependent on travel by private car. Terraced housing can be developed

with hard standing for cars on a forecourt. The 'town house' with an integral garage built into the ground floor was popular at one time. Such provisions, however, tend to be visually intrusive and damage the relationship of the house with the street. In many high-density areas of two- and three-storey houses, with good public transport, only kerbside parking is provided and this seems to function well.

Terraced housing, then, provides a standard of accommodation which is as good, or better, than the ubiquitous semi and has few relative disadvantages. Its success as a high-density form depends on efficient land use and planning.

TERRACED HOUSING – KEY VARIABLES

In the planning and design of terraced housing there are three key factors which can make a critical difference to the quality of housing it provides:

1   *Frontage width.* The narrower the width of terraced houses the more can be accommodated on any land area and the higher the density achieved. Some terraced housing has been developed with frontages as wide as 8 metres though this only reaches densities of about 45 units per hectare. At the other end of the scale experiments have been done with footages as narrow as 3.5 metres though this produces deep plans with narrow spaces difficult to light. Most terraces have frontages between 4 and 7 metres with most around 5 metres. These dimensions provide the optimum combination of efficient land use, economic construction and good internal planning.

2   *Overlooking.* To preserve the privacy of residents of buildings facing each other it is generally considered they should be kept a minimum of 21 metres apart. This distance might be reduced by placing windows at an angle or by screening devices. Separating houses by a reasonable overlooking distance provides a successful street width which is of good proportion while allowing for a carriageway, two pavements and a small front garden to each house. At the rear, each house can be provided with a 10-metre garden.

3   *Sunlight.* With a reasonable frontage width and a minimum distance between houses there should be no difficulty in providing adequate daylight to all main rooms. It is also important that all day rooms receive at least some sunlight. To achieve this, most houses using traditional plan forms need to receive sunlight on both sides. The optimum orientation is, therefore, east–west and this is a key constraint in planning developments of new terraced housing.

The traditional plan form works well and can continue to provide successful terraced housing. Some experiments in plan form have been made in recent years. One of these is the 'single aspect' house. This has all main rooms facing in one direction with only utility rooms and storage on the rear. This form is useful in addressing noise sources such as main roads or railways provided appropriate orientation can be achieved. Another innovation is to place kitchens on the 'front' or entrance side of the house so that living rooms can take maximum advantage of the rear garden.

Perimeter block flats

The problems associated with the large post-war housing estates have given flat living a bad image. Nevertheless, flats have proved a successful form of urban housing over a long period. Mansion blocks for middle-class occupation were built in London from the late nineteenth century and these were followed by similarly up-market developments in the first half of the twentieth century. The most desirable of these were in key locations such as on the borders of major urban parks or the esplanades of seaside towns. Tenement blocks have provided a common and enduring form of housing in Scottish cities. In recent years there has been large-scale growth in the provision of urban flats – many large-terraced houses have been converted into self-contained flats; tenement blocks have been successfully modernised and improved both by the public and private sectors; new flats have been provided for sale both by conversion and new construction.

What makes these developments successful is that they avoid most of the pitfalls which caused the large multi-storey estates to fail. Generally, they are modest in scale – flats of three or four storeys have commonly been built without lifts and many successful projects are within this height limit. Most blocks are built in tried and tested construction methods, avoiding the innovations which led to so many technical failures in the large estates. Most flats in successful blocks are small, recognising that flat living is more appropriate for small households rather than families with children. In their layout they generally avoid the complex networks of corridors, stairs and decks which are so often the location of abuse and crime. Above all, where the large estates ignored and destroyed the traditional street, successful flats work within the urban grain. Blocks of flats are set within the existing street pattern reinforcing the perimeters to street blocks. In large developments, the blocks themselves define and form coherent urban spaces – squares, courts or closes.

These modest and contextual flat developments sit alongside the large multi-storey estates. Their relative success is evident. But if small-scale flats are to be even more successful lessons can be learned from the shortcomings of the large-scale estates. These lessons fall into two key areas – the planning of blocks of flats and the choice of access systems.

BLOCKS OF FLATS – PLANNING ISSUES

Good planning and layout is essential in ensuring that flats make good housing. Three issues, in particular, need careful attention:

1   *Inter-relation of flats.* Many of the large estates were planned so that flats interlocked in a very complex manner. This resulted in living rooms and walkways being planned over, or next to, bedrooms so that noise transference became a major problem. Wet areas were placed over dry areas so that an overflowing bath or washing machine could cause havoc. Too often residents could not easily identify who their offending neighbours were. The solution is to plan flats in a simple repetitive manner stacking living rooms and wet areas above each other. Where this cannot be avoided, high-quality sound insulation and waterproofing would need to be installed.

2   *Outdoor space.* Too often outdoor amenity space was not provided at all. Where it was, balconies were often small and exposed. In large blocks, ground level outdoor space was a long way off and of poor quality. On many estates the occupants of ground floor flats had no access to the land outside their home. Ideally, all flats should be pro-vided with a garden, terrace or balcony. This should be generous enough to function as an outdoor room – to contain substantial planting, to use for sitting or eating out and for children's play. And it should be designed with a good degree of enclosure for privacy and shelter from the elements. In small blocks a communal garden can be provided at ground level providing a green space for the exclusive use of residents. Such an amenity is particularly valuable when children are to be housed in the block.

3   *Use of the ground level.* In many multi-storey blocks the ground was not used at all. This was often for reasons of architectural dogma – tower and slab blocks were supposed to 'float' above the ground allowing space to 'flow' underneath. Too often this 'flowing space' was dirty, windswept and totally useless. In fact the ground level is the most valuable and desirable part of a block of flats. In commercial areas it is highly valued for retail use. In purely residential parts there are competing demands from families with children, the elderly and

the disabled — all of whom value the ground floor for its accessibility and the opportunity of a garden. Any of these uses might be appropriate and the use of the ground floor must be considered in relation to the overall planning of a scheme and the mix of expected occupants.

BLOCKS OF FLATS – ACCESS SYSTEMS

Excluding the 'streets in the sky' approach which is now thoroughly discredited, there are three systems in common use:

1 *Gallery access.* From a vertical access point, which may include a lift as well as stairs, flats are reached from open galleries projecting from the face of the building. These have the advantage that they are open to light and air and readily observed. Their disadvantage is that some windows front onto the galleries and can be overlooked by residents and visitors passing by.
2 *Corridor access.* From a vertical access stack internal corridors are planned in the centre of the block to give access to flats on both sides. This system has the advantage that it can serve a large number of flats. However, the corridors are often long and featureless, poorly lit and ventilated. They are not overlooked by windows and this can encourage abuse.
3 *Staircase access.* All flats are reached directly from a vertical access point without the need for corridors or galleries. This system minimises the amount of communal space but, since each access point serves a small number of flats, it is expensive to include lifts in such a system.

Access systems were the most problematic aspect of large estates. The principle of 'defensible space' related the level of crime and abuse to the numbers of flats entered from each main entrance. Minimising the number of flats served by each entrance became a key issue in designing out crime. Staircase access was, therefore, by far the most effective from this point of view. If other systems are adopted there is likely to be a corresponding increase in the level of management and maintenance required for the common areas.[8]

A tower block revival?

For the most part, the post-war housing estates remain in bad odour and pose a continuing challenge for regeneration. Tower blocks, though, have enjoyed something of a revival. Several have been retrieved from stigma and renovated, often accompanied by changes in tenure and occupants (see Chapter 6, p. 133). Meanwhile, commercial developers have taken renewed interest in this type of housing. A few prestige schemes have been

▲ **4.12**   Montevetro, London

completed – most notably, perhaps, Montevetro on the banks of the Thames in West London. Designed by Richard Rogers this is a luxury development where apartment prices are measured in million. While not exactly a tower block the building ramps up to a height of 20 storeys from where residents can enjoy spectacular river views[9] (Figure 4.12).

More recently, there has been a flurry of proposals for new residential towers – these include 16-storey blocks of luxury apartments in Edinburgh;[10] a 23-storey residential block in central Manchester;[11] 28-, 29- and 30-storey residential tower blocks on the Isle of Dogs in London's Docklands;[12] and a 38-storey tower in the centre of Birmingham.[13] One of the most spectacular is a proposal for a 49-storey residential tower to be built at Vauxhall in central London. The tower would include green features such as wind turbines, and the use of geothermal energy.[14] By late 2004 very few of these schemes have got off the ground. It is too early to say whether homebuyers really do want to live high or whether a tower block revival is the stuff of architectural dreams.

HOUSING FOR NEW NEEDS

The changes in the population of Britain taking place at the turn of the new century means that there will be increasing numbers of elderly people and larger numbers of single people, many of them young. At the same time, mounting pressures to reduce travel, particularly to places of work, mean that many more people are likely to be working at home. Changing population and lifestyles create new housing needs. While many of these needs will continue to be met by the existing housing stock, they may be more appropriately accommodated in forms which are less conventional than the traditional family house.

The elderly and disabled

Self-evidently not all disabled people are elderly. Still less are all the elderly disabled. Nevertheless, it has long been recognised that many people do become incapacitated in various ways as they advance into old age and that their homes need to be designed to meet these changing needs. More recently, the 'Lifetime Homes' concept has been developed by the Joseph Rowntree Foundation. This took the view that any home might come to house someone who was permanently or temporarily disabled and a set of 16 design features was devised to ensure that new homes would meet the changing needs of most households. These included level or gently ramped access throughout; doors and corridors wide enough for wheelchairs; turning circles for wheelchairs in main rooms; socket outlets and switches at convenient heights; and bathrooms planned with side access to baths and toilets. In houses and maisonettes there should also be a toilet at the entrance level and provision for the installation of a lift or stair lift if required. Multi-storey flats also need to have lifts to met the 'Lifetime Homes' criteria.[15] Many of these requirements were incorporated into Part M of the Building Regulations in 1999, though the details of design for disability remain an area of specialist expertise.[16]

While the flexible design of all housing is a desirable aim, multi-storey forms are particularly suitable for housing the elderly. For most elderly people their space needs are modest and, with a need to increase housing densities, these can most easily be met in blocks of flats. Many elderly do not have the mobility to cope with gardening or the energy to manage external maintenance and flat living relieves them of these demands. Most importantly, perhaps, living off the ground creates much higher security. Ground level dwellings have windows and front and back doors which can be breached by intruders – a source of particular anxiety to vulnerable elderly people. An upper floor flat with a single entrance door and inaccessible windows is inherently much more secure. Common entrances can be secured by electronic locks and monitored by security cameras. In larger blocks, security and surveillance can be reinforced by concierge staff.

It is a short step from blocks of flats dedicated to elderly residents to 'sheltered housing'. At the most basic, these are simply blocks of flats which also house wardens – one for every 32 flats – which are on call in case of emergencies. More comprehensive sheltered schemes also include communal facilities such as a lounge and dining room. Bathrooms with specialist equipment and communal laundries may also be provided. These common and public areas are often grouped around the entrance and help to reinforce security. At the highest level of services and facilities for elderly residents are dedicated care and nursing homes. Again, the design requirements for such institutions are complex and specialised.[17]

Young people

In the past, most young people leaving home have rented their accommodation. This would usually be in general-purpose housing – a room in someone's home or a house or flat shared with others. Some would have moved into hostel accommodation whether provided by organisations such as the YMCA or by institutions for training and education. The student hostel is based on the college system which, in turn, grew out of the monastic tradition. Typically, each student is provided with a study/bedroom within a hall of residence in which communal eating and recreation facilities are also provided. The design of hostels and halls of residence is rooted in the need to control – to monitor comings and goings and enforce discipline. Contemporary approaches to student housing take a more libertarian approach. Students are housed in groups of three or four sharing a kitchen and bathroom, a form of housing which closely resembles a conventional flat.

The needs of most young people can easily be met by general-purpose housing. Like many elderly people, though, they neither want nor need the responsibilities of home and garden maintenance and are well suited to living in multi-storey flats. While many of the young will continue to find homes in the wider community, two new forms of housing have emerged in recent years specifically tailored to ease the transition into adult lifestyles:

1 *Foyers.* These emerged in France in the immediate post-war period. They provided basic accommodation for young single people backed up by common services. The *Foyer* idea did not come to Britain until

the 1990s. Their first aim is to provide a safe haven for young people in housing need. Residents stay for a limited period and during this time they are able to develop the social skills necessary to support themselves. *Foyers* provide high-quality accommodation in self-contained rooms or flats. Communal rooms are provided for recreation and training sessions. Most *Foyers* are newly built but they could easily re-use existing buildings adapted for their purpose[18] (see Case Study E).

Case Study E (p. 233)

2 **Caspar.** This concept was developed by the Rowntree Foundation and its full name spells out its purpose – city-centre *a*partments for single *p*eople at *a*ffordable *r*ents. Unlike *Foyers* they are not intended for young people in need of training and support. They aim to provide for people who can afford a sizeable cost rent but who wish to live in accommodation which is fully serviced and readily available on a short-term basis. They are intended to be located within easy walking distance of the work and leisure opportunities of urban centres. Two model schemes have been developed so far. Essentially these are developments of small flats, each housing one or two people grouped, around a secure common space[19] (see Case Study F).

Case Study F (p. 239)

Live/work

For some time, changes in technology and communications have made it much easier for people to work at home. That more people do not do so may, to a large degree, be due to the inflexibility of managers and employers. The pressures to reduce travel coupled with the shortcomings of the transport system are likely to make home working an increasingly attractive proposition. For many activities, working at home requires no special provision. For most desk-based activities the use of a spare bedroom or, at most, the conversion of a dining room, makes a more than adequate work environment. Such changes should be welcome since they intensify the use of urban housing. This increases effective density and supports a wider range of local services.

At the same time, there has been a growth in the construction of purpose-built live/work units. These might be dedicated developments built in areas previously scheduled for industry, or they might be included in predominantly residential projects in an effort to increase sustainability. Typically, these might include two storeys of domestic scale linked to a large double height well-lit space.[20] There seems to be a market for such units though it must be limited. These are, essentially, a revival of the traditional artists studio. Their appeal must be to those who need to work on relatively large-scale projects which may require an unusual pattern of working hours. Thus, the demand for purpose-designed live/work units is likely to remain small. It may be more important to develop workspaces alongside housing. This would allow more flexible patterns of living and working, and reduce the need for commuting.

THE PUBLIC REALM

It is both ironic and somewhat mystifying that, while the spatial and visual qualities of historic cities have had an enduring appeal, they have had so little influence on most new residential developments. For much of the twentieth century, new housing followed the principles of the garden suburb on the one hand and the 'radiant city' of towers set in parkland on the other. Both these approaches grew from theories – the Garden City ideal and the Modern Movement – which rejected the past and sought new urban forms to replace it. But history was not without its champions. In 1961 Gordon Cullen published *Townscape* – a cogent analysis of the elements of urban structure, finishes and features which together made old towns so attractive.[21] His work was widely admired but little acted upon. A little later came the *Essex Design Guide* which sought new standards in the spatial qualities of low-density housing based on the vernacular of traditional towns and villages.[22]

Creating successful urban housing depends on recognising and developing from the forms of housing which have endured. Making good-quality residential environments depends on a better understanding of how these forms fit together – the structure of the urban residential environment – and on a recognition of the importance of the traditional street.

The structure of urban space

There is now a general consensus that most successful urban environments are defined not by individual buildings but by a pattern of urban blocks. These blocks are delineated by a series of buildings joined up – more or less continuously – around the perimeter of a piece of land. The blocks delineate urban spaces. Between the blocks the fronts of the buildings face and define public areas – streets, thoroughfares and communal spaces. In the centre of each block the back of the buildings enclose space which has a relatively high degree of privacy and can be used for gardens or ancillary use. In residential areas it is the enduring forms of urban housing – the terraced house and perimeter blocks of flats – which most successfully enclose and define a pattern of public and private space.

URBAN BLOCKS – THREE VARIABLES

To effectively define coherent spaces it is essential that blocks are bordered by buildings which adjoin each other or are close together. Within this guiding principle, though, there is scope for conservable variation:

- *Size of blocks.* The minimum size of an urban block is defined by overlooking distance across the centre and the depth of building surrounding it. The effective minimum is, therefore, a block about 40 square metres enclosing an open space about 20 metres across. International comparisons suggest that many urban blocks range from small blocks near the minimum size up to about 150 × 180 metres.[23] Many Victorian-terraced streets were built in blocks of minimum width but up to 250 metres long. This type of block inhibits pedestrian movement. A pattern of smaller blocks is more permeable and encourages more journeys on foot.

- *Proportion of spaces.* The quality of a public space is partly a function of its size and scale. The ratio of the height of buildings to the width of the space is the critical factor. If the ratio is too low, a street may feel open and exposed though street trees can help to increase the sense of enclosure. If the ratio is too high, a street can feel canyon like and intimidating. Case examples suggest that comfortable street widths should be about twice the height of the buildings on either side.[24] Streets of two- and three-storey houses should therefore be 20 to 30 metres wide. The enclosure of squares and green spaces also needs to be of good proportion, though the layout of the space is also a critical factor.

- *Turning corners.* The design of corners for urban blocks is critical. Standard dwelling plans which repeat along the main frontages will not work on corners. Victorian terraces sometimes solved this with a corner shop of pub or avoided the problem altogether by leaving the corners open. Dwellings on corners need to face in two adjacent directions on the public side. Atypical house plans can be developed for corners.[25] In blocks of flats special type plans are sometimes designed for corners, but often the corner is turned by articulation of the entrance, lift and stairs. In urban design terms corners present an opportunity to introduce unusual and striking features.

The design of urban blocks is complex and it does not follow that they are best laid out, as a regular pattern of uniform blocks in rectilinear form. The introduction of variety and interest may be critical. Within the perimeter cartilage, buildings of different height and design can be introduced. Façades can set forward or back sometimes creating small squares off the main street space. The plan form of the blocks can be irregular. In many traditional towns the plan shape of blocks has developed organically with a high degree of irregularity. This helps to create spaces of varying height and width. It also introduces 'closure' where a vista is stopped by another street or building turning the corner. In any successful urban environment, it is also important to create landmarks and focal points which help people relate to, and identify with, their locality. Finally, the detail is important. The choice of paving materials, the appropriate selection and integration of street furniture and signs, the introduction of planting and street art, can critically affect the quality of urban space.

The importance of the street

One of the key factors in the design of twentieth century urban housing was the vogue for separating vehicles and pedestrians. This was promoted on the grounds of safety but its real purpose was to cater for increased motor traffic. Dedicated highways were created on which motorists could drive at speed unencumbered by the need to pay heed to pedestrians. The corollary was networks of pedestrian-only spaces which were often dirty, windswept and vandalised. Outside peak hours many pedestrian ways were little used and became the focus of crime and antisocial behaviour.

Belatedly, the traditional urban street has been discovered to have inherent virtues. Streets are usually lined by homes or shops which have windows overlooking them. They frequently have a large number of entrances with people coming and going. They are traversed by a mixture of pedestrians, cyclists, commercial and public service vehicles. This combination of overlooking, and the passage of traffic in a variety of forms, creates a pattern of visual supervision at most times of the day which is an effective deterrent to wrongdoers. While many streets are successful, on many there are conflicts mainly between the danger and pollution caused by vehicles, and the needs of pedestrians. But there are ways of improving streets so that they can be more pleasant but still function well.

Traditional streets provided space for a number of activities, including journeys on foot and by bicycle, social interaction, children's play and, if course, vehicle access and parking spaces both for goods and personal transport. With the growth in car ownership the needs of vehicles have come to dominate – parking consumes most of the space; high traffic levels and excessive speed creates dangers for pedestrians especially where streets are allowed to become 'through' routes. The balance needs to be redressed, reducing the dominance of the motorcar and allowing a wide range of street activities to function well. In Holland, the development of the *Woonerf* or 'residential precinct' established the principle of balance between vehicles and pedestrians in the 1970s, and similar innovations have been introduced in other European countries.[26]

In Britain, a range of measures have been carried out to reduce the volume and impact of traffic in residential areas, with a more comprehensive approach recently being introduced: the Transport Act of 2000 gave local authorities the power to designate 'home zones', and a number of pilot projects have been implemented.[27]

HOME ZONES – KEY ISSUES

To create a home zone, changes to the typical layout and use of urban streets are needed. These can include:

- *Speed restriction.* Local councils have the power to impose speed limits of 20 miles per hour and lower limits can be introduced with government approval.
- *Reducing through traffic.* Closing streets to through traffic and creating traffic 'mazes' are long-established tools for environmental management. Traffic reduction is also central to home zones.
- *Traffic calming.* The use of speed humps, width restrictions and abrupt changes of direction are established means of reducing vehicle speeds. These may be supplemented by features to mark the entrance to a restricted area; changes of paving surface and 'rumble strips' to slow vehicles; and by the introduction of surfaces designed to be shared by vehicles and pedestrians.
- *Environmental improvements.* Space can be set aside for street trees, shrub planning and seating areas to improve visual quality and encourage greater use of the street.
- *Play space.* Streets used to provide space for a wide range of children's play. A safer, shared environment would provide more scope for informal play. Designated play areas can be located off or adjoining streets reached by safe pedestrian routes.
- *Parking.* Streets will continue to provide parking for residents and visitors but this should be well planned and integrated into the design of the street. In areas of high demand, it also needs to be managed and this is best done through the introduction of a 'controlled parking zone'.
- *Resident involvement.* Local people's needs and aspirations are best understood through an effective consultation process. Community involvement is also key to promoting more use of the street and maintaining planting and other environmental improvements.

Home zones can be created in existing residential environments. The principles, however, can equally well be applied to new development where opportunities exist to purpose design well-balanced mixed-use residential streets. A key factor in creating successful urban residential areas is to limit car parking which consumes so much space in low-density suburban areas. In areas of terraced housing, on-street parking can provide for more than one car per house. In flat developments, kerb-side parking would provide less than 100 per cent. Nevertheless, in high-density urban areas with good public transport, car ownership rates are generally quite low. They might be reduced even further by the shared ownership and use of cars – 'car clubs' – which is now being piloted in several urban areas. Reducing the space for storage of cars increases that available for the communal and recreational use of streets (see Case Study G).

Case Study G (p. 245)

Security and design

Crime and antisocial behaviour are serious urban problems though there is plenty of evidence to suggest that they are not confined to the cities – rural and suburban areas are experiencing increasingly rising crime. The key to a safer urban environment is natural surveillance. Behaviour on the streets is observed by many eyes – from overlooking windows and entrances; from passing vehicles; and from those on foot. High levels of activity and surveillance make the urban street a relatively safe form of environment. It is important, though, to ensure that high levels of surveillance continue at night by provision of high levels of street lighting. In designing the urban environment it is important to avoid certain pitfalls – pedestrian-only routes, particularly alleys flanked by blank walls; sharp corners where sight lines are blinded by high walls; large shrubs planted against pedestrian ways. All these can present hiding places for felony and hazards for the unwary.

In response to rising crime – or more particularly the growing fear of crime – there has been increasing reliance on security. Houses are routinely fitted with alarms and security lights. Blocks of flats are now, almost invariably, provided with security systems ranging from electronic intercoms at entrances through to surveillance by closed circuit television (CCTV) and main entrances staffed by security guards. Such systems can be strongly justified in blocks accessed by stairs and corridors which are not overlooked and are traversed by relatively few people. They are not socially divisive, and are seen equally commonly in blocks of luxury flats and as a solution to the problems of run-down multi-storey social housing estates. The same cannot be said of the gated communities which are becoming increasingly widespread in urban areas.[28] Where residential streets become enclosed by fences and gates it draws attention to privilege and may actually invite crime. The urban street has inherently strong security which is evidenced by the fact that many of the most wealthy citizens live on streets with open public access.

Good design can help produce safer environments and security systems can harden the targets of criminals. But none of this is proof against crime, still less against environmental degradation as a result of anti-social behaviour. The prevalence of litter, dumped rubbish, abandoned cars and domestic appliances, vandalism and graffiti, is all too evident in many urban areas. Design cannot be a substitute for good urban management and policing. This requires regeneration measures to redress social exclusion and low attainment. It requires maintenance teams to clean and repair the built environment. And it requires patrols to deter and punish miscreants. All this is expensive and requires good organisation. Recognising this is as much a part of an urban renaissance as is an awareness of security in the design of urban space.

KEY POINTS

- The form of urban residential areas is rooted in history, often based on old street patterns and land boundaries. Much is the result of responses to the slums of the nineteenth century. This includes by-law terraces and different types of multi-storey flats. Many estates of flats failed but some still offer viable models.
- The most enduring types of urban housing are terraced houses and modest-scale blocks of flats in 'perimeter block' form. Both types can provide good-quality accommodation.
  - Small-terraced houses offer similar accommodation to the modern semi-detached but can be built to higher densities. New-terraced houses need to be well planned in relationship to each other with orientation carefully considered.
  - Most successful blocks of flats are of modest scale and provide mainly for small households. Blocks need to be well planned internally and flats need to be provided with outdoor space. The choice of access system is critical.
- With increasing numbers of the elderly it is important to recognise that any dwelling might come to house someone who is disabled.

New housing needs to be flexibly designed to make it adaptable to the need of the handicapped. Multi-storey flats are, in many ways, well suited to the needs of the elderly.

- Today's larger numbers of young people can also be well housed in flats. Many will share general needs housing. The more vulnerable will need hostel accommodation – students just leaving home, the homeless who might need the support of a 'foyer'. Some need purpose-built small serviced flats.

- Housing needs to be designed as contiguous buildings which define urban blocks. These enclose semi-private space on the inside. On the outside they can shape and define well-proportioned streets, squares and other urban public spaces.

- The traditional urban street is important because it provided a public space which was secured by the surveillance of overlooking windows and doors, and passers by. It provided a space for walking, casual meetings and children's play. These uses now need to be encouraged by restrictions on the use of motor vehicles.

5

CONSTRUCTION

THE GREEN AGENDA

SUMMARY

Given the threat to the global environment, there are four main issues that the large quantity of housing to be constructed in the near future will need to address. The first is conserving energy – ensuring that housing consumes less energy in its day-to-day use. Urban housing has inherent advantages in conservation but there are key innovations to be made. These include the achievement of higher levels of insulation, garnering the benefits of solar gain and improving the efficiency of ventilation. The second issue is to develop the generation of energy from renewable sources. This is partly a matter for public policy but new means of gathering and generating energy can be built into houses or groups of homes. The third issue is water management. This is likely to become an increasingly serious concern and should mean changes in the way homes are used. Less water needs to be used and more collected and recycled. A fourth, overarching issue is the conservation of scarce resources and the protection of the wider environment. This has critical implications for the selection of suitable materials for house construction. At the same time, good design should ensure the promotion of a healthy and diverse environment. Alongside these concerns there is a renewed emphasis on 'off-site construction'. System building has a chequered history but new approaches may have benefits in reducing waste, improving quality and speeding the production of the many new homes needed.

ENERGY CONSERVATION

The green agenda for housing design and construction has been set largely by a number of small-scale one-off projects. These include a range of individual house types built at Energy World, Milton Keynes (1988);[1] Brenda and Robert Vale's Autonomous House (1994);[2] the Oxford Solar House by Susan Roaf (1995);[3] and the Integer House pioneered by the

Building Research Establishment (BRE) and realised in two demonstration houses built in Wiltshire (1999).[4] Abroad, small settlements have been developed as low-energy prototypes such as 'Sun village' near Lund in Sweden[5] or the Solar Village at Amersfoort in Holland.[6] Similar settlements have been proposed for Britain and such communities seem to hark back to a long-held idyll of rural self-sufficiency. What these projects have in common is that they are low destiny and sited in relatively remote locations. The innovations they embody are not necessarily applicable to urban housing design.

The first major difference is transport. Research has shown that a family living in a very energy-efficient house in a remote location will use more energy overall than a similar family living in a wholly un-insulated traditional house in the inner city simply because of their dependence on the private car.[7] High-density urban housing makes a substantial contribution to reducing carbon emissions simply by engendering more efficient transport. The second major difference is inherent in the form of urban housing. It has been estimated that a two-storey house in the middle of a terrace uses 30 per cent less energy that the equivalent semi-detached house simply because of its smaller proportion of external walls. A flat will show a more or less similar reduction depending on its position in the block.[8] Urban housing, then, has inherent energy advantages over the low-density forms prevalent in the recent past. There are lessons, though, from the green agenda which can be appropriately applied to make these advantages even greater. Energy consumed in the use of housing can be reduced by making best use of orientation and by improving insulation and ventilation.

Passive solar gain

The orientation and design of buildings can result in considerable heat gain from sunlight. Some energy may be absorbed in the building fabric but the main gains are through glazed areas. Solar radiation is of short wavelength and can pass through glass – energy reflected off internal surfaces is of longer wavelength and cannot. Radiation cannot escape and heat thus becomes trapped in glazed spaces. Any large glazed area can trap solar energy within buildings.[9] However, conservatories are significant design elements which can be used to maximise the collection of solar gain. 'Sun spaces' – smaller glazed enclosures attached to the south faces of houses – can have a similar effect. This can include enclosed balconies placed at higher levels of buildings. Once gained, it is important that buildings have sufficient thermal mass to absorb the heat and allow it to be released slowly. This usually means high-density materials such as masonry, concrete or dense blockwork.

To the proponents of maximising solar gain, orientation is of critical significance. As Brian Edwards put it in his book on sustainable housing:

> *Since passive solar gain can make an important contribution to reducing energy consumption in housing (by as much as 18 per cent without house type change) orientation of dwellings should be up to 30° either side of south. Coupled with this, the area of glazing should be restricted on the north and enlarged on the south. As glazing areas are partly a function of room needs this results in houses of different layout according to the aspect... To achieve solar penetration between houses an unobstructed angle of 10° is needed on south elevations.*[10]

The ideal, then, would be housing built in parallel rows all facing south and widely spaced enough to allow maximum penetration of sunlight in winter, though this would vary with latitude.

It would be difficult to form well-functioning streets on this basis since they would be fronted by living rooms and bedrooms on one side and by utility rooms on the other. South elevations can also experience very high heat gains in summer that necessitate shading and heat extraction measures. In hot climates it is customary to protect south façades from the sun. In the design of urban housing there are multiple constraints to address, and a range of priorities of which maximising passive solar gain is but one. The need to define coherent urban blocks, and to create well-defined spaces and streets which are safe, is probably of greater importance. This may mean compromises on solar gain. It is certainly important to avoid placing large glazed areas or main living rooms on north elevations but placing them on the east or west side is acceptable. This should provide some solar gain while avoiding the high levels of exposure in summer.

Higher insulation levels

To conserve energy in the use of housing it is important to ensure that as much as possible of the heat produced within the home is retained. Insulation acts as a barrier between the inside and the outside reducing the rate at which heat is lost. The means and methods of insulation have long been well understood. What has changes is the intensity. There has been a focus on raising the standards of insulation both through regulation and through the incentive of grants programmes. There have been successful experiments in creating 'super-insulated' houses. In these, insulation levels are very high – reducing heat loss so much that conventional heating systems can be dispensed with altogether. Sufficient heat is generated by the use of appliances and by human activity to make

HOUSING AT STADLAU, VIENNA

▲ **5.1** The south façades have large areas of glazing to maximise solar gain

This development of social housing in the Viennese suburb of Stadlau, completed in 2000, was designed to high environmental standards by architect Wolfgang Reinberg. The triangular site is laid out strictly in accordance with the aim of maximising solar gain. Along the northern edge of the site is a linear block of four-storey flats. In front of this are a series of short terraces of two-storey houses. All the blocks are set in parallel rows running east–west. The blocks are spaced apart so that winter sun can penetrate to the base of the buildings. The houses are designed with the living rooms and bedrooms on the south side. These have large windows and sun spaces to gather maximum heat from the sun. The north sides have kitchens, bathrooms and utility rooms. These have small windows to minimise heat loss.

The core of the houses is constructed of in situ concrete. This includes the basement, ground floor and internal walls. The external walls are built of concrete blocks insulated with 100-millimetres mineral wool. The house

▲ **5.2** Utility rooms on the north side have small windows to minimise heat loss

walls thus have a high mass, which helps to store and retain much of the heat gained from the sun. The houses have green roofs finished with soil covering and turf, providing some earth sheltering. To meet the ecological aims of the design considerable emphasis is placed on the use of natural and non-toxic building materials. The main construction is of timber and concrete avoiding the use of brick which, in Austria, is regarded as energy intensive in manufacture. Internal finishes are mainly wood sealed with natural oils.

good the small amounts of heat lost – except perhaps in the very coldest weather when small unit heaters may be required.

In urban housing the need for insulation is less because of the extent to which dwellings are joined together. It is generally assumed that housing will be occupied for most of the time and that thermal insulation between dwellings is not necessary. Insulation must, therefore be concentrated on the parts that are not joined. In traditional construction, roofs have been the weakest point in terms of heat loss and increasing quantities of insulation have been incorporated into roof structures to combat this. Heat loss from external walls has been reduced by higher-insulation standards in the fabric and by the incorporation of double or even triple-glazed windows with insulated frames. Generally the proportion of external wall is low in urban housing but particular attention must be paid to 'flank' walls – the end of a terrace or the side of a block of flats. Dwellings in these positions are not protected by an adjoining building and there is a particular need to achieve high levels of insulation in these walls. Ground floors have not always been insulated. Though it is now normal to include an insulation layer, the principle of 'earth sheltering' must be taken into account.

The earth can act as a stabiliser helping to prevent extremes of temperature in housing. In winter, it acts as a heat store releasing warmth into the house, in summer it absorbs heat and helps to keep the building cool. This principle has been used in the design of several individual houses which are partly or wholly underground. It is one of the features of the Hockerton Energy Project in Nottinghamshire where 50 per cent of the roofs and walls of the houses are earth sheltered.[11] Large-scale earth sheltering is impractical in high-density urban housing but basements and semi-basements were common features in much traditional housing. They were often blighted by dampness but modern water-proofing methods make partial earth sheltering a viable proposition, particularly on sloping sites. Planted or 'green' roofs involve partially covering buildings in earth.[12] Their main attraction in urban housing is in providing planted areas at high level. Soil depths are normally not much more than 100 millimetres – too thin to provide full earth sheltering – but they do have some effect in stabilising internal temperatures.

Improved ventilation strategies

Good ventilation is essential to remove stale air, to provide air for combustion for boilers and cookers and, perhaps most important, to remove moisture which can cause condensation and seriously affect health. Most traditional houses are well ventilated. Air passes in and out through flues, extractors and permanent vents and also through gaps in ill-fitting windows and doors. Air leaking in can cause cold draughts and discomfort. More importantly, air vented out takes with it a substantial amount of heat energy generated within the house. On top of this, mechanical extracts themselves consume electrical energy. The solution is to devise a ventilation strategy for the whole building which is natural, avoiding the use of fans, and well-controlled, minimising the heat carried out by vented air.

Natural air movement has two main causes. One is the pressure difference created by wind. The other is that as air is heated it expands and becomes lighter. Warm air tends to rise, causing convection currents. The combination of negative wind pressure and convection creates a phenomenon called 'stack effect'. A ventilation system based on these natural movements is known as 'passive-stack ventilation'. It has three essential components:

1 *Air inlets,* usually at low level which can be opened and closed. These can include trickle vents in windows. Alternatively, fresh air can be ducted into the building from high level.
2 *Air outlet points* in key locations, probably in all main rooms but particularly kitchens and bathrooms. The outlets also have adjustable controls and feed into a duct system which conducts the air up through the house.
3 *An outlet at roof level.* The action of the wind causes negative pressure which supplements natural convection to suck out air. This process can be aided by cowls at roof level which turn with the wind to maximise the effect.

For maximum benefit the air leaving the building passes through a 'heat exchanger'. This contains a series of hollow tubes and fins that extract heat from the outgoing air and redirects it back into the building[13] (see Case Study H).

Case Study H (p. 251)

RENEWABLE ENERGY SOURCES

Reducing the amount of energy used in housing would make a considerable contribution to cutting carbon dioxide emissions. But if nothing else were done most of the remaining energy required would still need to be provided by burning fossil fuels. There is a need to invest in alternative systems which will provide energy from natural or 'renewable' sources. Some of these alternative sources – wind power for instance – can most effectively be provided on a national or regional scale. Others can be incorporated into houses or groups of homes. Most alternative energy sources require considerable investment and it may take a long time to gain a significant return. As these systems come into more common use, though, they will become cheaper and economically viable. These alternative sources can be divided into those that provide heat, those that provide electrical power, and those that provide both – combined heat and power (CHP).

Heat sources

Alternative heat sources basically feed into conventional systems that provide piped hot water and space heating by hot water radiators. There are three main alternative sources:

1 *Solar power.* Heat from the sun can be garnered using solar panels. These have various designs but the most effective consists of a metal collector plate to which tubes are bonded or incorporated containing heat transfer fluid. This fluid is circulated by a small pump to transfer heat to a conventional hot water cylinder. The optimum size for a solar collector is about 4 square metres – enough to provide hot water needs for the average household in summer. Collectors need maximum exposure to the sun. They should be mounted facing somewhere between south-west and south-east, and at an optimum angle of 34°.[14]

2 *Biofuels.* Heat energy can be provided by burning organic fuels. These can be provided from crop and forestry residues, animal waste, sewage or suitable municipal waste. Raw material can also be purpose grown as energy crops. These include coppiced willow, rape-seed oil and straw. Wood and straw-based fuels can be burned to provide hot water and space heating. They need special boilers, though, and for this reason are best used in systems serving groups of dwellings. It is also possible to turn biomass into gas or to extract heat by fermentations. Although biofuels still produce carbon dioxide emissions in combustion they are produced from sustainable sources which makes them 'carbon neutral'.[15]

3 *Geothermal energy.* Volcanic areas such as Iceland provide a rich source of geothermal energy. In Britain the opportunities are limited but there are two possible sources. In some areas it is possible to tap into deep geothermal aquifers to provide hot water and heating on a district basis. Elsewhere ground source heat pumps may be possible. These involve circulating water in a coil buried deep in the ground and through a heat pump. This extracts heat using the small temperature difference between ground level and the earth deep below. These systems can only be used to supplement other heat sources.[16]

Electrical energy

Alternative sources of electric power are generally not stand-alone systems, certainly not for an individual house. They can only work successfully when connected into the national grid. This requires an input–output meter, which can accept and measure flows both ways, and a supportive pricing system. In this way natural sources can be used to provide power to homes when available and any surplus fed into the public system. When the natural sources are inoperative the homes can take electricity from the public supply in the normal way. There are three possible sources of alternative electrical power:

1 *Photovoltaics (PV).* PV cells absorb light and convert it to electrical energy. They are combined in panels which can be incorporated into buildings as roof or wall cladding, roof tiles, glazing, roof lights or sun-shading devices. They work best when facing south and mounted at an angel of 30° to 45°. PV is an effective way of garnering electricity even in temperate climates. The modules used to be expensive but are rapidly falling in price.[17]

2 *Wind power.* Wind turbines are an efficient form of energy generation but they are not generally viable for housing schemes, still less for an individual house. In certain areas wind turbines may be helpful in providing supplementary electricity to homes on a district basis. Proposals have also been developed for mounting wind turbines on top of housing tower blocks in Bradford.[18]

3 *Fuel cells.* These are devices similar to a battery, and which produce energy through electrolytic action. They draw on a store of hydrogen, usually in liquid form, and combine it with oxygen from the air to produce electrical energy. Water vapour is produced as a waste product. Due to their small size they are commonly thought of as an alternative source of energy for vehicles. If they become viable, though, there seems no reason why they should not have applications in buildings.[19]

CHP

The process of generating electricity produces surplus heat on a large scale. In the past this heat has been dissipated into the air via cooling towers or washed away in nearby rivers. The wastefulness of this process is self-evident. As long ago as the 1940s the large housing scheme at Churchill Gardens in London (see Chapter 4, p. 83) was provided with heat from the waste produced by the nearby Battersea power station. CHP units neutralise this waste by providing both heat and electricity. Basically, they consist of a generator powered by oil or gas which has a means of collecting heat by a water circulatory system – in principle similar to a vehicle engine. Strictly speaking, they are not an alternative source of energy since many are run on fossil fuels. They can be run, though, on biofuels. Solid fuels can be burned in a gasifier to produce a hydrogen rich gas that can be used to drive CHP units.[20]

CHP for housing is most effectively used on a group or district basis. Small units are now being developed, though, which can be installed in individual houses. Basically, the units are calibrated to provide for the heating needs of the housing they serve. Electricity is generated at the same time which also serves the housing but any surplus can be fed into the national grid. The attraction of CHP systems is that, while they may still produce carbon dioxide emissions, they are far more efficient that conventional systems of power generation and heating provision. Using CHP ensures that a far higher proportion of the energy released from fuel is put to beneficial use.

WATER MANAGEMENT

It is generally recognised that, with a growing world population, water will increasingly be seen as a scarce resource and may well become a cause of conflict. It may seem perverse, though, to be overly concerned about water in a country like Britain which has high annual rainfall. There are, however, three reasons why better water management is highly desirable. First, climate change has brought more extreme variations. There may be periods of exceptionally heavy rainfall and, equally, prolonged dry spells when drought can become a problem. Second, there is rising demand for water. Between 1985 and 2000 domestic water consumption increased by nearly 40 per cent per household and if current increases are maintained demand will outstrip supply by 2012.[21] Finally, the collection, treatment and distribution of water is costly and consumes considerable quantities of energy. Using treated water for all purposes is wasteful and unnecessary.

There are some low-key methods of reducing water consumption. Metering is increasingly common and is likely to act as a curb on demand. Reductions in water consumption can be made by the use of more efficient domestic appliances. These include low-flush or dual-flush toilets; water efficient showers; and low water-consuming washing machines and dishwashers. A positive impact can be made on water management by considering installations for the collection and recycling of water. Both these have an impact on water use and also reduce the quantity of liquid waste leaving homes. This, in turn, reduces the energy costs involved in wastewater collection and treatment. Alternative methods of sewage treatment can reduce these still further.

Water collection and recycling

There is a long history of collecting and storing rainwater and, until relatively recently rainwater butts to collect water from roof drainage were a common domestic feature. Simple mechanisms can now be installed to divert a proportion of rainwater from downpipes to fill storage tanks. These can be connected to external taps which allow the water to be used for washing cars and watering gardens. The collection of rainwater can be supplemented by recycling 'grey water'. Water used for washing can be collected from sinks, washing machines, basins, baths and showers. It is then passed through a simple filter to remove any large solid particles, and collected in a tank. Grey water is very suitable for flushing toilets and can be used for other purposes such as watering plants. It requires a dedicated distribution system within each house which can be gravity fed or pumped.[22] The collection and recycling of water within homes reduces the need for waste management but also contributes to reducing the rate of 'run off' which has been a significant contribution to increasing flooding.

Sewage treatment

Measures to reduce demand for piped mains water are desirable and probably necessary in all forms of housing. A number of housing projects which aimed at full self-sufficiency have also installed alternative methods of sewage treatment. There are three basic types:

1 *Composting toilets.* There are several types which use a variety of methods to aerate and sterilise sewage in a small chamber. The compost can then be removed for use as fertiliser. Little or no water is used.[23]
2 *Reed beds.* Wastewater and sewage from a group of homes is fed into a series of ponds planted with reeds. These filter and aerate the effluent allowing aerobic decomposition and absorption of organic material. Clear water flows out of the system.
3 *Bioworks.* This uses the principle of hydroponics. Waste is pumped into a treatment tank. Plants are supported by a mesh above the tank with their roots growing in the water. Waste is processed both by plant and bacterial action. The whole system is contained in a greenhouse so that water can also be collected by transpiration and condensation. Water emerging from the bioworks is clear and of 'grey water' quality.

The practicality of these alternative methods for urban housing schemes is questionable. The composting toilet requires considerable dedication on the part of the users. Reed beds are effective but space consuming. Bioworks systems may be practical for serving small groups of homes. There really is little incentive, though, either for individuals or landlords to install such systems as an alternative to mains sewerage.

CONSERVING ENVIRONMENTAL RESOURCES

Environmental concerns in the development of new housing fall into two areas. The first concerns the conservation of both energy and scarce resources. It revolves around the concept of 'embodied energy', the proper consideration of which has a considerable impact on the selection and use of materials in the construction of housing. The second concern is the maintenance of a healthy environment and the creation of health and well-being in new residential areas.

Embodied energy

The energy 'embodied' in a building is all that used in the production of its materials and components, and in their incorporation during its construction. For example, the energy embodied in sawn timber would include that required to fell the tree; to transport it to a timber mill; to saw it into sections; to kiln dry it; to treat it with preservative; to transport it to the building site; and finally to cut and fix it in position. Timber is one of the most low-energy materials available. Others, particularly those involving minerals, require a much more complex process of extraction, manufacturing and transportation. The measurement of embodied energy is complicated. A number of different methods have been used which produce considerable variation in their results. Further, refinement of this relatively new field is likely to lead to consensus and greater consistency.

There is also inconsistency in the estimates of the amount of embodied energy in buildings. Traditional thinking held that the amount of energy involved in construction was relatively small compared with the energy consumed in building use – 20 per cent or less. Recent research into energy life cycle analysis (ELCA) suggests that embodied energy may be as high as 50 per cent of a building's lifetime energy use. This would include construction, maintenance and demolition. Whatever the true figure it is clear that embodied energy is a major part of the total energy used in housing. Reducing embodied energy can make a significant contribution to cutting greenhouse gas emissions. This can be done by using low-energy materials, making greater use of local materials, and recycling:

- **Low-energy materials.** Some building materials have lower embodied energy than others. For example, an aluminium window frame has almost three times more embodied energy than a timber one. Even taken over a 50-year life span, the aluminium frame will consume almost twice as much energy as timber. UPVC window frames also have high embodied energy and, since they are manufactured from fossil fuels, also draw on non-renewable resources. This is a new field with limited information at present. Developed countries are beginning to assemble databases and it is likely that increasing information will become available. In Britain, 'environmental profiles' can be obtained from the BRE giving relative energy implications of a range of building materials and components over their whole life cycle.

- **Local materials.** With globalisation it has become increasingly common to transport building materials and components long distances. Partly this is a result of specialisation, but for the most part it is cost driven. Most forms of transport do not meet their full environmental costs and this is particularly true of aircraft. Cheap freight transport is creating a large amount if international traffic. Using local materials can much reduce the transport costs embodied in building construction. It may also have the advantage of restoring the distinctive character of different localities. In the past, the quality of the built environment in different regions was often shaped by the use of local stone or brick or by vernacular construction such as shiplap boarding, tile hanging or textured render.

- **Recycled materials.** Recycling is a means of conserving a proportion of the energy embodied in salvaged and re-used materials. Salvaging attractive artefacts – such as fireplaces, panelled doors, railings – from old buildings is established practice. But bricks, timber and steel sections can also be salvaged and re-used. Masonry can be crushed on-site during demolition providing landfill or, more importantly, aggregate for new concrete. Concrete is one of five building materials containing the highest embodied energy. The use of recycled aggregate reduces energy with no loss of performance. Other materials can be re-processed. These include glass – to produce blocks and tiles; newspaper – to produce thermal insulation; plastics – to produce pipes, containers and components; rubber – to produce sheeting and flooring; and aluminium re-smelted and re-used.

The reduction of embodied energy in housing construction could have a major impact on reducing greenhouse gas emissions, and in these terms is second only in importance to greater energy efficiency in building use. But it also has a significant impact on the environment. Reduced transport and lower levels of manufacturing means a consequent reduction in damage to the natural environment. The use of recycled products and lower-energy building products reduces the demand for scarce resources and the environmental impact of the extraction and manufacturing of materials for building.[24]

A healthy environment

In protecting the global environment the major concern is the impact of high energy use. But sustainability also requires a concern for health – the health of the wider natural environment and the health of the residential environments we create for ourselves. The mining of metal ores, and the quarrying required to extract stone and gravel for building, destroys large swathes of the natural environment and the habitat it provides for wildlife. The transport of these materials creates noise, atmospheric pollution and erosion causing wider damage to natural habitats. The manufacturing of many building materials causes atmospheric pollution and often results in the release of damaging and toxic chemicals as a by-product. The disposal of waste from manufacturing and construction processes creates further environmental damage – despoilation through the use of landfill sites or atmospheric pollution through combustion.

Part of the answer to these problems is the greater use of recycling. Most metals can be re-used, reducing the need for mining. Glass can be reprocessed and gravel substitutes created through crushing and recycling masonry. Both of these reduce the need for quarrying. Recycling is expensive but the costs can be offset by making mining and manufacturing companies meet the environmental costs of their operations. Better regulation is beginning to enforce this, as is the increase in landfill taxes. Another part of the answer is greater concentration on materials from renewable sources. Examples of these include rubber, which can be continuously harvested and straw, a by-product of agriculture, which can be processed effectively to provide insulation panels for building. The most important renewable material, though, is timber.

In principle, trees can be grown and re-grown on the same land and thus provide continuous cropping. But there are severe limitations. The use of hardwoods in building has been partly responsible for the destruction of tropical forests. Once destroyed, rainforests are hard to re-grow. Some estimates suggest that, at the present rate, almost all commercially exploitable forests will have disappeared by the mid-twenty-first century. In recent years an international independent body – The Forestry Stewardship Council – has monitored hardwood forests and given certification for sensitive management and good practice. Millions of acres of forests in Europe and South America are now subject to monitoring and there is a similar scheme in the USA. Given good management, hardwood forests can be continuously managed to provide a source of building materials. In the UK and Europe, oak, beech and chestnut are available from renewable sources.

The use of hardwoods needs to be very carefully controlled and managed. Softwood production is much less sensitive. Tree species such as pine are fast growing and can be harvested regularly in large quantities. Softwood has been commonly used for house building worldwide and high-quality timber framed and clad houses are characteristic of North America and Scandinavia. Timber is both low energy and sustainable and its greater use in housing construction is to be encouraged. It can be used structurally to support quite large multi-storey buildings.

As well as consideration for the natural environment it is important to consider the well-being of the environments we create. The issue of health in housing has a long history. A key concern of nineteenth century reformers was the disease created by overcrowded housing conditions and poor construction. These problems created a drive for higher space standards and also better buildings. Reforms concentrated on better damp-proofing and ventilation. Even so, many health problems persisted until the late twentieth century. Often these were the result of condensation caused by poor insulation and cold bridging and inadequate ventilation. Coincidentally, the new concern for energy conservation should also produce more healthy buildings. Better insulation standards should reduce or eliminate condensation problems. Better controlled and more effective ventilation should remove moisture along with dust and allergens. There remains concern about the toxins contained in some paints and stains and some particles and fibres in insulation and board materials. The use of many harmful elements such as lead or cadmium is no longer generally permitted, though some are still being used in some plastics production for components such as water pipes. Organic solvents can cause problems and water-based paints are generally considered less harmful to health.

Greening the built environment is an important concomitant of urban housing development which can affect health and well-being in a number of ways. Most obviously, planted areas provide spaces for outdoor play

FLATS AT CHORLTON PARK, MANCHESTER

▲ **5.3** The five storeys of this development are the maximum permitted with a timber structure

This development comprises 20 one-bedroom flats for shared ownership and seven two-bedroom flats and maisonettes for private sale. It was designed by architects Stephenson Bell and completed in 2002. The L-shaped building is mostly three-storey but rises to five with the addition of four duplex units on the main façade. The project is notable for two reasons. The first is its construction. The project has a level of insulation high enough to eliminate the need for conventional heating but its key feature is its structure. All of the main load-bearing elements are timber. The floors are of 300 millimetres deep engineered timber joists and these are supported on load-bearing braced timber stud walls. Bracing is provided by a 'glulam' timber ring beam around each flat at each floor level. The most prominent structural timbers are the framing to the private balconies. These are 300 × 300 green oak sections sourced from hurricane-flattened forests in Northern France.

The second issue of note is the location. The development is built on a 'brownfield' site – previously occupied by a petrol filling station – but it is in a suburban location. The surrounding buildings are all two-storey semi-detached houses with a density of around 30 to the hectare. The new building reaches a density of 180 per hectare. It is a demonstration of how the suburbs can be intensified. The area is currently poorly served by public transport and residents are dependent on cars. More development of this sort would help to boost public services.[25]

and recreation. Urban planting has a 'green lung' effect, converting carbon dioxide to oxygen. While this is by no means sufficient to counteract fossil fuel emissions, it is some help in mitigating their impact. Tree planting can also provide shelter. Belts of trees, strategically planted can protect housing from excessive wind. Trees planted along streets and walkways help to protect pedestrians and cyclists from light rain or from the heat of the sun. Planting also provides succour and support for a range of wild life.

A central aim of sustainability is to maintain the diversity of biological species in the environment – 'biodiversity'. This is a concern of conservation generally but has implications for urban housing. Concern has been expressed that many 'brownfield' sites have spontaneously generated plant and animal ecologies of considerable diversity. Building on them will destroy many of these natural habitats. Some of them could be preserved as wildlife parks within urban developments. The concern to maintain natural ecosystems has sometimes led to the view that only native species should be planted in urban landscaping. This is probably excessively purist. The wide variety of garden plants introduced from abroad is a rich source of diversity in itself, and domestic gardens are known to support a wide range of animals, insects and birds.

In addition to gardens and landscaped areas, buildings themselves can contribute to biodiversity. Balconies and flat roofs can provide space for planting in pots and containers. These can be supplemented by green roofs and terraces. Generally, these comprise a layer of soil spread over a waterproof deck to provide support and drainage. The soil, if planted with grass species or sedum, will support a range of insects and act as a food source for birds. A recent innovation is to cover roofs in steel wire cages containing loosely compacted rubble. This acts as a medium for wind-borne seeds and gradually becomes a mass of planting. One housing scheme in Montpellier, France takes this to the ultimate conclusion by covering most of the walls in contained rubble. Eventually the entire building will be clothed in greenery.[26]

OFF-SITE CONSTRUCTION

The greater use if prefabrication in buildings has long been on the agenda of designers and technologists though, on the face of it, off-site construction does not form part of the green agenda. There is, however, increased awareness of the problems of waste. Construction is estimated to generate 16 per cent of total waste in the UK. House building contributes a large proportion of this partly through packaging. There is also waste in the off cuts and surplus mixed materials generated by crafts such as carpentry, bricklaying, plastering and decorating.[27] In its report of 1998, the Construction Task Force – chaired by Sir John Egan – drew attention to the waste involved in traditional construction. It also noted that up to 30 per cent of construction costs were incurred to remedy poor workmanship or design, and that site-based labour was being managed at only 40 to 60 per cent of potential productivity.[28]

The Egan report recommended greater efficiency in construction by making it more like manufacturing. This would not only involve a greater proportion of buildings being produced in factories, it would also mean the end of traditional practices such as competitive tendering. The engagement of developers, producers and suppliers in 'partnership' agreements was seen as improving quality and reliability and reducing delay. The proponents of off-site construction saw it as a great advantage to have the major part of buildings made in factory conditions. This would allow components to be accurately made and assembled in clean conditions by skilled people. Both waste and defects would be reduced and the finished products would have greater quality and precision. This, it was claimed, would result in lower building costs. More, the reduction of on-site time would speed the development of sites and the production of housing, thereby reducing finance and management costs. This prospect was seized on by a government anxious to boost production to meet the projected growth in households. Off-site construction was actively promoted and in 2004/2005, 25 per cent of the budget for new social housing would be spent on homes that used some element of prefabrication.[29]

Forms of prefabrication

An admiration for industry was one of the hallmarks of the Modern Movement in architecture and there was a strong desire to see greater precision and the production of more buildings and building components in factories. Various experiments with prefabrication were carried out during the 1930s and in the post-war period the building of housing using industrialised systems became widespread, particularly in Scandinavia and Eastern Europe. In Britain, a large number of multi-storey social housing estates were built using 'heavy panel' systems. These used pre-cast concrete panels joined together at the edges so that they formed a series of rigid boxes that would stand up without an independent structural frame. These systems became discredited in the 1970s partly because of inherent defects and partly through association with unpopular large housing estates.

In the current revival of prefabrication there has been a concentration on 'lightweight' systems. Experimental schemes have been carried out which mainly use three basic methods:

1 **Timber frame.** Timber is a low-cost, low-energy material, which can be supplied from renewable sources. Its widespread use in housing is to be promoted by innovative and more efficient building methods. A pioneering method of timber construction was the Segal System developed from the 1980s onwards. This is not actually prefabricated but uses standard-sized materials in a simple method of construction which has been widely used in self-build schemes (Figure 5.4).[30] A prefabricated timber frame system has been developed by the Timber Research and Development Association (TRADA) and this has been used in the prototype Integer house.[31] The Swedish Huf'n'Puf system has been used in a development in Dulwich. This uses a factory produced post and beam system built over a basement constructed of precast concrete panels.[32] Timber frame systems can be faced with a variety of materials to meet weatherproofing and fire resistance standards.

▲ **5.4**   Timber-framed terraced houses in North London self-built by residents using the Segal system

2 *Steel panels.* Pressed steel is the archetypal material for factory production. It is lightweight and malleable and is produced in a wide range of shapes in vehicle manufacture. The size of pressed steel panels is limited by the need for rigidity. Larger panels need to be profiled to ensure stability. Nevertheless, some prefabricated systems have been developed. A prototype 'flat pack' house has been developed in Teeside. It is constructed in single-leaf steel sheet panels finished in waterproof insulated render. These are fixed to a framework of lightweight load-bearing steel studs. The interior is finished with conventional plasterboard lining and the void filled with mineral wool insulation.[33] A similar system has been used to construct part of the second phase of the Greenwich Millennium Village with a factory purpose built on site to produce the pressed steel panels.[34] Manufacturers such as Fusion, Terrapin and Haironville TAC also produce panel systems based on steel framing or pressed steel technology.[35]

3 *Modular construction.* Modular construction involves prefabricating whole rooms or groups of rooms ready for assembly on site. Their form gives them inherent structural stability. They can be taken to site, placed in position, connected to services, jointed and sealed, all with a minimum of on-site labour. This means factory finishes and fittings can be maximised with the achievement of high quality. Particular attention was attracted by the Murray Grove scheme completed by the Peabody Trust in 2000. This scheme contained thirty flats in a five-storey building. Each flat comprised two prefabricated boxes designed to the maximum size to fit on the back of a lorry. The boxes are built of steel construction and each is fully fitted with doors, windows, fittings and finishes (Figure 5.5).

As with the pioneering low-energy developments, many of the innovations in off-site construction have focused on individual houses at low density. Systems suitable for urban housing must address the problems of building at high density. Prefabricated timber frames can be used successfully to build terraced housing – though special attention needs to be given to separating them with fireproof construction. For multi-storey flats modular units can be stacked to achieve high density. Flats are usually repetitive in plan and this makes them particularly suitable for production-line manufacture. Added to this, the modular form offers speed of erection. It has subsequently been used in several multi-storey developments (see Case Study I).

Case Study I (p. 257)

The lessons of history

The issue of prefabrication in housing construction is not new. In Britain we have been down this road before. From the early 1960s there was a

▲ **5.5**   Murray Grove, pioneering project using modular construction

concerted drive to solve the long-standing problem of housing shortage by increased production. Industrialised methods were seen as the key. Then, as now, it was promised that these would provide lower costs and increased production. The government invested heavily in research and development. Experiments were made with various approaches. Eventually, a large-scale programme was implemented using precast concrete panels. Mostly these were used to construct blocks of multi-storey flats for local authority tenants. The whole programme came to an abrupt halt with the Ronan Point disaster in 1968. As a result of an explosion in a tower block, concrete panels collapsed like a pack of cards, killing several people.

The immediate issue was 'progressive collapse'. The dangers of this required retrospective strengthening to most buildings of 'heavy panel' construction. But subsequent investigation revealed more far-reaching problems. In many such blocks there were technical shortcomings caused by poor construction of the panel joints. This resulted in water penetration into flats and rusting of reinforcement. This deterioration, together with poor specification, caused erosion and spawning of the concrete. These technical failures proved costly to remedy. But even without that, subsequent analysis showed that the supposed cost advantages of system building was largely illusory. The cost saving over traditional construction being estimated to be less than 3 per cent.[36] To an extent this seems to be true of contemporary developments with some of the pioneering prefabricated schemes running into delays and cost overruns and containing significant defects.[37] Proponents of off-site construction argue that such problems will reduce once production volumes reach higher levels.

Even more serious than high costs are the possibilities of technical failure. The consequence of the disasters of the 1960s was a much more cautious approach. Prefabrication was introduced into building construction but gradually in an incremental manner. Off-site fabrication of components such as trussed rafters and factory finished window and door composites are now commonplace, and there is scope to increase the number of prefabricated components and assemblies. The lesson of history is that there are no panaceas. All innovations need to be thoroughly tried and tested before they can be successfully absorbed into the construction process. This is true both of off-site construction and of many of the other new approaches offered by the green agenda.

KEY POINTS

- The use of energy in housing can be reduced by taking advantage of heat collected from the sun. The achievement of 'solar gain', however, is only one of a multiple of considerations necessary for successful urban housing design.
- In reducing the waste of energy, insulation acts as a barrier between the inside and the outside by reducing the rate at which heat is lost. Good control of ventilation is also necessary to minimise the escape of heat in expelled areas.
- Alternative sources of energy extract heat or electricity either directly from the sun or from energy trapped by organic or geological processes. These sources create no carbon dioxide emissions. CHP does create emissions but uses fossil fuels much more efficiently.
- With climate change water supplies are uncertain. Greater demand for water consumes increased energy in treatment and distribution.

Both problems can be mitigated by better management and by increased water collection and recycling.

o— A substantial proportion of total energy use in a building is 'embodied' through extraction, processing and transport of materials used in construction and through demolition at the end of its life. This 'embodied energy' can be reduced by greater use of low energy, and locally sourced materials, and by recycling.

o— The health of the natural environment can be protected by the greater use of materials from sustainable and renewable sources. The most important of these is timber. The health of the built environment can be enhanced by the greater use of planting which acts as a 'green lung' and promotes biodiversity.

o— Off-site construction has the potential to reduce waste and speed production. Its use in high-density housing, however, has a history of technical failure. The increased use of prefabrication needs to proceed with caution and in an incremental manner.

6

RECLAMATION

RE-USING BUILT SPACE

SUMMARY

Existing buildings are a valuable resource. Part of their value is that they shape the established and familiar urban environment; part that they contain embodied energy and their re-use reduces the costs and time involved in new build. Realising this value means improving old buildings and adapting them to new uses. Existing housing is responsible for a high proportion of greenhouse gas emissions. Reducing this involves improvements in energy conservation through better insulation and ventilation. It also means greater energy efficiency in the way existing homes are used. The improvements possible in occupied homes are limited, but there is greater scope for change in the relatively high proportion of homes which change hands or become vacant. Many of these empty homes can be converted and adapted to new patterns of occupation. This applies both to older, larger houses and to multi-storey social housing estates which have become stigmatised and unpopular. There are also opportunities to create new housing by re-using and adapting buildings originally used for other purposes. Industrial buildings of various kinds can be converted to housing. Urban commercial buildings also provide such opportunities and a particular resource is the often-unused space over shops. Re-using this redundant space can make a major contribution to meeting the high demand for new homes.

THE IMPORTANCE OF EXISTING BUILDINGS

During the middle part of the twentieth century the inner areas of Britain's cities were torn apart by redevelopment. In urban centres hundreds of Victorian commercial and industrial buildings were demolished and replaced by modern shops and office blocks. In the areas around the urban centres hundreds of thousands of homes were cleared away – terraced housing in the English cities run down, neglected and often multiple occupied; overcrowded tenement flats in the cities of Scotland. In their place rose estates of multi-storey social housing which promised better homes but proved unsuitable for their occupants. In their turn they, too, became neglected and run down. The process of redevelopment too often proved negative and destructive. Established communities were broken up and dispersed, their networks of social contact and interaction destroyed. Equally important, the buildings and streets which made up the familiar urban fabric also disappeared.

Fortunately it is now recognised that wholesale clearance is not the way to create successful cities. The social and economic life of urban neighbourhoods develops slowly over time. Making prosperous and vital urban environments means building on what is there. A neighbourhood may be unpopular; its buildings may have deteriorated into disrepair. Some may need to be replaced through selective renewal. But most can be preserved, repaired and rehabilitated or converted to new uses. In the process the established social and economic life will be preserved and enhanced by new residents and new businesses. The best of the familiar buildings, streets and landmarks will be retained and restored, and can be supplemented by carefully designed new infill.

Preserving and enhancing existing urban environments is highly desirable, but it is not the only importance of existing buildings. In the context of the Kyoto protocols they are also important for the energy embodied in them. The adaptation and re-use of existing buildings saves some of the energy that would be required to construct their replacements. True, even in demolition some of the embodied energy can be retained through salvage and recycling of components and materials. But much more can be saved through rehabilitation and conversion. Even the most comprehensive refurbishment process involves stripping a building out, but keeping its basic structure. The foundations and superstructure of a building represent about 20 per cent of the total construction cost. This is an indication of the minimum embodied energy which can be saved through building re-use. In most cases it would be more because most buildings can be converted and renovated without totally gutting them. There is also the added advantage that building re-use reduces the time taken and the disruption caused by new construction.

While preserving the energy embodied in existing buildings is important, it is an even greater priority to reduce the energy consumed by the existing stock in its day-to-day use. In terms of perceived housing need, 3.8 million new homes will be required in England by 2020. If this target is achieved these new homes will certainly be built to higher standards of energy conservation than in the past. It is unlikely, though, that they will be to such a standard as to have a neutral impact on energy consumption. Even if they were, this would make a minimal reduction to the energy consumed by housing. In 2002 the existing housing stock was about 21.5 million homes and this was responsible for 27 per cent of the nation's carbon dioxide emissions.[1]

Reducing the environmental impact of the existing housing stock is a major priority. But it is much more difficult than achieving higher-energy conservation standards in new construction. The improvements that can be made in occupied homes are limited. Greater opportunities sometimes arise when houses are vacant. In the owner-occupied sector about 1.4 million homes change hands each year.[2] A substantial number of tenancies in rented housing also change. When homes change hands there may be an opportunity for improvements to be made. More significantly, most housing needs major refurbishment every 30 years or so. The greatest opportunities to improve the environmental performance of existing housing lies in that part of the stock which is already in need of major renovation.

Vacant and unpopular housing

In 2003 it was estimated that 3.4 per cent of the housing stock in England was vacant – about 740 000 homes. Some of this was empty during sale or transfer or while awaiting planned modernisation, conversion or redevelopment. Other stock was simply not being marketed because of poor condition, disputed ownership or abandonment.[3] At the same time, there was a great deal of unpopular housing. Nearly 1 million homes were estimated to be in areas of low demand. There is some overlap in these figures since some of the vacant houses are also in areas of low demand. Nevertheless, this substantial quantity of existing housing in need of renovation represents both a resource – a contribution to meeting housing need – and an opportunity to carry out major improvements.

Unpopular housing does not have a distinctive character. Low demand affects all types of housing and all forms of tenure. Over half is houses and bungalows with the remainder multi-storey flats of various types. About half of it is private sector stock. The remainder is social housing, though the majority (about 380 000 homes) is owned by local authorities, with a smaller amount (about 90 000) in the hands of housing associations. Unpopular housing is characterised in the public sector by lack of waiting lists and high transfer requests, and by high levels of vacancy and tenancy turnover. Unpopular private housing is typified by low and falling values, high levels of empty and abandoned homes and by high population turnover. The causes of unpopular housing and its nature varies considerably between the north and south of the country.

In the north of England unpopular and abandoned housing is widespread in many cities. One of the main causes is economic decline. This results in high unemployment, low wages and reduced spending power which is reflected in the neglect of housing and the environment. It is also a cause of population decline. This creates a housing surplus in which people have more choice. Once unpopular areas go into decline houses become boarded up and vandalised, forcing long-term residents out and causing more abandonment. Nevertheless, unpopular areas are often very localised with only a few streets vacant and boarded up. Such areas will not regenerate spontaneously. Even in places with high levels of owner occupation the action of individuals cannot arrest decline. Public intervention and finance is needed, aimed both at improving housing conditions and creating a better social mix. This was the approach of the government's Housing Market Renewal initiative of 2003. This established nine 'pathfinder' projects in areas of low demand in cities of the North and Midlands. Early results of such regeneration schemes suggest selective demolition has been necessary when there is a clear surplus of homes. Sometimes housing needs to be replaced with more attractive stock. Renovation has also been effective with conversion or major rehabilitation of the housing and enhancement of the quality and security of the environment.

In the south of England there is generally high demand for housing. In the past poor quality housing was associated with large houses rented in multiple occupation and some of these remain today. Most unpopular housing is now in inner-city social housing estates and is, again, concentrated in small pockets. Many estates are associated with crime, antisocial behaviour, deprivation and low attainment which stigmatises them and makes them hard to let. Many are also of bad design and in poor condition. Addressing these problems is partly a question of management changes to introduce a more mixed population and more suitable housing. But investment and physical improvements are also vital. A range of approaches has been carried out to improve and regenerate unpopular estates.[4]

IMPROVING THE EFFICIENCY OF EXISTING HOUSING

There may be many changes that are needed to adapt existing buildings to new uses and to bring the older housing stock up to modern standards.

But to meet the public policy objective of reducing greenhouse gas emissions it is a high priority to make existing housing more energy efficient. The scale of this task is immense and, in many ways, energy efficiency is more difficult to achieve in existing buildings than in new constructions. Even in the most thorough-going refurbishment, there may be constraints posed by the existing structure which prevent the achievement of high levels of efficiency. In most vacant housing the improvements required fall well short of comprehensive and the possibilities for raising energy standards will be limited. Most limited of all is the improvement of occupied housing but, even here, a range of modest changes can be made to considerable benefit.

In principle, the key concerns are the same as in new construction. On the one hand, there is the need to minimise waste by reducing the amount of energy lost in heat escaping from buildings. On the other hand, it is important that the consumption of fossil fuels is reduced by ensuring that the installations and appliances in buildings are using energy in the most efficient way. In reducing waste the most significant change is to install much improved insulation to existing buildings. But it is almost equally important to improve ventilation since a great deal of energy is lost in warm air leaking out of buildings. All these changes come at a cost but they also bring benefits to householders through reduced energy bills. Some improvements bring very rapid financial benefits though more complex changes may have a much longer 'pay back' period. In overall terms it was estimated in 2004 that improving the least energy-efficient homes would cost about £5 billion but would result in savings of running costs of £1.2 billion annually.[5]

Improving insulation

Most heat is lost from buildings by conduction through the external envelope. The aim of better insulation is to improve the thermal performance – the *u*-value – of the outer skin. Each of the elements of this skin – roof, walls, windows and floor – require a variety of approaches depending on the nature of the existing construction:

- *Roofs.* In much existing housing the roof is responsible for the greatest proportion of heat loss. At the same time, most roofs present opportunities for improving insulation simply and effectively. Simplest are pitched roofs where the loft space is unused. Insulating quilt can be easily laid between or over the ceiling joists. Most pitched roofs already have some insulation but contemporary standards suggest this should be increased to 150–200 millimetres. Habitable loft spaces are a little more complex, but insulation board can be fixed between or over the inside of the rafters. Flat roofs present, perhaps, the greatest challenge.

Internal insulation is disruptive and often impractical. If the roof covering needs replacing, an insulation decking can be laid as a base for the
new roof finish. If the existing asphalt or felt is good, new insulation
can be laid over the top. This comprises preformed expanded poly-
styrene boards with an integral mortar topping. These need to be
weighted down at the edges and at abutments. The roof needs to
have an adequate kerb surround and care needs to be taken in
providing appropriate drainage.

- **Walls.** Existing walls can be insulated externally, internally or within.
  In most housing of traditional construction built in the last 50 years, the
  external walls will be of cavity construction. Mostly this will be a small
  cavity of 50 millimetre rather than the wider cavities needed for contemporary insulation. Nevertheless, insulating cavity walls is simple
  and provides significant thermal improvement. New insulation can be
  injected from the exterior with no disruption to the residents. Internal
  thermal lining using insulation board or a similar new insulating layer
  can also be effective. It is highly disruptive, however, and care needs
  to be taken to avoid 'cold bridges' at beams and partitions. Internal insulation reduces room sizes to a degree and this may be significant. In older
  housing it may obliterate original features such as mouldings and create
  difficult junctions where it meets window and door openings. Externally, a basic form of insulation can be provided by fixing insulating
  slabs which are then rendered over. This obliterates the original
  materials and details and is usually of bland appearance. It is inappro-
  priate for frontages which have significant architectural quality. A
  range of proprietary systems of external 'over-cladding' have now
  been developed which provide both insulation and rain protection.
  These are of good appearance but need to be used on a large scale
  with a high degree of standardisation. They have been successfully
  used on large multi-storey blocks.
- **Windows.** A great deal of heat can be lost through windows particularly through the glass. Frames can transmit heat and materials, other
  than timber, need to be insulated. Double glazing is desirable and, on
  exposed façades, triple glazing. Existing casement or fixed windows can
  usually be re-glazed with sealed double-glazed units. Sash windows are
  more difficult unless purpose made for double glazing. Replacement
  windows may be the most effective way of reducing heat loss though
  this is disruptive and costly. If replacement is impractical, some benefit can be gained from insulated and well-fitting shutters or by hanging
  curtains with thermal lining. The addition of conservatories, or glazing in
  of balconies, has become increasingly common. Very often, though,
  this is done to increase living space. There may be little benefit if the

glazed extensions are poorly orientated and a net disbenefit if they are heated in winter.

- **Floors.** Generally the ground floors of houses are the least exposed in terms of heat loss. Insulating them is invariably highly disruptive. Suspended timber floor can be effectively improved by fixing insulation slabs between the joists though since it involves removing most of the boards it is not often done. Solid floors can be insulated with propri-etary boards and then resurfaced with a new finish. This usually involves raising the floor level which creates difficulties around thresholds and involves removing all fittings.

Insulating existing buildings can usually be done effectively where major refurbishment is carried out. Where work required is less comprehensive, and particularly in occupied buildings, there are much greater difficulties. A pragmatic approach is required which involves implementing the simplest improvements and identifying and remedying the greatest areas of heat loss.

Controlling ventilation

Good ventilation has long been seen as critical to good health, removing stale air, and providing an input of oxygen. Flues and chimneys provided valuable ventilation in older buildings. More recently, regulations have required the installation of permanent vents to guard against condensation and the installation of mechanical extracts to remove moisture from kitchens and bathrooms. Effective ventilation is still needed but, in a more energy-conscious era, there is concern about uncontrolled air move-ment. Warm air leaks out of uncontrolled vents and flues. Cold draughts leak in through gaps around doors and windows, and service entries.

The aim of controlling ventilation is to prevent the unwanted passage of air in and out of the building while, at the same time, being able to pro-vide all the ventilation necessary for health and comfort. It is possible to install a ducted system of ventilation which passes through a heat exchanger at roof level. For most existing housing this is a far too com-plex approach. Good control can be achieved by a number of small-scale improvements which involve minimal disruption and modest cost:

- **Draught stripping.** A good deal of air leaks around door and win-dow openings. This can usually be stopped by a range of proprietary draught-stripping products, though there are some problems fitting effective seals to sash windows. Openings to unheated spaces such as loft hatches should also be sealed. Draught stripping may be supple-mented by fitting of additional lobby doors which are particularly effective at front entrances.

PRIORY COURT, WALTHAMSTOW

Priory Court estate was built in the early 1950s and comprised mostly six-storey slab blocks. The flats were of generous standards but were poorly insulated and constructed. By the 1980s technical shortcomings had led to condensation problems and extensive water penetration – both through leaking roofs and cracking walls. A regeneration scheme started in the 1990s involved the redevelopment of some blocks but fourteen of the slab blocks were comprehensively refurbished. This involved new lifts, internal improvements and the development of unused ground floor space to provide flats for disabled tenants.

The technical problems were addressed by giving the buildings an entirely new external envelope. A proprietary over-cladding system was installed to provide a rainscreen and insulation to the outside of the existing walls. New double-glazed windows were built into the new external skin. On top of each block innovative barrel-vault lightweight roof shells were constructed. These prevented rain from reaching the existing roof covering which was topped with new insulation panels. The scheme ensured that the blocks were given a high level of thermal protection entirely by adding insulation externally. This meant the improvement work could be done with little disruption to the internal space.

▲ **6.1**   Typical block before improvement

▲ **6.2**   An identical block after addition of new external skin

- **Controllable vents.** Permanently open vents should be closed and fitted with grilles which can be opened and closed. Chimneys should be sealed and fitted with dampers or vent grilles. Trickle vents can be installed in window frames to help combat condensation. These adjustable vents can provide close control of air movement, though the ability to open windows and doors provides control of large-scale ventilation.
- **Air extract.** In areas of high humidity it may be necessary to use extractor fans. To reduce energy use these should be closely controlled by a timer or a humidistat. Linking the fan to the lighting circuit is an effective way of controlling bathroom fans. There are proprietary 'trickle vent' systems which use little energy. A range of passive vents is now available which could be effective in replacing powered extractors altogether.
- **Venting appliances.** Gas burning appliances, particularly boilers, require a supply of oxygen to operate. Providing oxygen is essential to prevent an unhealthy build-up of carbon dioxide. To prevent combustion air being drawn in without control it is helpful to provide fresh air ducted directly to boilers and, perhaps, to cookers. Boilers are also available with 'balanced flues' which drawn in and expel gases simultaneously direct to the outside.[6]

In most existing buildings it is impractical to install complex air handling systems. It is important, though, to devise a ventilation strategy which can be implemented through a range of simple measures. This will identify what level of air change is needed in each room and provide the necessary inlets and outlets to achieve it without causing excessive air movement throughout the house.

Using energy more efficiently

It is important to reduce the waste of energy in existing housing by better insulation and ventilation. It is also important to ensure that the systems and appliances that use energy in the home do so in the most efficient way. Partly this efficiency lies in using each source of energy for its most appropriate purpose. For example, electricity is not efficient when being used to produce heat. Its use for heating and generally for cooking should be avoided. At the same time, it is the only practical method of providing lighting and powering household appliances. Greater efficiency should be a key consideration when adapting or installing energy-using equipment:

- **Heating.** One of the consequences of reducing the waste of energy is that more heat is retained within the home and heating systems can be smaller. If they need to be replaced the sizes of radiators and boilers can be reduced. Greater efficiency can be achieved by having good controls on heating systems including programmers and thermostatic valves. But the greatest potential is in the heating source. Modern condensing boilers use less energy by re-absorbing some of the excess heat. For the future combined heat and power (CHP) may be a viable option. At present, this is only practical if it serves a substantial number of homes and this provides an option for the refurbishment of multi-storey blocks. Small CHP units are becoming available which could be used in individual homes.

- *Lighting.* The use of electric lighting can be reduced by making maximum use of natural light. At night greater use could be made of task lighting rather than more extensive general lighting. More attention could be given to turning off unwanted lights and to installing more efficient fittings. Most homes are lit by tungsten filament lamps. These are highly inefficient with most of the energy being converted to heat and only 5–10 per cent into light. Compact fluorescent 'bulbs' are five times as efficient and last seven to eight times longer. Quartz-halogen lamps are more than twice as efficient and long-lasting as tungsten lamps. Simply replacing tungsten lamps with more effective forms could make a considerable reduction in energy use.

- *Domestic appliances.* Purchase price is often the main consideration when installing a new domestic appliance. In terms of lifetime efficiency, though, the key concern should be energy in use. Electric cookers are cheaper than gas cookers but use far more energy and cost much more to run. Many computers and television sets are now equipped with 'standby' modes which are supposed to save energy though many of these are not very effective. Kitchen appliances such as washing machines, dishwashers and refrigerators have been fairly profligate in their use of energy. More efficient models are now being developed and most appliances are now given a graded rating on their energy efficiency.[7]

More efficient use of conventional energy in the home will save on gas and electricity use and reduce carbon dioxide emissions. In addition, there is some scope for the garnering of renewable energy in existing housing. Solar hot water panels are relatively easy to install though they need to be linked into an existing hot water storage system. The use of photovoltaic (PV) panels may be viable, particularly if roof replacement is being carried out. The use of such systems may be most appropriately considered where large-scale refurbishment or substantial adaptations are being made to existing housing.

CONVERSION AND MODERNISATION

The great majority of existing housing is in need of improvement to make it more energy efficient. This can most effectively be done when houses are empty or in such bad order that they must be made vacant to allow major refurbishment. Under these circumstances there is often an opportunity to improve housing quality and increase the numbers of separate dwellings by conversion. This can be done in four ways:

1 *Subdivision.* Large houses or other buildings can be subdivided by new construction to create several separate self-contained homes. This often involves upgrading and improvement of the common areas of the buildings.
2 *Combination.* Small flats can be combined either vertically or horizontally to make larger self-contained dwellings. This can make older blocks suitable for a different mix of households and family sizes.
3 *Re-planning.* Older housing often had low space standards and poor kitchen and bathroom facilities. This can be remedied by changing the use of part of the space to create modern sanitary and cooking facilities, and reducing the number of bedspaces.
4 *Extension.* Housing space can be increased by extension. This may involve an addition to the roof or conversion of an unused loft. It could mean building out with new construction of one or more storeys or enclosing an existing terrace or balcony.

These approaches have been applied to a range of older housing usually combined with improvements to standards of construction and energy efficiency. Older large houses have been converted and modernised as have a substantial proportion of the multi-storey flats built during the twentieth century.

Large houses

One of the most significant causes of housing deprivation in nineteenth and twentieth century cities was multiple occupation. In London and other large cities houses of four and five storeys, originally designed for wealthy families with servants, were divided up into several lettings. Commonly, each tenant would rent one or two rooms which might house a whole family. All the occupants would share a kitchen, toilet and bathroom – if there was one. In the four-storey tenements typical of Edinburgh and Glasgow large flats intended for middle-class occupation were 'made down' into separate lettings with similarly poor standards. During the 1950s and 1960s many of these overcrowded buildings were condemned as slums and demolished to make way for new multi-storey housing estates.

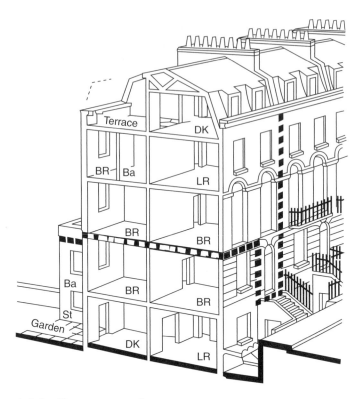

▲ **6.3**   House conversion

From the early 1970s there was a renewed emphasis on reclamation, largely generated by the introduction of improvement grants and the intervention of local authorities to ensure comprehensive regeneration of the worst areas. In each house the original tenants would be re-housed. The entire building would then be comprehensively refurbished and divided up into a number of self-contained dwellings. Figure 6.3 shows the conversion of five-storey Georgian houses in Islington. The original house is divided into two large family maisonettes. The lower one is entered from the basement and has sole use of the garden. The upper one is entered by the original street door and has an open-air terrace at roof level. In other conversions the upper floors might be converted into smaller flats, one per floor.

Renewal of the building fabric, creating separate dwellings and ensuring good space standards, were the main priorities. But there were some key planning issues. One was the efficient provision of services and this involved placing kitchens and bathrooms above each other, usually in the centre or at the back of the house. Another was minimising noise transference. This could be partly achieved by 'stacking' – placing living rooms over living rooms, bedrooms over bedrooms (in Figure 6.3 the bedrooms are zoned together). Where this could not be achieved sound reduction construction was incorporated in the floors. A final issue was the management of the common areas. Where there were several flats on the upper floors the main entrances were provided with electronic intercoms. This secured the building against intruders and allowed upper floor residents to speak to visitors without descending several flights of stairs.

Tenement housing

Tenements were most common in Scotland and these were built for a wide range of income groups. Many of the worst problems were in the larger flats which had been subdivided, such as those in the Gorbals demolished in the 1960s. But the much smaller flats designed for low-income tenants were little better. When clearance became discredited tenement blocks began to be retained and improved. Working class flats in the Govan area of Glasgow were among the first to be rehabilitated in 1972. These blocks contained three tiny two-roomed flats on each floor, all sharing a single toilet on the common staircase. There were no bathrooms. The solution was to re-plan the three flats to form two of reasonable size providing each with its own bathroom making them self-contained.[8]

Tenement-type blocks were also built in English cities – first by the philanthropic housing societies in the nineteenth century, later by local authorities. Mostly these took a similar form. They were four or five-storey high with flats on each floor usually reached by access galleries. These estates were built to re-house the occupants of the most seriously overcrowded multiple-occupied houses. When complete they provided self-contained flats to a much higher standard than the old housing that surrounded them. Over the years the services and fabric of the buildings deteriorated and the standard of space and facilities had been overtaken by rising aspirations. Many such blocks became unpopular and hard to let.

Figure 6.4 shows the conversion of a typical tenement estate in London in the early 1980s. The five-storey blocks contained mostly two-bedroom flats with tiny kitchens and bathrooms. The tarmac courtyards were of bleak quality and completely open to public access. On the ground and first floor flats were combined vertically to make family maisonettes, each with their own garden and separate entrance. On the upper floors flats were re-planned, making one bedroom into a bathroom and enlarging the kitchens. This made them into small flats suitable for households without children. Lifts were installed and the staircases secured by electronic intercoms. The courtyards were landscaped to form communal

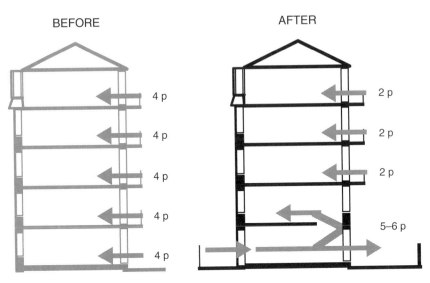

BEFORE

AFTER

▲ **6.4**   Conversion of a tenement block

gardens private to each block. These changes meant that almost all the children in the blocks were accommodated on the ground and excluded from the upper floors. They also meant that all the entrances to the flats were turned outwards recreating the form of the traditional street.[9]

These schemes show that tenement flats can be converted to make very successful housing. Many have been modernised by community housing associations or by local authorities. Others have been sold to developers for improvement and sale. Regrettably many have been demolished and there are many blocks, particularly in London, which remain unimproved. Modernising tenements does not add to the total stock of housing. It does ensure that substantial and familiar buildings are retained and their improvement involves considerably less construction energy than redevelopment.

Post-war housing estates

As a result of large-scale slum clearance more than 600 000 high-rise flats were built in the inner areas of Britain's cities during the 1950s and 1960s. From early on these estates of tower and slab blocks were criticised as unsuitable for families. This was partly because of the safety of children in high buildings and partly because the young families were isolated from the ground. The relationship between indoors and outdoors, and the supervision of children, which was an integral feature of the traditional street, had been destroyed. These criticisms led to the inception of high-density/low-rise estates. In these the flats were reached by open pedestrian decks – 'streets in the sky'. More than 300 000 flats were built in such estates in the late 1960s and 1970s.[10] But the high-level 'streets' proved no substitute for their ground-level counterparts.

In all types of multi-storey housing, problems developed in the common areas – the lifts, stairs, corridors and walkways as, on the whole, these were not overlooked or supervised. On many estates children began to vandalise and abuse these areas from an early age. This syndrome of anti-social behaviour escalated as children grew into teenagers and, at its worst, this resulted in serious personal crime, drug abuse and gang culture. Early efforts to tackle these problems focused on security issues and electronic intercoms – which had proved successful on small blocks – were introduced on a wide scale. In large blocks these simple entry-phone systems invariably failed. More sophisticated systems were developed where security doors were supplemented by CCTV surveillance cameras monitored by 'concierge' security staff. Peace could be bought, but at a heavy price.

The problems of many multi-storey estates did not end with social instability and serious management difficulties. Many had been built through innovative building systems using precast concrete panels. These often developed technical problems which led to water penetration, spawling concrete and condensation. By the mid-1980s a counsel of despair had developed. Many estates were in poor condition and were evidently unsuitable as the housing for low-income families. The apparent solution was to tear them down and replace them with new family houses with gardens. The London Borough of Hackney became expert in blowing up tower blocks, while the government sponsored housing action trusts (HATs) became vehicles for large-scale demolition and redevelopment of multi-storey estates in London and Liverpool.

Local authorities all over Britain have reached for the dynamite option to solve their problems with multi-storey estates. But it is a mistaken policy for three reasons. First, demolition repeats the errors of the past – it destroys communities. The attachment of residents to multi-storey estates may be weak but many people do like their homes and are prepared to work to improve them. These community values provide a good basis for successful regeneration. Second, redevelopment is no guarantee of harmony. Many low-rise housing areas have serious social problems, and serious management difficulties have developed on many new housing association estates of social housing. Finally, multi-storey living may not be suitable for low-income families with children but for other social groups it might prove highly appropriate. This is particularly true of the growing numbers of single-person households whether they are young or old.[11]

Multi-storey estates represent a resource which can be re-used with considerable cost saving and social benefit. Much of the post-war social housing was built to good standards of space, facilities and construction. For those blocks with technical problems there are usually viable solutions. Much of the housing can be re-designated for new user groups – sheltered housing for the elderly; student hostels; accommodation for childless key workers, etc. Tower blocks are particularly suitable for such re-population. The flats in most tower blocks are small – one or two bedrooms – making them very suitable for small households. With a single point of entry and all windows well off the ground they provide a high level of security. On top of that there are often spectacular views. Tower blocks have proved popular with a range of childless households and are particularly suitable for the elderly. Throughout the country tower blocks have been re-designated and adapted as sheltered housing.

But the potential for renewal does not end with towers. Many of the more difficult slab and deck access blocks can be remodelled, making them suitable for family occupation. This does not just involve refurbishment, it often means extensive re-planning of the access systems to reduce the unsupervised stairs and corridors. Such blocks can make successful housing if the flats are re-arranged in small groups reached by easily controlled entrances. With the potential for considerable remodelling of existing social housing the emphasis of regeneration has moved away from wholesale demolition. The contemporary approach is selective renewal to create mixed communities. Some blocks can be improved and, perhaps, dedicated to new occupants. Others can be redeveloped to provide a mix of family houses and small flats. The most successful schemes keep the best of the old while partially redeveloping with the aim of recreating traditional streets inhabited by communities which comprise a mix of ages, household structure and tenure (see Case Studies J and K).

Case Study J (p. 263)
Case Study K (p. 269)

USING REDUNDANT SPACE

The conversion, adaptation and modernisation of older housing provides considerable cost and energy savings when compared with redevelopment. It does not, however, add significantly to the total numbers of homes. The change of use of other existing buildings can provide net additions to the

GRANGE COURT, HACKNEY

▲ **6.6**   The new secured main entrance

▲ **6.5**   The improved tower block reserved for older residents

Grange Court is a 20-storey tower block in Hackney, East London. The block was one of several residential towers on the Holly Street Estate. Hackney Council had made a name for itself by dynamiting several tower blocks. As part of its programme to rid itself of its troublesome multi-storey housing the council planned to demolish and rebuild the Holly Street Estate. When the plans were announced in the early 1990s a substantial number of long-term residents protested that they were very attached to their high-level homes. After a long campaign by a group of tenants, many of them elderly, the Council eventually agreed to save one of the tower blocks.

Grange Court has been extensively refurbished – internally and externally it has been improved to modern standards. The building is now surrounded by new low-rise housing which helps to enclose and secure the approach to the building. The common areas of the block have been improved and provided with a secure entrance staffed by a 'concierge'. The basement of the building has been converted to provide a lunch club, a resource centre and a health club. Flats in the block are now let only to tenants over 50. Excluding children and young people from the block has reduced the potential for conflict and helped to secure the residential environment.

housing stock. Such opportunities may arise because buildings become redundant through changes in the economy. In areas of high demand it may simply be that house prices are so high that it become financially advantageous for owners to convert buildings to housing.

It is an old maxim that no site is too small or too difficult for housing. Homes are complex but flexible and adaptable amalgams of small spaces. It may well be that the more difficult the site the more interesting the housing that can be built on it. Much the same is true of existing buildings – there is almost none which cannot be conversed to housing. Among the urban building types which have been turned into apartments are:

- *Offices.* Office blocks have open floors ready for subdivision and can easily be divided into flats. They have readymade service cores of lifts, stairs and sanitary facilities that can readily be adapted to domestic use. The external envelope may be less suitable, particularly if it includes curtain walls. Some re-cladding may be necessary to produce a domestic pattern of windows and solid walls, and to add balconies (Figure 6.7).
- *Schools and colleges.* Some older school buildings can be successfully adapted for residential use. The old London Board Schools, for example,

▲ **6.7**   The Aspect Cardiff – former offices of the AA Insurance Service converted into flats. The project was completed in 2002 and comprises 99 one, two and three-bedroom apartments. Two new floors have been added to provide penthouse maisonettes

were built with large classrooms with high ceilings to maximise light and air. Each of these rooms can make a very attractive flat by the insertion of a mezzanine at the rear to provide bathroom, kitchen and bedroom. This leaves a double-height living space with large high windows.

- *Churches.* A number of urban churches have been converted to housing. This involves inserting new floors into the body of the buildings and often into the steep pitched roofs. Again, mezzanine floors and double-height spaces may be necessary to accommodate large windows. All this creates domestic spaces of great variety and interest.
- *Pubs.* Urban pubs are closing their doors in increasing numbers. These buildings are already part residential and the upper floors can easily be converted to self-contained flats. The bars often have high ceilings which make attractive and unusual domestic spaces (Figure 6.8).

The opportunities for converting these building types, and others, arise fairly frequently but they are unlikely to provide a large supply of housing. Far greater quantities of homes can be created by converting redundant industrial buildings and making better uses of shopping centres.

Industrial buildings

Manufacturing industry has been in decline in Britain since the mid-1970s and was particularly hard hit during the recession of the 1980s. Changes in the transport of goods, including the development of containers and air freight, have made the storage and handling of goods at docks and

▲ **6.8**   Conversion of a listed hotel to flats – Part of a complex of new housing at Graham Square Glasgow. A two-storey infill block has been built between the two existing buildings to provide more accommodation and a new main entrance

BOX WORKS, MANCHESTER

Box Works was a canal-side factory in Manchester's Castlefield district. Like much local industry it closed during the recession of the 1980s and fell into marginal use. In the 1990s the factory was acquired by developers Urban Splash as one of a number of innovative housing projects they were carrying out in the area. Some of these involved redevelopment, others were able to re-use and adapt the redundant industrial buildings. The Box Works building was structurally sound and its high ceiling heights made it suitable for subdivision into generous-scale apartments.

The existing building was divided up with a central corridor arrangement served by new lifts and stairs. New glazed façades were added on two frontages to provide balconies and sun spaces. A two-storey extension was added on top of most of the existing building. The apartments were originally designed as 'lofts' – serviced shells in which the room divisions and fittings were carried out by the purchasers to their own designs. The market for this proved to be limited so the developers appointed interior architects to design three prototype apartments. Purchasers were able to choose one of these designs as an alternative to an unfinished 'loft'.

The conversion was completed in 2002 and contains 75 apartments. Most of these are with two bedrooms. A few are single-bedroom units and there are penthouse flats at roof level. Urban Splash sets a premium on good design and the building is designed and finished to a high standard. The open-plan layout of the standard apartments, though, has limited appeal. The lack of full separation between rooms means a high level of sound transference which would not suit all lifestyles.

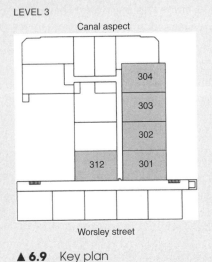

LEVEL 3

Canal aspect

304
303
302
312 301

Worsley street

▲ **6.9** Key plan

Balcony

Entrance

Sun space

▲ **6.10** Typical flat plan

▲ **6.11**   The factory before conversion

▲ **6.12**   The completed project

waterways unnecessary. These made a large number of industrial sites and buildings redundant. Many of these became derelict or were put into marginal uses. These redundant premises provided development opportunities on a significant scale and their use has accelerated over the past 20 years. Generally speaking, factories built during the twentieth century were large, lightweight sheds with roof lighting. These were designed to be serviced by motor vehicles and were often surrounded by large areas of land. Such buildings are usually unsuitable for conversion to housing – though a former handbag factory in North London has recently been turned into houses.[12] Rather, these large sites more often provide opportunities for 'brownfield' redevelopment.

Older industrial buildings, though, have often proved highly suitable for conversion. At the height of the industrial revolution factories were often housed in multi-storey buildings in or near city centres. Transport needs made this essential – workers had to travel on foot and the carting of fuel, materials and finished goods was slow and cumbersome. Many were built along canal sides to take advantage of water transportation. Warehouses near docks were also multi-storey to ease the manual transfer of goods from ship to shore, and their subsequent storage. These buildings were sturdily built to carry the weight of heavy machinery or large quantities of stored goods. Many were also of striking design.

Many Victorian industrial and warehouse buildings were of very solid construction and often had generous fenestration designed to provide good daylighting. Their conversion involved the insertion of new lifts and stairs together with the installation of new services – gas, water, electricity, sanitation and communications. Quite often conversion meant the provision of 'loft apartments'. In New York, these originated in the adaptation of warehouses – each building was subdivided into large spaces which were provided with services but otherwise unfinished. The occupiers were left to complete the dwellings to their own designs with spatial sub-division, finishes and decorations. In other projects conversion took the form of fully finished flats.

In certain areas the conversion of industrial buildings has been carried out on a large scale. In London there is a particular focus around Shad Thames on the south bank near Tower Bridge and on the opposite side of the river in Wapping. A large number of six- and seven-storey warehouses have been converted to flats, many of which enjoy river views. These sell for high prices and are particularly attractive to well-paid employees working in the financial institutions of the City of London nearby. In Manchester industrial buildings have been re-used as homes, both by conversion and redevelopment, all along Whitworth Street and into the canal-side area of Castlefield. Similar conversions of factories and mill buildings have been carried out in most of the old industrial cities of the north.

Shopping centres

There are three ways in which shopping centres can provide more housing. First, shops themselves can be converted into homes. Many Victorian residential areas were generously supplied with small shops. With the development of modern large stores many of these have become redundant. They can be readily converted to homes though to do this properly requires considerable investment. The shopfront needs to be rebuilt to provide domestic fenestration and the street frontage needs to be reclaimed and enclosed as a front garden. Sometimes large commercial buildings can be converted to provide apartments (see Figure 6.13).

▲ **6.13** The new atrium in Smithfield Buildings – an apartment block created by the conversion of a former department store in central Manchester

The second way to bring more housing to shopping centres is to make better use of the existing space over shops. Many older shopping centres were built with residential space above in which the shopkeepers originally lived. Living over the shop has become less common and, over time, the upper space has often become used for ad hoc storage or disused altogether. A report in 1990 estimated that, in many shopping centres, 40 per cent of the space above-ground level is unused or underused. In some places this was thought to be as high as 90 per cent.[13] A recent government report estimated that such redundant spaces could provided over 300 000 new homes.[14] Since most were built as residences, these spaces would be relatively easy to bring back into use. Some might require conversion to make them self-contained. Others might need work to make new separate entrances to the street. Many would be on major roads with heavy traffic. They would need sound reduction measures, including secondary glazing and artificial ventilation, to make them into good-quality homes.

A third way in which shopping centres could help to meet housing need is by making better use of the airspace above. Many modern stores and supermarkets built in high streets are of only one or two storeys while the surrounding buildings might be several storeys higher. Recent research for the Housing Corporation has shown that extending upwards over existing large stores could provide 10 000 new homes. Many more could be provided if housing was designed into new shopping developments.[15]

Additional housing in shopping centres is unlikely to be suitable for families – there would generally be a lack of outdoor space and a safe residential environment. But it could be developed as small flats which would be highly suitable for young single people and childless couples. This is one of the largest categories of new household formation and an area of strongly growing demand. Such residents are among those most likely to benefit from city-centre living. Their introduction into town centres would help to bring life and activity after dark. In many places this is serious lacking. More residents in commercial areas would help to make them safer, more vital and more pleasant to visit.

KEY POINTS

- Wholesale redevelopment destroys communities and familiar environments. The physical fabric and the social and economic life of urban neighbourhoods develop slowly over time. Successful regeneration means building on what is already there.

- The adaptation and re-use of existing buildings preserves some of the energy embodied in them. This is equivalent to a minimum of 20 per cent of the construction cost and, in most cases, considerably more. There are also savings in time and finance costs.
- It is a high priority to make existing houses more energy efficient. In older housing this can be difficult as full-scale improvement might compromise use and architectural quality. Generally a pragmatic approach is required, implementing the easiest improvements and focusing on the greatest areas of heat loss.
- Large older houses have been successfully modernised and subdivided to form self-contained flats. Tenement blocks can also be successfully converted, often by combining small dwellings horizontally and vertically to make flats and maisonettes of good space standards.
- Modern multi-storey estates often present serious technical and management problems. Demolishing them may destroy communities and remove buildings that can be remodelled successfully. Contemporary approaches favour selective renewal and the creation of mixed communities.
- Many urban building types can be successfully converted to housing. This is particularly true of older industrial buildings. Many have been converted to make generous-scale apartments, often as loft developments.
- There is scope for using space over shops as housing – partly by converting unused and redundant space; partly by using the air space over large stores. Such housing properly designed would be very suitable for small households and would help to revitalise town centres.

7

DESIGN QUALITY

A QUESTION OF TASTE

SUMMARY

*People generally have little influence on the design and quality of the build-
ings they use. In housing, though, they are usually able to exercise choice.
This choice is not unlimited. The appearance of housing has been con-
strained both by tradition and popular expectations. It has also been influenced by competing architectural theories and different approaches to
design. At root, though, there are certain basic qualities which can give
unity, coherence and functional effectiveness to the residential environment.
These can be set down in standards for new housing and can be enshrined
in 'codes' which set the parameters for a successful new development. After
completion, these standards can be enforced by a range of regulations and
restrictions. Within a framework aimed at improving the environment,
householders can be offered more choice to customise their living space.
This can be done before construction by offering choices of internal layouts
and finishes. Homes can also be designed so that they can be adapted as
needs change over time. Within a pre-established structure, whole
dwellings can be purpose designed to meet individual needs and tastes.
Beyond these mechanisms for individual choice, the quality and nature of
development or improvement can be shaped by collective discussion and
debate. This democratic approach to design probably gives people the
greatest influence over the quality of their own homes.*

THE IMAGE OF THE HOUSE

It is a foremost priority that the design of any building should ensure
that it is soundly constructed and that it works well. But its visual quality is also important. On the whole, people cannot influence the design
and appearance of the buildings they use. Most buildings are designed
by architects and developers without reference to the people who will

work in them or visit them as part of their daily lives. Of course, these designs are subject to the regulation of the planning system, which includes certain obligations to consult, but this process does not touch the majority of people. Sometimes, in the case of a major public building, a public consultation exercise is mounted. Too often, though, this is a hollow sham. In 2002, a Liverpool regeneration agency conducted a public poll on four short-listed schemes for a major project on a waterfront site. The poll produced clear preferences but the agency did not reward the most popular scheme. They awarded the contract to the project, which had least support among the public.[1]

Research shows that people do care about the quality of design. A study for the Commission for Architecture and the Built Environment (CABE) suggests that three quarters of the public believe the quality of a new school affects the quality of a child's education. More than half of those polled thought there was a relationship between a hospital's design and how quickly patients recovered.[2] There should be ways in which people can influence the design of such buildings – mostly there are not. But if the design of social buildings is important, how much more important is the design of housing where most people spend the majority of their time. In housing, at least, people are offered choice. For the great majority who are owner-occupiers this choice is made available through the housing market. Even for those who rent, though, there is usually a degree of choice on offer.

In terms of the types of homes people prefer there is some evidence from market research. A recent survey showed that, given a choice of where to live, most people preferred a bungalow or village house. Second preference was for a Victorian terrace and this was followed by the modern semi-detached. Most people were not attracted by multi-storey housing.[3] However, other surveys have shown greater support for high density. In one, almost half of young people (aged 16–34) were interested in high-density city housing; in another, residents of Ashford supported high-density housing around the town's railway station.[4] To a degree, prevailing attitudes reflect what is familiar and the fact that the overwhelming majority of housing built in the past half century has been low density. This is particularly true of housing built for sale by private developers. Nevertheless, these surveys do reveal a substantial demand for urban housing forms – terraced houses and flats. New housing of this type has, only recently, begun to be built by private developers.

In many respects, expressed preferences reflect the benefits people expect to derive from living in a particular form of housing. They are only partly concerned with appearance and the quality of the built environment. The importance of visual qualities is hard to measure and some indications is given by the market. Houses which sell well are generally of traditional appearance though it is not clear that visual qualities are the chief attraction. Choice is often limited and architects have repeatedly criticised developers for their conservative approach to design. Many established urban areas have become highly valuable in market terms. A lot of these have high environmental quality and are accredited with 'conservation area' status. Visual factors are important though they may not be as significant as factors such as location. To get a better understanding of visual quality in housing it is worth reviewing some of the theories, which have helped shape housing design over the period of urban growth.

Traditionalism versus modernism

Traditional housing design is rooted in simplicity. It was based on the use of local materials, which would be readily available, and simple construction techniques, which could be easily mastered. Such simplicity was essential for the construction of large-scale mass housing. Rare and expensive materials, and highly skilled craftsmanship were preserved for the houses of the wealthy. The same was true of advanced design ideas. From the eighteenth century onwards the homes of the rich were designed with the principles of the classical revival of the renaissance. This was true of both the fine country houses and the town houses. The squares and crescents of Georgian Bath and the Nash terraces in London were the prototypes for high-quality urban houses in neo-classical style. As it became more common, more down-market, the Georgian house became simpler, more traditional in its use of materials and techniques.

The Arts and Crafts Movement of the late nineteenth century was founded on dislike of Victorian urbanity and machine mass production. It looked to a revival of traditional crafts and building practices which, it was felt, had been obliterated by the classically inspired Georgian and Regency housing. In their pioneering suburban houses for wealthy clients Arts and Crafts architects revived such features as steep-pitched roofs, half timbering, tile hanging, bay windows and side-hung casements. All of these had been features of the pre-industrial architecture of Britain. These design features were incorporated in several pioneering developments such as the model towns of Burnsville and Port Sunlight and the first Garden City at Letchworth. These traditional features were absorbed into the suburban housing of the 1930s and have continued to influence the design of low-density housing. Arts and Crafts ideas also found expression in the design of early multi-storey housing. This included 'mansion' blocks for the wealthy and tenement blocks for the deserving poor.

The Modern Movement rejected the traditional approach. It had a quite different form of expression – flat roofs instead of pitched; white painted walls instead of brick or tiling; flat façades with strip windows in place of bays and turrets; an absence of decorative detail. The earliest expression of this aesthetic was in the individual houses of Le Corbusier and others built in the 1920s. During the 1930s a few houses in the Modernist style were built in Britain for individual clients. But, on the whole, Modernism had little influence on the design of houses. With blocks of flats, though, it was a different story. Apartment buildings by Modernist architects became an inspiration to housing designers. None more, so, than those by Berthold Lubetkin, particularly the pioneering 'Highpoint' development in Highgate which is still highly regarded.

Many blocks of flats were built under the influence of Modernism. Most are regarded as failures, if only for social reasons. Some people do appreciate the openness and good light in Modern flats provided by large areas of glazing. In particular, the large sliding windows giving on to generous terraces were a key innovation of lasting value. Modernism still finds favour in the design of some large new apartment blocks but many of these are now clad in traditional clothes. It is something of a paradox that while Modernism has, over the past 50 years become the dominant style for the design of public buildings and it has had relatively little lasting influence on housing design. There has been some rationalisation, some simplification but, in the main, it is traditional styles and materials, which characterise the design of homes.

Formalism

The conflict between 'formalism' and what might be described as a more pragmatic, problem-solving approach to design has lain beneath many of the conflicts between architectural theories for a long time. It symbolised the difference between Classicism and the Arts and Crafts movement; it has been part of the conflict between different branches of Modernism; it has characterised contesting approaches to architectural education. It is an important issue in housing design.

Formalism can be defined in at least three ways:

1 *The application of rules.* Classicism had a clear set of rules, including the use of the three classical orders, the proportions of the

▲ **7.1** Northdown Street, London N1 – Classical formalism. Four houses are designed as one giant portico with each owner given care of a giant pilaster. Even then the entrances are not symmetrical

'golden section', and the importance of symmetry. These rules could be made to work in the design of grand houses but became inhibiting when applied to repetitive urban housing. For example, terraced housing cannot be designed effectively within the constraints of symmetrical planning (Figure 7.1). Modernism also had rules, which laid down the basic appearance of buildings regardless of local climate and vernacular traditions.

2 *Pattern making.* This can apply to plans – landscape designs are often based on patterns which look good on paper but which mean nothing when viewed from ground level. In housing, designs are often compromised by 'façadeism' – the desire to treat an elevation as a pattern rather than functionally. The strip windows in Le Corbusier's houses were pattern inspired and were often blanked behind. Pattern making is commonly found in Lubetkin's façades. For example, on the Hallfield estate balconies are used purely to create a façade pattern. Some flats get them and some do not when self-evidently the functional requirements are the same[5] (Figure 7.2).

3 *Preconception.* Designs are often based on a pre-conceived idea or shape. Sometimes this can be simplistic. A recent example is the

▲ **7.2**   Hallfield estate, London W2 – Façadeism. Balconies are used chiefly to make a façade pattern so only some of the flats in the block have the benefit of private outdoor space

'gherkin' office block in the City of London where the shape takes precedence over the functional requirements of the building. In social housing there are many instances of design ideas overriding user needs. An outstanding example is the development at Marne-la-Vallee near Paris where housing is built in a grandiose and bombastic neo-classical style with one apartment block taking the shape of a huge disc.[6] Ricardo Bofill has more recently completed a similar scheme in Montpelier where the buildings are so strongly dominated by a pre-conceived style that they are barely recognisable as housing (Figure 7.3).

The alternative to formalism is a more carefully considered and open-minded approach. This starts without preconceptions and analyses of the functional requirements, site conditions, orientation and the local context. It may also include a range of project objectives in terms of energy conservation, use of materials, flexibility in use, maintenance considerations and so on. Design is a matter of considering and resolving these requirements many of which may be contradictory. Formalism is often inimical to the proper resolution of the functional requirements and may prevent them being met. At the same time, there may be room for some aspects of formalism. The use of formal shapes in planning such as squares and circles may give clarity to the urban environment and help people relate to it. The existence of some rules may provide a framework, which gives consistency and order to residential development.

▲ **7.3**   Antigone, Montpelier, France – Preconception. Ricardo Bofill's development is based on a formal geometric ground plan. The appearance of the buildings is dominated by a heavily stylised neo-classical approach which makes them almost unrecognisable as housing

A FRAMEWORK FOR QUALITY

A set of rules may be beneficial if they are not rigidly applied. They can form part of the brief and sit alongside of the other constraints to be resolved in the design process. Standards have played a big part in raising quality in housing design. The most recent standards, though, are now more than 40 years old. The Parker Morris Report[7] set high standards but it has long since ceased to be mandatory and much housing fails to meet its bench-marks. It was, in any case, aimed primarily at individual houses at relatively low density. Its application to multi-storey housing may have caused more harm than good in that it failed to address the problem of common areas.

With the change of emphasis from low-density developments of individual houses to higher density developments it may be time to consider a new set of standards for urban housing. A recent research project suggested some of the issues which might be considered. This pinpointed noise and privacy as key issues in high-density housing. Residents were concerned about intrusive noise from their neighbours and high levels of sound insulation in party walls – or floors in the case of flats – is a key issue. They were also concerned with noise transference within the home from members of their own household. Better insulation would help but planning is also an issue. People living in town houses cited privacy as one of the key benefits of the division of space over three or four storeys. On the other hand people seem less concerned with visual intrusion. It may be that a more relaxed attitude is needed in defining overlooking distances or allowing windows to be placed on to public thoroughfares.[8]

In any review of standards for high-density housing a number of issues concerning construction and internal layout could be considered. This could include the complex question of access systems in blocks of flats, which have caused so many problems in the past. Standards in the external layout and appearance of housing have long been the subject of design guidance and this is increasingly being used to set the framework for new development.

Design codes

The process of setting a framework for the design of new housing was pioneered in the 1970s by the *Essex Design Guide*.[9] Concerned about the poor visual quality of the amorphous suburban housing being developed in their area, Essex County Council set out guidance which would revive the qualities of traditional villages. These required good grouping and massing of houses, tighter street layouts, and the use of vernacular materials and techniques. The guide was highly influential and inspired a spate of similar initiatives by other local authorities. All these, however, were aimed at improving the quality of the low-density housing which was then the norm.

As part of its policy shift in favour of higher-density urban housing the Government issued new design guidance. This included the recommendation that planning authorities should set out urban design frameworks for areas undergoing change or significant development. These frameworks should establish the local context for developments and 'bring forward ... design codes' to establish the quality of the built environment.[10] Design codes were influential in the design of West Silvertown

Urban Village (see Case Study C, p. 221). They were also developed for the new housing in the regeneration of Marquess Estate (see Case Study J, p. 263). These codes set design standards for a number of issues including:

- Land use and the location of community facilities/services.
- Storey height, scale and massing of new buildings.
- The establishment of a traditional street pattern.
- Relationship of buildings to the pavement including footpath widths and the extent of front gardens.
- Dealing with rubbish including refuse storage and recycling.
- Dealing with the design of buildings at street corners.
- The extent of green verges and open spaces.
- A palette of materials and colours.

The criteria contained in a design code give the completed development unity and coherence regardless of the detailed design of the individual bullrings.

In France the establishment of design codes has a long history dating back to the development of the *grandes boulevards* of Paris by Baron Haussman. Then rules were set down to govern building heights, cornice levels and certain other design aspects to ensure a unified approach to urban design. Similar principles were used in the development of new housing at Bercy in the early 1990s (see Case Example 7A). Drawing on the approach used in earlier developments in Paris a *cahier des charges* – or book of rules – was drawn up for the design of new housing. These rules ensured that the new buildings had a coherent scale, massing and appearance despite the fact that the blocks were designed and built by several architects and developers.[11]

Maintaining quality

If design quality can be achieved through the application of an urban design framework and design codes there remains the problem of ensuring that this quality is maintained in perpetuity. In the Bercy scheme the rules set out for the development became legally binding requirements with which subsequent owners of the land have to comply. This is similar to the restrictive convenants, which many landowners applied to their developments in Britain. The owners of large estates that developed such high-quality environments as the urban squares and terraces of Belgravia and Chelsea often imposed binding obligations on the subsequent occupiers of the buildings. These would restrict changes, which might damage and diminish the high quality of the buildings. In some cases these went so far as to set down the colours in which the buildings were to be painted.

HOUSING AT BERCY, PARIS

The Bercy regeneration covered an area of 51 hectares in the south-east of metropolitan Paris. The area had consisted largely of wine warehouses, which had become run down and marginalised. The focus of the regeneration was the development of a large park alongside the dual carriageway road, which borders the bank of the Seine. Around the

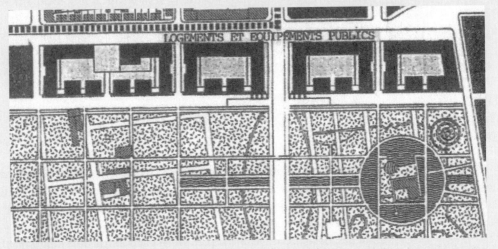

▲ **7.4**   Location plan showing housing on north-east side of park

▲ **7.5**   A design code created visual harmony in the housing lining the edge of the park

park a range of recreational and community facilities were developed together with a new centre for employment. On the opposite side from the river, sites were designated for housing much of which would enjoy a south-westerly aspect overlooking the park.

The housing was to be designed and built by several different architects and developers. To ensure coherence a framework was set out for the scheme by architect Jean-Pierre Buffi. The development was divided into four large street blocks, each of which was to have buildings arranged around a courtyard with openings on to the park. Between the blocks were pedestrian ways lined with housing which had the benefit of oblique views into the park. The façades along the park were to have a sequence of solids and voids linked together by balconies.

To develop a high degree of visual unity between the eight or nine separate developments a *cahier des charges* (book of rules) was set down. This prescribed the form of the blocks, their overall height and the height of interior floors, the form of elements such as balconies, the materials to be used in the façades, the proportion of glazing and the form of planting of external spaces. The housing development was completed in the 1990s and has now matured along with the landscaping. The finished product shows a high degree of consistency in its overall impact, while allowing considerable scope for variation and diversity within each of the separate developments.[11]

▲ **7.6** The housing blocks are penetrated by pedestrian ways

▲ **7.7** Flats in the pedestrian ways have an oblique view of the park

Many of the most attractive areas of older cities and towns have been preserved and enhanced by the power of planning authorities to declare 'conservation areas'. In these, demolition and the felling of trees are controlled and there are special procedures for planning applications. A conservation area plan must be prepared to define the framework for any new development. It is unlikely that any new residential area would quickly acquire conservation area status. It is not unreasonable, though, to expect that local authority planners should exercise a similar degree of sensitivity and constraint when considering changes to any urban area of high quality. In particular, it could require that any new development must be designed in a sensitive manner, which reflects and respects the special character of the area.

CUSTOMISATION OF HOUSING SPACE

Urban design guidance and design codes help to establish consistency and quality in the design of residential areas. But they do not offer to the individual householder any degree of influence or choice in the appearance and quality of their own homes. Generally, such freedom has been the preserve of the rich who were able to commission the design and construction of their own homes. Inevitably, these were mostly individual houses on large sites. The idea of 'customising' mass housing lies deep in architectural thinking of the twentieth century. In 1932 Le Corbusier proposed, for Algiers, a multi-storey linear structure composed of serviced decks. Within these decks housing would be developed by individual householders in a variety of styles reflecting their own culture and taste.[12]

In 1961 Dutch architectural theorist John Habraken published a critique which derided the prevailing approach to the design of mass housing – providing homes in which the occupants had no means of shaping their own environment or expressing their own preferences. Habraken proposed separating the structure and services – 'supports' – and the enclosures forming the dwellings – 'infill'. Urban support structures could be built providing multi-storey serviced decks. People could rent or buy space on these decks and have their own homes built into them. A variety of manufacturers would be able to offer the infill components for a new home, custom planned using prefabricated elements. Having selected a supplier, customers could:

> … visit the showrooms of the manufacturer of their choice. With the help of a representative of the firm an effective arrangement of dwelling is decided upon. The representative invites [the] customers to return in a fortnight.

The dwelling will be ready for inspection in the showrooms. At the appointed time they see a full-scale model of their dwelling. They walk about it, test doors and windows, visit kitchen and bathroom, and try the usefulness of rooms and cupboards. After suggesting a few alterations they decide to buy. The manufacturer transports the parts to the support structure where the dwelling is finally assembled in a short time.[13]

This was a high ideal and an important aspiration. People should have the right to plan their own homes and to choose what they look like. The result would be satisfied customers and an urban environment enriched by the variety produced by individual self-expression.

Adaptability

Habraken's ideas were never realised in their literal form. But they did influence two housing projects, which experimented with the idea of adaptability:

1 *Primary System Support Housing Assembly Kit (PSSHAK).* During the late 1960s, two young architects – Nabeel Hamdl and Nic Wilkinson – developed an application of Habraken's 'supports' concept. This idea for flexible housing was dubbed the PSSHAK. Unlike Habraken's original concept, PSSHAK did not use a large-scale support structure but concentrated on housing which could be adapted to individual needs within a small-scale standardised shell. Only one significant scheme was built using this concept. At Adelaide Road, North London, eight three-storey blocks of local authority housing were built (Figure 7.8). Each block comprised a 'primary support' shell consisting of floors, roof, external walls, windows and doors and ducts to serve bathrooms and kitchens. The blocks could be subdivided in a number of ways to provide different mixes of dwellings. Within each home a variety of layouts was possible using prefabricated modular partitions. Prospective tenants were allocated housing space and each was invited to design their layout using an instruction manual. The layout could be designed to suit each tenant's choice of the relationship and size of rooms and also to accommodate the furniture and fittings they already had. Once tenants moved in they had the chance to have the layout re-arranged after a trial period and the system allowed for further changes in the future.[14]

2 *Diagoon Houses.* The Dutch architect Herman Hertzberger was influenced by the general interest in Holland in user participation in design, and by the work of Habraken in particular. The idea of people interacting positively with the buildings they occupy influenced many of his projects. During the 1960s he planned a development of adaptable

▲ **7.8**   Adelaide Road, North London, late 1970s. Adaptable housing designed using the PSSHAK concept

houses at Delft. The full scheme was never realised but a pilot project of eight 'Diagoon' houses was built in 1971 (Figure 7.9). The design of the houses was flexible so that the occupiers themselves could decide how to divide the space and live in it. If the composition of the family changed the house could be adjusted and, to a degree, extended. Each house consists of two fixed cores containing stairs and drainage/services. These connect with several half-storey levels, which can accommodate a wide range of different uses and spatial sub-division. The interaction between the half levels creates unusual visual connections between different spaces and activities. The occupants of each house were offered a range of options for its layout and division. The houses can also be extended by enclosing the car-port space at ground level to make a garage, office or other usable space; by enclosing the roof terrace to make a sun space or an extra bedroom; or by infilling the recessed parts of the plan at front and back.[15]

▲ **7.9**   Diagoon houses, Delft 1971. Housing which could be adapted and extended to meet the changing needs of its occupants

Both these projects were a limited realisation of Habraken's ideas. His intention was that individual preferences would be expressed externally in variations in window types and sizes and in different cladding materials. In the PSSHAK scheme tenants had some choice in location and in the planning of their homes, although they had no control over the form of housing or over its external appearance. In the Diagoon housing the basic form and appearance of the buildings was determined when they were built. Residents did have freedom to adapt the interior and they had the opportunity to influence the external appearance when carrying out extensions.

The principle of adaptability is a good one and it can fairly easily be applied to the design of individual houses. Purpose designed into new urban housing, though, it presents two difficulties. The first is the question of density and intensity of development. Adaptability has been presented as a model for 'starter' homes, which can be expanded as families grow. This requires that initial developments are quite low density allowing for a build-up over time. Developers would be required to build housing which was, in effect, only partially finished. In a market situation this would mean selling at a price well below that of a normal development. The second difficulty concerns how easily adaptations could be made. Even with demountable partitions there would be considerable disruption to lifestyles and to finishes and decorations. It is questionable whether adaptable housing could be changed any easier than, say, the typical Victorian terraced house. The ability to adapt and extend these older houses has been one of the reasons for their popularity.

Degrees of choice

Adaptability means giving householders the means of changing their homes as their families grow or their lifestyles evolve. But an equally important aspect of customisation is to give residents more choice in the way their homes are designed before they move in. In the comprehensive modernisation of housing estates carried out by many local authorities it has been common practice to give residents a considerable degree of choice. These choices can include:

- Layout and finish of kitchen units
- Colours of floor and wall tiles
- Colours of internal paintwork
- Wallpapers
- Front door colours

All these choices can be given with virtually no cost and with no significant variation to the general specification. It would be relatively easy to extend these choices to include sanitary fittings, glazing to doors, light fittings and other internal design issues. These choices are not always given in new-build private housing. There seems no reason, though, why developers should not offer such customisation at minimal cost.

The next level of choice is the internal layout of homes. Some choice can be offered in the layout of houses but the greatest scope is in development of multi-storey flats. The basis of such developments is to provide the superstructure, the external envelop, the access system and the services. Within this there is a high degree of scope for variation in the internal layout of the dwellings. Some developers are now offering choice of room sizes, numbers of bedrooms and layouts, etc. The greatest choice, though, is offered by 'lofts'. These are serviced shells without internal division. The purchasers are left to arrange their own partitions, fittings and finishes. There are some limitations on the location of sanitary fittings but, beyond that, residents have a high degree of freedom to design the layout and appearance of their homes.

The ultimate in customisation is the ability to determine the design of the whole house. In the past this has only been possible with the detached villa. In a recent Dutch scheme, though, they have found a way to apply such choice in urban housing. The Borneo development in Amsterdam is, in part, an experiment in housing design (see Case Example 7B). In one long terrace each owner/occupier and their architect has been given the freedom to develop highly individual designs. A strong framework was defined which set out the building's perimeters and established certain key functional requirements. Within this there has been a great deal of scope for the expression of personal preferences in both the functioning and the appearance of the houses.[16]

DEMOCRATIC DESIGN

It is important to give people more influence in the design of their homes, and customisation is a significant part of this aim. Based, as it is, on individual choice it can only have an effect on the interior and, to a limited degree, the external appearance of each dwelling. If user involvement is confined to customisation, the form of a development, its housing mix and the design of the external environment would be left entirely to professionals. These issues can be influenced by the participation of householders in a collective debate about the design of their homes. The demand for democratic participation in housing design and development issues grew out of the community movement of the 1970s. Then whole swathes of inner city housing were being swept away by comprehensive redevelopment. The communities of people who lived there were broken up and dispersed. Before long, threatened communities began to protest at this destructive approach and to demand involvement in the decision-making process.

An early model for a more democratic approach to design was the Byker redevelopment in Newcastle. The scheme was designed by Ralph Erskine in 1970 and constructed over a period of 10 years or more. From the start residents were invited to participate in decision-making both informally – through visiting the site-based design office – and in a more structured way through attending liaison meetings. The scheme's most prominent feature is the 'wall' of multi-storey flats, which snakes along the northern edge of the site. The wall was a critical first step in the development

BORNEO, AMSTERDAM

The Borneo development is part of the regeneration of Amsterdam's eastern docks. It is a strip of land projecting into the sea either side of a narrow dock. Most of the area has been developed as housing designed in a conventional manner. But a land fronting the north side of the narrow dock was reserved for an architectural experiment. Sixty plots were defined and designated for individual houses. The form of the houses was governed by a strict framework. Each was to more or less fill the plot in each direction and all were to be topped by a flat roof at a standard level. Gardens would not be provided; instead each house would have a sun terrace at roof or second floor level. Most houses were required to have a garage or parking space on the frontage facing the street. On the other side, the houses front directly on to the dock with access to the water.

▲ **7.10** The street frontage provides vehicle and pedestrian access

▲ **7.11** Houses front directly on to the water on the dock frontage

The result of the experiment is a terrace of houses which has an unquestionable urban scale and form. Its appearance, however, is a patchwork of materials and architectural elements. Working with their chosen architect, each building owner has been able to express their preferences both in the way the house is laid out internally and in its external appearance. These preferences are not just cosmetic. Some have chosen to recess part of the façade to provide a small outdoor space or to give more privacy to a large picture window. Others have chosen to add balconies or oriel windows at upper levels and there is considerable variation in the design of the upper level terraces. The Borneo housing does not have the unity and coherence of the traditional urban terrace. Instead, it has the richness and variety generated by the expression of individual choice.

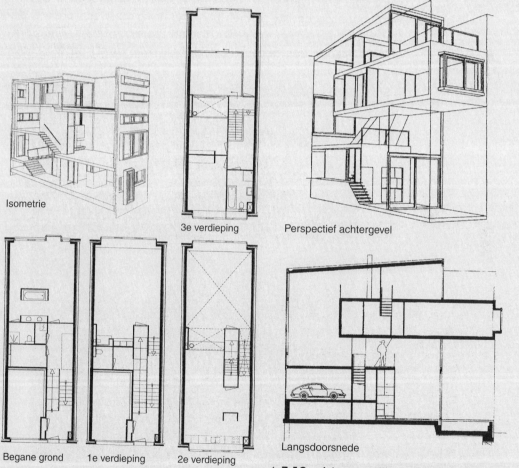

Isometrie

3e verdieping

Perspectief achtergevel

Begane grond   1e verdieping   2e verdieping

Langsdoorsnede

▲ **7.12** A typical house showing changes of level and roof terrace at the front

▲ **7.13** A house with most of the façade recessed. Note garage at rear and terraces at ground and upper levels

process. It meant that a large amount of housing could be built on a small amount of land, preserving the great majority of the existing terraced housing. Once complete, clearance and reconstruction could proceed on a phased rolling programme, rehousing the existing residents street-by-street. After the wall the reminder of the site was rebuilt as terraced houses and small-scale flats in accordance with residents wishes.[17]

Keeping communities intact became a key aim of a more democratic approach to housing design and development. But it also ensured that the improved housing – whether achieved through reconstruction or refurbishment – met the needs and wishes of the people who were to live in it. Democratic discussion and debate-produced solutions, which were different from what might otherwise have happened and which were more appropriate to their purpose. Being more appropriate, democratic solutions are more likely to stand the test of time. The principle of participation has become established over time and it is now an

▲ **7.14**   Byker, Newcastle, 1970s. A project which pioneered participation in design. The 'wall' became a key to keeping the existing community intact

integral part of the improvement process for social housing estates. Techniques have matured and now involve a complex mixture of communication and decision-making processes involving people both as individuals and engaging them in the activities of small and large groups.[18] The processes involved in estate improvement, however, are not necessarily appropriate to the contemporary agenda of new housing construction on 'brownfield' land.

Housing co-operatives

During the 1980s a considerable number of housing co-operatives (co-ops) did develop new housing for their own members and their experience might be applicable to the processes necessary today. Typically, a co-op would consist of 40 to 80 households. The first steps involved establishing funding, the support of an umbrella organisation and the identification of a site. A project committee would then be elected. This would appoint an architect and set a brief in terms of the numbers of dwellings required and their size mix. Through discussion, research and feedback with members, the committee would decide on the form of the housing, the layout of the site and the details of materials and components, which affect the appearance of the buildings. Individual households were then offered choice in the layout and finishes in their homes. Quite often the completed schemes were distinctively different from what might otherwise have been built.[19]

There were housing co-ops in most major British cities but they flourished particularly strongly in Liverpool. In 1982, eight co-ops were already established and more were to follow. The established pattern of social housing in the city had been to build low-scale walk-up blocks of flats of three or four-storeys. The co-ops all broke with this pattern, choosing instead to develop family houses with a few small flats for the elderly. The layout of the new housing varied considerably, however. Some co-ops chose conventional low-density patterns, others went for more urban layouts of courts and alleys or houses ringing a central green space. In appearance there was a general preference for tradition with pitched roofs, timber windows and walls of brick or render finish.[20]

A recent scheme in which co-op members were influential in designing their new building is the Homes for Change project in Manchester (see Case study D, p. 227). Apart from their value in democratising the housing design and development process, co-ops have an important continuing role. They are responsible for managing the housing in perpetuity. Thus, the co-op has an important function in maintaining quality. If the occupants of housing are responsible for the maintenance of buildings

▲ **7.15**   Weller Street Co-op, Liverpool. The first of the Liverpool co-ops developed houses in a simple traditional style with pitched roofs, red brick and stained timber windows. The scheme was also notable for its generous landscaping

and the public environment and for controlling antisocial behaviour it is more likely that the integrity of the development will be sustained. Sometimes, for this reason alone, co-op management is introduced after a scheme is completed. This was the basis of the Iroko scheme at Coin Street (see Case study A, p. 209).

Democracy in new housing

Co-ops were never numerous and are unlikely to be. Most new housing will continue to be developed by social landlords or private developers. However, a degree of the democracy inherent in co-ops could, with benefit, be injected into this process. A key feature of democratic design was that the future occupants of dwellings were known well in advance. This meant they could take part in the design process and their homes

▲ **7.16**   Bramley Co-op, West London. This co-op, founded on a squatters group, developed a mixture of family houses, shared houses and small flats for single people. At the centre of the scheme is a communal garden shared by all the residents

could be customised for them. This is much more difficult with most new housing developments and may be impossible. Some effort could be made though.

Social landlords usually have waiting and transfer lists. They may well be able to pre-allocate new homes. Even if they cannot, they do have existing tenants who would be highly likely to have pertinent comments to make on the design of new housing. It should be perfectly possible to form a panel or committee to advise on new developments. Democracy is more difficult for private developers. Homes are often sold well before completion, though, which should make a considerable degree of customisation possible. Schemes are subject to the planning process, though this is dominated by professionals and their concern for technical and urban design issues. Developers could help their cause, both in public relations and in their planning applications, by recruiting advisory panels or 'focus groups'. These could include housing specialists as well as ordinary people resident in similar types of housing. Concerted moves to bring greater democracy to the development process could have a significant impact on the quality of new housing.

KEY POINTS

- People's preferences in housing design are conditioned by familiarity. The vernacular approach developed by the Arts and Crafts movement has had a continuing influence on British housing design. It is Traditionalism rather than Modernism, which characterises the design of most housing.

- 'Formalist' approaches to design are often inimical to the proper resolution of functional requirements. A more carefully considered and open-minded approach is preferable which analyses the functional requirements, site and environmental condition and local context.

- It is desirable that a new set of standards for urban housing should be developed. This should address the problems of privacy and noise transference. It should also examine critically the key factors in the layout of new multi-storey flats paying particular attention to access systems.

- 'Design Codes' have been used both historically and more recently to provide a set of rules which give a completed development unity and coherence. Within this framework there is considerable scope for variation in the design of individual buildings.

- Adaptability is a good principle that allows people the opportunity to re-shape their homes from time-to-time to meet changing needs. However, it has proved difficult to achieve – initial development is costly and changes to the layout cannot be made easily at a later date.

- In housing which is newly built or extensively refurbished, customisation should be possible. This can include giving each prospective householder choices of finishing materials and colours. Choice could also be fairly easily extended to fixtures and fittings.

- Individual choice is important but collective decision-making can have a more far-reaching influence on design. Democratic discussion and debate can produce design solutions, which are more appropriate to their purpose and are more likely to stand the test of time.

8

CITIES OF TOMORROW

SUMMARY

With an increasing proportion of the world's population living in cities the challenge is to create settlement patterns which are sustainable – in balance with the environment in the broadest sense. Low-density housing and dispersed development – characteristic of much of the developed world – are a major contribution to pollution and climate change. Even if these problems can be ameliorated by technical innovation, such land-use patterns do not provide a viable model for the many regions which are set to become increasingly congested. In some areas the high-density, high-rise city has developed in response to such pressures. These, however, have their drawbacks both technically and socially. A more viable model is provided by the cities of Europe. These are relatively high density but built to a more human scale, providing an environment which has both high amenity and cultural vitality. European cities have had their problems of urban decay and poor housing quality. Many still have stresses caused by social polarisation. But they have a heritage of strong street and neighbourhood patterns and viable servicing systems. These provide a good basis for successful urban regeneration. These strengths provide a model for urban development which has made progress in addressing the problems of population change and global warming.

A WORLD MORE URBANISED

At the start of the twenty-first century the world is becoming increasingly urbanised. More people, it is said, now live in cities than in the countryside. Greater urbanisation is, perhaps, an inevitable consequence of economic progress. As more people earn their living from industry, commerce and services rather than from agriculture more will become dependent on the cities. Urbanisation, though, is a vague concept. Cities vary enormously in size, form and in the way they function. Many are beset with problems of overcrowding, poor quality buildings, environmental degradation and ineffective transport systems. For future urban growth, what is important is to create cities that provide a good environment for people to live, work and take their leisure; which have effective systems of servicing and management; and that are in balance with the natural environment. If sustainability is to be achieved, it is necessary to draw from this diversity of contemporary cities the elements of urban form and function which can address both population change and environmental challenges.

The American way

Given its high profile in the visual media, Manhattan seems the archetype of the American city. But this impression is misleading. There are a few centres of high density living like New York and San Francisco. For the most part, though, the American city is characterised by a densely built core where commercial buildings rise high but almost nobody lives. Around this is an inner ring, with low population and employment density, characterised by marginal uses – warehouses, parking lots and the like. Beyond are the residential areas. These are largely very thinly populated, reaching densities which average only 12 persons per hectare.[1] The development of many suburbs was based on the plot system where sites were divided up and sold for the development of individual houses. Such housing is inherently difficult to insulate and is often equipped with expensive heating and air conditioning systems. It also makes its residents highly dependent on the private car which Americans are said to use for even the shortest journeys.

This combination of housing which consumes copious quantities of energy, low-density sprawl which necessitates long distance commuting and heavy dependence on the motor car are all major reasons why the USA is the world's biggest polluter. This entrenched lifestyle also makes it extremely difficult to address the problem. Rather than commit to the policy protocols of the Kyoto accord, the USA places its faith in technology. Commercial organisations in California are investing heavily in renewable energy provided by PV panels, an investment largely stimulated by the failure of conventional power generation. There is also considerable faith in the benefit in more efficient cars, in particular, the powering of vehicles by a combination of solar power and 'fuel cells'. These generate electricity by processing hydrogen and oxygen, and produce only water as a by-product. These systems are said to be pollution free though they would cost a great deal to implement and the long-term implications are unclear.

The American way is based on individual rather than collective solutions to the provision of housing and transport. Much the same could be said for other developed western countries. Australia has similar patterns of settlement and travel while in Canada, cities are more dense but considerably less so than in Europe.[2] It may be that there are technologies which will make low-density lifestyles sustainable. But the big issue is land. One thing the New World countries have in abundance is space and this has been a key factor in allowing the spread of low-scale land-use and transport systems. Such dispersed individualised systems cannot operate in regions which are more congested and heavily populated. They do not offer a development model for the many countries of the world with high population densities.

The developing world

The countries of the developing world – Asia, Africa, Latin America – remain largely agrarian communities. There has, though, been considerable urban expansion. In some cases this has been fast and furious – the rapid growth of Sao Paolo and Mexico City, for example, are legendary. Often such expansion is fuelled by population growth and is accompanied by rural–urban migration. The housing systems in agrarian communities are strong. Most houses are 'self built' either by families or collectively by villages. Construction is based on the use of local materials and simple techniques. This approach has often been taken to the cities by migrants. Around many third world cities there are large squatter colonies where families have built their own shelters from any available materials. These are often tightly packed on hillsides, homes clustered around narrow alleys with inadequate sanitation and water supplies. Their inhabitants scrape a living from causal labouring or from selling goods and services on the roadside.[3]

The cities of the developing world are often based around an historic core. This may be an informal traditional city or a planned centre of imperial origin. Around this core the new city has grown, often by piecemeal individual developments along main roads. Many third world cities are characterised by a viable central area surrounded by a motley development which is largely unplanned. Much of this is low scale, of poor quality construction and poorly maintained. At the edges, the cities peter out into scattered individual houses and smallholdings. Commonly the road system is inadequate and there is poor public transport, resulting in serious traffic congestion. In many ways, this is another manifestation of individualised solutions to housing and transport but concentrated in higher population densities. Such cities have a low impact on greenhouse gas pollution but they fail to provide an adequate environment for their inhabitants. For the future, better models of high-density cities are needed.

The high-rise model

One area of the world which has achieved relatively high economic development, but which has not followed the American pattern of urban settlement, is the Pacific Rim. The countries of the eastern and southern seaboard of Asia are dominated by the economic power of Japan but they have many things in common. They are relatively densely populated with limited surplus land and they have experienced rapid economic and urban growth. Much of this growth has been concentrated into large dense cities. In the wealthiest and most developed cities there has been considerable investment in making high density work well. This has necessitated a considerable degree of public intervention in the provision of both transport and housing. While many of the cities of this region are high density not all are high-rise. In Japan, in particular, the height of buildings is restricted to minimise the impact of earthquakes.

The most potent models of the high-rise city are probably Singapore and, particularly, Hong Kong which has an unmatched intensity of development. Both are island states with limited room for expansion. Like the American cities the commercial buildings are high rise. But so too is much of the housing. The room for suburbs and individual houses is limited so that much of the population lives in high-rise apartment buildings. As land is at a premium space standards are often low both in terms of the size of dwellings and the levels of occupancy. But minimum standards are maintained by the intervention of the state in providing a significant proportion of social housing. Effective networks of public transport are needed to make such cities work. These are based on multi-modal systems providing frequent and rapid transit for both short and long distances. In compensation for the limitations of living space, public intervention ensures a high level of communal open space both in urban hard space and green parkland. As seaboard cities, the water itself plays a large part in both transport and recreation.

In many ways these high-rise, high-density cities are highly successful. There are high levels of employment and relative prosperity. The transport systems work well with the high level of public provision ensuring that traffic congestion is minimised. The public environment is attractive and well maintained. All this is achieved with a high level of urban management and institutional control. To some this is one of the drawbacks of the high-rise model – the degree of control is so high as to border on repression. And there are other drawbacks. In housing there are severe limitations on personal space which is not fully compensated by public amenities. The maintenance and management of high-rise housing is also complex and costly. In environmental terms such cities are highly dependent on energy-consuming technologies such as lifts, artificial lighting and air conditioning. While the high-rise city has appeal and can be made to work, a better model might be found in the cities of Europe. These average more than three times the density of American cities but are far less intensively developed than many of the cities of Asia.[4] Their more human scale offers a better quality of life but is dense enough to realise many of the benefits that the high-rise city offers.

THE CITY IN EUROPE

Europe has a heritage of fine cities. Some of these are ancient foundations and many more date from the pre-industrial era. The economies of these old cities were based on craft production or on trade. In this, water transport was important so many were established on the coast or on navigable rivers. Lift technology was, of course, unknown. The need to climb stairs, coupled with the limitations of traditional construction methods, limited the height of buildings to three or four storeys. Transport of goods and people was slow and difficult and these problems were eased if buildings were close together. For the same reason people lived near their work. Often this meant living over the shop or work-shop. A strong common pattern emerged in Europe's pre-industrial cities. They were modest in scale but compact and a tradition had emerged of multi-storey living – the origination of the modern flat.

On this pattern of traditional cities was overlaid the changes generated by industrialisation. This stimulated both massive population increases and large-scale urban growth. Britain led the way in this – urban indus-trialisation started earlier and went further than on the rest of Europe. Eighty per cent of Britain's population lived in cities by the end of the nine-teenth century. Urban growth was slower in Europe but by the 1930s half the population of France lived in cities. In Germany two-thirds did; and in the Netherlands the proportion was even higher.[5] Industrialisation had much less impact on Eastern Europe and almost none in the southern countries. In the cities of North and Western Europe the burgeoning new urban populations had to be housed, and many crowded into mul-tiple occupied existing buildings. In the great cities, during the nine-teenth and early twentieth centuries, new tenement blocks were built by private developers. These were often six- or seven-storey high and built around courtyards linked together. Mostly they contained one and two-roomed dwellings which were of mean space standards and lacked light and air.[6]

These overcrowded and unhealthy conditions gave rise to serious health concerns and led to public intervention. Most industrial countries in Europe introduced initiatives in social housing in the twentieth century. In the inter-war period these largely took the form of demonstration projects. These were mostly small scale but highly influential. The programme of social housing estates in Vienna was widely admired, as was the 'New Town' at Drancy-la-Muette in France. At the same time, architects of the modern movement were developing their ground-breaking housing ideas.[7] Before these could come to fruition, however, the Second World War intervened. The war caused destruction to European cities on a massive scale making millions homeless. The post-war settlement also divided Europe and for several decades east and west were to follow different paths. The West was developed under the social market economy; while the east was dominated by state socialism and central planning.

The West

After 1945 most of the countries of Western Europe faced serious problems in urban housing. These had their origin in the long period of urban growth which resulted from industrialisation. The rate of house construction had consistently failed to keep pace with population increases, which meant that much urban housing was overcrowded and multiple-occupied. Low space standards and shared facilities led to deterioration and neglect, which left much urban housing in poor physical condition. These problems were intensified by losses due to the war. Most European cities suffered war damage but it was probably at its worst in Germany where more than five million homes were destroyed.[8] A bad situation was made worse by continuing urban growth. In France the urban population expanded from 50 to 60 per cent in the 10 years after the war. Many families lived in hotels and furnished rooms. Several hundred thousands settled in self-built shanty towns on the edges of large cites – a pattern which prefigured that in many third world cities today.[9]

By the 1950s most countries had initiated intensive efforts to eliminate bad housing conditions and increase the supply of urban homes. These efforts were led by substantial programmes of social housing constructed or funded by the state. In Britain this took the form of decentralising population to new low-density housing outside the existing urban areas. Inner

THE REGENERATION OF KREUTZBERG, BERLIN

The West Berlin district of Kreutzberg was an area of six-storey tenements similar to much of the city's older housing. In the nineteenth century residential areas were laid out in large urban blocks. Flats had elongated plans which extended deep into the blocks and were provided with light and air only by narrow courtyards. Kreutzberg was situated against 'The

▲ **8.1**   New housing in scale with the existing environment

▲ **8.2**   New housing by Herman Hertzberger

Case Example Continues . . .

Wall' which divided the city during the cold war and was a neglected residential backwater on the periphery of West Berlin. It had been the focus of a squatter's movement and had since come to house as a large low-income Turkish community. In the 1980s a major urban renewal programme was carried out. This involved substantial amounts of demolition and the construction of high quality new housing and communal facilities. There was also a large programme for the rehabilitation of more than 5000 flats. This work involved demolishing parts of buildings so that the interiors of the housing blocks could be turned into communal gardens; and the careful adaptation and modernisation of the flats with the help of the residents.[11]

The regeneration included the designation of one urban block, housing over 1000 people as a testbed for the application of 'green' principles. This involved early experiments with ideas which have since become more widespread. Some of the power requirements were provided by a CHP unit and photovoltaic panels. Water conservation measures included rainwater collection and 'grey' water recycling in an innovative vertical stack of plastic dustbins planted with swamp grasses. The courts and terraces were extensively planted and 40 per cent of the roofs covered with grass. Environmentally friendly materials were used in the construction and a refuse recycling scheme introduced into the completed project.[12]

▲ 8.3   Existing housing renovated with court-yard opened up to give light and green space

▲ 8.4   New community centre

city slum housing was then cleared and replaced by multi-storey estates. In Europe the pattern was generally different. Most new social housing was built on the outskirts of big cities, often in the form of large estates of high-rise flats. The aim of this approach was to relieve overcrowding in the housing of the inner cities. At the same time, there was a desire to clear chaotic marginal land and provide better housing for the migrant communities which had settled there. The regeneration of the inner cities was largely achieved through rehabilitation and small-scale infill development. This process was mainly left to the private sector though with the support of government regulation and some finance.[10]

Over a period of 20–30 years of intensive activity most of the housing problems of Western European cities seemed to have been addressed. Their inner areas had been regenerated on the traditional pattern of streets, squares and other urban spaces, defined and enclosed by contiguous buildings of relatively modest scale. The housing in these buildings generally took the form of flats though the pattern of ownership and development created a mixture of size, quality and tenure. This traditional urban form, once restored and renovated, proved highly attractive. Many of the wealthy made their homes there alongside lower income households rehoused in good standard accommodation. These mixed communities have created economic vitality and cultural diversity. Most of the problems that remain are in the high-rise estates on the urban periphery. These have become ghettos of the poor and disadvantaged and, despite considerable investment in their improvement, continue to present a plethora of social problems.

The East

Eastern Europe had a heritage of old cities similar to that of the west. The key difference was that the pace of industrialisation and urban growth was much slower. In most of the cities there was little of the poor quality mass housing which had accompanied industrialisation in the west. The impact of the war had a mixed pattern. There was serious destruction in East Germany and in Poland where Warsaw was almost entirely destroyed by the retreating German army. Elsewhere most of the old cities escaped unscathed. In the post-war settlement the countries of Eastern Europe came under the domination of the Soviet Union. Soviet communists had great faith in the power of industrial development to liberate impoverished peasant societies both politically and economically. Much emphasis had been placed in industrial development in Soviet Union in the years following 1917. These policies were subsequently applied to the largely agrarian economies of Eastern Europe.

Industrialisation meant urban growth and, in housing, there was a one-dimensional policy. There was a negative attitude to rural areas and no interest in their housing problems. Housing in the old cities were seen largely as outmoded accommodation and, though most of it was brought under state control, there was no attempt to carry out improvements or significant maintenance. Instead, all workers of the new industrial society were to be housed in new flats. Some quite innovative model flats had been developed in the early years of the Russian revolution and during the 1930s, experiments had been carried out with prefabricated construction alongside similar innovations in Scandinavia and France. The need for mass housing developments was made much more pressing by the terrible destruction wrought by the war when 25 million Soviet citizens were made homeless. In 1954 a massive programme of prefabricated construction was introduced, state funded and centrally directed. Standard designs were produced by a Central Institute in Moscow and built by local administrations under a system of central approval and inspection.[13] Similar programmes were implemented in all the Eastern European countries under which large numbers of multi-storey blocks were constructed using precast concrete panel systems. Mostly these were in large estates of 2500–10000 people built on the outskirts of the old cities. These came to comprise a substantial proportion of the housing stock estimated at 70 per cent in some regions and cities.[14]

Following the collapse of communism in 1989 the majority of housing in Eastern Europe has been privatised. The provision of new housing has also been left largely to the market. To a large extend the old cities, which had been neglected and run down, have been regenerated. Mostly this has been done by the private sector though there have been some significant public interventions. The problem remains with the prefabricated flats. The standards of construction of these estates deteriorated over time and by the 1980s they were very poor. Inadequate construction has been exacerbated by lack of maintenance. Many now have serious problems of water penetration, low levels of insulation, inadequate services and a poor environment. Some of these estates could be renovated using techniques such as 'overcladding', successfully developed in the west. Others are beyond salvation. For the most part, though, neither renovation nor reconstruction has been possible. Privatisation has not provided the organisational means and the economies cannot afford the massive investment needed. Regeneration of the concrete estates remains a massive challenge for the cities of Eastern Europe.

HOUSING IN LATVIA

▲ 8.5   Old urban housing Riga

▲ 8.6   Mezciems estate 6 km from city centre

Latvia was part of the old Russian empire. After the Bolshevik revolution in 1917, the country, along with the other two Baltic states – Estonia and Lithuania – became independent. As part of the 1945 post-war settlement the Baltic states were reintegrated into the Soviet Union. From then on they were subject to development and housing policies similar to those implemented on other Eastern European countries. Industrial development meant substantial immigration. To house the new workforce large concrete panel estates were built on the outskirts of major cities. The scale, form and materials of this new housing were all alien to local traditions. The concentration of resources on building new estates also meant that much of the old urban housing became neglected and run-down.

With renewed independence in the early 1990s came a change in the political and economic system. Much of the existing housing was privatised and both improvement and new development were left to the private sector. Within a 10-year period most of the

Case Example Continues . . .

▲ **8.7**   House in the resort of Jurmala

old urban housing had been renovated and restored by private investment. New housing projects have been built and these could not be less like the earlier large panel estates. They have revived local vernacular traditions both in building scale and the use of materials. Timber was abundant in the Baltic states and a significant amount exported. It was used on a large scale for the construction and external cladding of houses. Major problems remain with the large estates. Many of these were poorly built and have suffered from lack of maintenance. While new investment has gone into renovation of the old cities and the construction of new housing, very little has been done to the concrete estates. Substantial improvement or redevelopment is needed which requires large-scale organisation and financial investment.

▲ **8.8**   New housing development clad in timber

EUROPEAN URBAN ISSUES

In their built form and functioning the cities of Europe provide good illustrations of many of the issues in urban housing design addressed in earlier chapters. Housing form has followed the traditional pattern and is usually relatively high density. There is commonly a strong pattern of streets and neighbourhoods with a mix of uses and services. Most have effective systems of public transport which has ensured ease of movement and kept traffic in check. There are good models of regeneration both of poor quality old housing and the re-use of 'brownfield' sites. There remain, however, current and potential problems of social polarisation and urban management difficulties created by ghettos of the disadvantaged.

Housing form

The suburban belts of sprawling low-density houses, common in many parts of the Western world, are not to be found in Europe. On average the outer areas of European cities are more than three times as densely built as those in the USA.[15] There are suburbs, and many of them are ill planned. But they generally consist of relatively small numbers of individual houses often grouped around satellite towns. Alongside these are blocks of multi-storey flats. Some of these are private. Many are in large estates of social housing. Many people, of all social groups and household structure, live in urban housing in or around the established cities. This housing might be old, refurbished to modern standards and replanned to meet contemporary expectations of space and self-containment. It might be new, in which case it will probably have been designed to fit in to the established urban pattern.

In most cities the traditional pattern is of terraced buildings designed to form or define urban spaces. These terraces are often low in scale – two, three or four-storey – but because of their layout they provide relatively high residential densities. In some cities, particularly those expanded during the nineteenth century the buildings are higher – five, six or even seven storeys along main boulevards or around large squares or open spaces. Much of this housing, particularly in the higher blocks, is apartments. The numbers of people living in flats in European cities is high. But there are houses too. In some areas, as in England, the traditional preference is for houses. This is particularly true of Holland where high densities are mainly achieved though terraced housing. This has a long tradition rooted in the tall narrow houses of Amsterdam and Rotterdam (Figures 8.9–8.11).

▲ **8.9**   Street in central Tallinn

▲ **8.10**   Residential area in Paris

▲ **8.11**   Merchants houses in Amsterdam

The choice between houses and flats is an oft-debated issue. It has much to do with established mores and expectations. The traditional character of many European cities shows that both forms can achieve good urban qualities at three and more storeys and both can be built to relatively high densities. In many countries the constraints of flat living are relieved by the existence of 'secondary housing'. In France and Southern Europe, urban migration has been relatively recent and many urban dwellers can travel freely to visit families in the country. In Scandinavia, there is a tradition of owning 'summer houses' in the country or on the coast. In Vienna and Berlin many city dwellers have allotment plots where they can spend weekends in self-built chalets. It may be no coincidence that the preference for houses has persisted most strongly in parts of Europe which are most densely populated and the opportunities for secondary housing are more limited.

Streets and neighbourhoods

Most European cities are made up of 'urban blocks'. The shape of these blocks may be rectilinear, in the planned areas of the eighteenth and

▲ **8.12**   Urban block in Prague

nineteenth centuries; they may be irregular in the more organic pattern of older urban areas. Whatever their shape, urban blocks fulfil the same function – they are terraces of buildings which form an enclosure. Inside the enclosures there were often courtyards providing light and air, and communal open space. Outside the blocks define streets (Figure 8.12). The streets are a hierarchy – access roads, secondary roads and main roads. The main roads are the arteries carrying traffic through the city. Often these are wide boulevards carrying several lanes of mixed traffic. In some places this function is performed by canals. Whether paving or water, the main arteries are effective barriers difficult to cross. They divide the city up into clearly definable neighbourhoods.

Though physically defined these neighbourhoods perform economic and social functions. Round the neighbourhoods, along the main roads, the buildings are usually higher. They often contain a range of commercial and industrial premises. These are uses most suitable for the busy and noisy environment. They provide a range of shops, services and opportunities for employment for residents. Within the neighbourhood social facilities are often provided – nurseries, primary schools and small parks. Most neighbourhoods are small enough that all these services and facilities can be reached on foot. They are also the smallest unit of administration for various aspects of urban management. Each neighbourhood is commonly given a name. They have become a means of defining the traditional city and breaking it down to an easily comprehensible pattern.

Movement

Many parts of European cities are pleasant places to walk. The streets have a proportion which relates to the human scale. The enclosing buildings are attractive and there is vitality and interest given by the shop frontages and street life. Walking is encouraged by the relatively high density which means that many destinations are within a short distance. Short travel distances also make cycling popular, particularly in countries like Holland where the flat terrain saves the trials of hill climbing. Many cities encourage cycling by the provision of dedicated and prioritised road space. Good route definition and signposting do much to encourage health-inducing and non-polluting modes of movement. Where walkers and cyclists do experience some danger and discomfort is on the main streets, which are often wide and heavily trafficked. But these main boulevards also provide access to other transport modes.

As well as private and commercial vehicles these main streets carry a wide range of public transport. Alongside private cars all cities have taxis. Many also have shared taxi systems operated by minibuses which vary their route according to their passengers' requirements. There are bus networks everywhere and many cities have tram systems as well. The junctions of the main streets are also commonly access points to the underground railway systems which most large cities have. For longer journeys there are surface railways which link urban centres to the suburbs and beyond. In Western Europe there has been large-scale investment in these public transport systems. As a result they are frequent, fast and comfortable. The stations are well designed and maintained. Many have also been provided with wheelchair access which makes them easier to use for all travellers. Public transport was also a high priority in Eastern European cities. Most have good systems which are well-used and function effectively. Some have, though, become rather run down and in need of modernisation.

The effectiveness of public transport systems in European cities has led to less use of the private car. Car ownership rates in Western Europe are often higher than in Britain, but car use is less. Intensively used mass transit systems use fuel much more efficiently. Higher densities also mean that most journeys are shorter and that more intensive public provision becomes possible. Research suggests there is a threshold density of about 30 persons per hectare above which diverse, less motorcar based, personal transport systems become viable. This threshold coincides with the density of a group of European cities such as Paris, Stockholm, Hamburg, Frankfurt and Amsterdam. These cities proved to have personal transport costs which were less than one-third of those in low-density North American cities. Lower transport costs mean less fuel consumption and less emission of greenhouse gases.[16]

Regeneration

Most of the cities of Western Europe have carried out regeneration schemes. In the 1950s and 1960s these were aimed at making good war damage or renovating areas of old urban housing. Renovation was accompanied by the development of new peripheral estates to relieve overcrowding. Mostly the improvement of the old urban areas was achieved without the large-scale redevelopment which was carried out in Britain's inner cities. Much regeneration was achieved by private initiatives but some areas were improved by planned and concerted action. A relatively recent example of planned housing regeneration is the mixed approach taken in the Kreutzberg scheme in Berlin (see Case Example 8A, p. 190). In the past 20 years economic changes have led to industrial areas becoming redundant and derelict. The large-scale development at Hammarby Sjöstad in Stockholm (see Case Study L) and the scheme at Bercy in Paris (see Case Example 7A, p. 168) are examples of approaches to the regeneration of these 'brownfield' sites. By the 1980s many of the large peripheral estates had significant problems of social distress which necessitated large-scale improvement schemes. All these large regeneration schemes have key factors in common:

Case Study L (p. 275)

- They were all initiated by intervention from central or local government which established the framework.
- They all involved the setting up of umbrella organisations to plan and co-ordinate the development.
- They all required the establishment of transport and services infrastructure, and the development of social and recreational facilities alongside housing.

- The construction projects were divided up and implemented by a mixture of agencies and developers.
- There was a mix of management systems for the completed development.

This co-ordinated multi-agency approach is in contrast with the more monolithic methods of the past. Most social housing was developed directly by the agencies of central or local government; most private housing complexes by developers acting alone. The contemporary approach produces a more balanced mixture which is more likely to succeed.

Such an approach might be adopted more widely in Eastern Europe. Since the introduction of the new political and economic regime there has been excessive faith in the power of the private market to regenerate housing. The old areas of historic cities such as Tallinn in Estonia, and Riga in Latvia, have been improved by private initiatives. But privatisation alone cannot ensure the improvement of large areas of run down housing. There has been recognition in Budapest of the limitations of the private sector. The success of the Ferencváros scheme (see Case Study M) shows that planned intervention and a co-ordinated approach can regenerate a large inner city residential area and, at the same time, preserve its essential character. The biggest problems, though, remain the large panel estates. They have a multitude of constructional problems and poor social provision. They cannot be improved without public intervention to plan and co-ordinate investment and action.

Case Study M (p. 281)

Social polarisation

The large-scale multi-storey estates which were built on the edges of cities in Western Europe had a monolithic social profile. They were all social rented dwellings. Almost all of them were designed for families with children. There were high child densities from the start. The form of the housing meant large unsupervised access networks and communal areas. Such networks provided abundant opportunities for antisocial behaviour and the estates quickly became vandalised and degraded. Those who could, moved. The estates became hard to let. Increasingly, they became occupied by the recent immigrants who were mostly in poorly paid employment. The estates became ghettos of the poorest and most disadvantaged and the focus of serious social problems and criminal activity.[17] Public concern led to large-scale improvement programmes. These concentrated on physical improvements and better management. They have brought some benefits but overall have a mixed record of success and failure. More recent approaches have concentrated on creating a better mix of household structure, housing types and tenure.

By contrast, the large concrete estates of Eastern Europe were designed to house all household types and occupational groups. When they were built they were regarded as the most desirable form of housing – a distinct improvement on the cramped poor quality flats of the old cities. Time has taken its toll. The estates suffered through deteriorating construction standards and poor maintenance. The new market economies have created increasing social stratification. Those who can choose their housing are moving out of the estates. Those who are left will be those with least choice. Unless there is action to improve them, the mixed communities, which used to characterise the concrete estates, will be no more. The estates will go the same way as their western counterparts.

TOWARDS SUSTAINABILITY

The new agenda for urban growth set out in Chapter 1 focuses on the need to strive for environmental balance. It meant better use of land by achieving higher residential densities. It meant more efficient transport systems and better land-use planning to reduce the need for travel. The cities of Europe have inherent advantages in meeting this agenda. Their traditional living patterns are more suited to the new agenda and, over the past 50 years, substantial investment has been made to reinforce them by improving both housing and transport. There are still problems: many cities have too much traffic causing too much pollution; there are still too many poor and dysfunctional communities; too much crime and antisocial behaviour. But on balance they work well and have vibrant cultural and economic activity. They provide a viable model for urban sustainability.

Progress in Britain

The pattern of urban growth in Britain over the past half century has been more like that in America than in Europe. It is true that the low-density housing environment has its roots in the English 'garden city' movement. Nevertheless, if the new agenda is to be addressed, Britain's cities need to become more like those in Europe. In response to the new agenda set by increased housing demand and by climate change, the British Government introduced new policies. These would affect the form of future urban development by increasing the supply of new housing which would be built to higher densities, by concentrating new development on 'brownfield' sites, and by improving the efficiency of the transport system.

By the end of 2003 there had been mixed progress on these initiatives:

- *Housing supply.* New housing was to be concentrated in the South East of England where demand was highest. Four new growth areas were designated based on existing urban areas. There were efforts to increase the rate of housing supply.[18] These good intentions had not been realised. For more than 10 years annual housing output had remained below 200 000 and, in 2001 fell to a 50-year low of 175 000. It was estimated that an extra 39 000 houses were needed each year 70 to 80 per cent of which would need to be 'affordable' or social housing.[19] At the same time, demand remained high and the growth in house prices seemed relentless.

- *Density.* The new higher densities required by PPG3 had been built into planning policy. Nevertheless, some considered the new range of 30 to 50 dwellings per hectare was still too low and that higher densities were needed.[20] There was some evidence that developers were building to higher densities. Between 1999 and 2002 the proportion of flats built in England almost doubled increasing from 17 to 32 per cent of housing completions. For the first time there were more flats built than detached houses.[21]

- *Brownfield development.* The policy of concentrating new housing development on previously used land seemed to be an unqualified success. The 60 per cent target has consistently been exceeded. In 2002 the proportion of new homes built on 'brownfield' sites reached 64 per cent.[22] This doubtless made a considerable contribution to urban intensification and the more efficient use of land. There were some concerns over the supply of suitable sites but success invited speculation that the target might be increased.

- *Transport*. There has been little progress in this area. More money put into public transport failed to address years of under-investment with the railway system proving particularly troublesome. By 2001 road traffic had increased 15 per cent in 10 years. With 72 per cent of work journeys being made by car and people making longer journeys it was predicted to go on increasing. The government was obliged to renege on its target of reducing congestion and scrap its moratorium on road building.[23] The one positive development was the introduction of a 'congestion charge' in central London which had significantly reduced traffic. Such charges were under consideration for other parts of the country.

Moving Britain's urban areas towards sustainability is a major challenge. There are critical structural problems. Britain has too much low-density housing, too much separation between work and home. Land-use policies are needed which intensify housing density and introduce more employment into residential areas. This would reduce both the need for commuting and the demand for travel in general. In the main, policy has moved in the right direction though the changes need to go further. At the present rate of progress positive change will be very slow indeed.

The continuing environmental agenda

Given its land-use pattern Britain would seem to be at a disadvantage in meeting the Kyoto targets for reducing greenhouse gas emissions. Ironically it seems that Britain and Sweden are the only European Union countries which are likely to meet the targets for 2010.[24] The answer to this apparent paradox seems to be that much of Britain's progress has largely been achieved through changes in energy generation. This coupled with the fact that the base year for measuring emissions was 1990. At that time much of Europe, with its more efficient land-use and transport systems was probably already causing less pollution than Britain. However, by 2004 there was, in any case considerable doubt about the future of the Kyoto accord, which had not been ratified by enough countries to make it legally binding.

With or without an international agreement global warming remains a reality. Urban growth continues to pose a challenge. There will still be a need to try to get human settlement in balance with the environment and with scarce resources. This means we will still need more dense urban development. We will still need housing forms which work well and which create successful and attractive urban neighbourhoods. We will also need to build new housing to higher standards of energy efficiency and to make more effort to improve the mass of existing housing. Most important of all, perhaps, we need to build on the models of the most successful cities to create urban areas which attract people to them. The best of cities can provide a good quality of life as well as address the environmental agenda.

KEY POINTS

⊶ In the new world, where there is abundant land, urban residential development has been very low density. The pattern of extensively serviced separate houses, whose occupants are highly dependent on the motorcar, makes for high energy use and high pollution.

- High-density cities of the Pacific Rim are, in many ways, very successful with good transport systems and high levels of public provision in housing and recreation. They are, though, dependent on energy-consuming technology and pose limitations on personal space and freedom.

- In many of the cities of Northern Europe dense housing was developed during industrialisation. The response to poor living conditions was to develop social housing. Unlike in Britain, this was generally built on the urban periphery. Many outlying multi-storey estates are now the focus of continuing social problems.

- The inner areas of European cities were regenerated piecemeal preserving the established urban form. This comprises a mixture of houses and flats of modest scale. These take perimeter block forms, enclosing urban space of good proportion and visual quality. They are the model to be emulated.

- Most European urban areas have a hierarchy of dense but well-defined streets which makes movement on foot easy and pleasurable. Major roads define identifiable neighbourhoods and also provide the network for efficient, multi-modal public transport.

- Recent large regeneration schemes in Europe are characterised by initial intervention from government and the setting up of a co-ordinating organisation. They all involve early establishment of infrastructure and they are all implemented and managed by a mixture of agencies and developers.

- Britain has, over the recent past, followed the 'new world' pattern of low-density residential development. The necessity to move towards sustainability requires that future development is closer to the European model. Some progress has been made but much more needs to be done.

PART TWO
CASE STUDIES

High-Density Social Housing
Iroko, Coin Street, London

▲ **A1**   Communal garden and four-storey houses

BACKGROUND

The Coin Street area lies behind the complex of theatres and concert halls on the south bank of the Thames in Central London. The strip of land – more than 5 hectares in all – had become run down and was ripe for redevelopment for several years. By the end of the 1980s two schemes were in contention. One was a very dense development of high-rise commercial offices. The other was a much lower-scale proposal by a consortium of community organisations for social housing, light industry, shops, restaurants and public open space. Both schemes were granted planning permission. Most of the land was owned by the Greater London Council which came under a radical administration in 1982. The new

Council favoured the community scheme and set up Coin Street Community Builders – a 'not-for-profit' organisation – to carry it out. In 1984 ownership of the site was transferred to the new organisation and funding arranged for the development.

Progress was slow, but by the late 1990s Coin Street's new owners had carried out several projects. These included a shopping area, a new public open space fronting on to the riverbank, and the conversion and rehabilitation of an industrial building to provide flats and a rooftop restaurant. The projects also included two new-built social housing developments. These schemes were low density and low scale – mostly only three-storey high. The modest scale of these schemes prompted

▲ **A2**   The 'hard' public face of the scheme clad in brickwork

criticism that they could not provide an appropriate model for urban housing and that many more people should have been accommodated in such a desirable location.[1] The Iroko Scheme can be seen as a response to such criticism.

THE SCHEME

The Iroko project, completed in 2002, is bigger in scale than its predecessors – four- or five-storey high throughout. It is also of a form which makes more intensive use of the urban site and creates good-quality housing which is easy to manage. The site had been used as a temporary car park for several years and the new development includes a commercial car park in its basement. The revenue from this subsidises the management and maintenance costs of the housing. The new building occupies three sides of a square – the fourth side is reserved for a new community resource and training centre.

The built form has a number of advantages. If repeated it can successfully define well-proportioned streets and urban spaces. The horseshoe form encloses an interior space which can be treated quite differently from the public domain. The façades facing the street are more vulnerable to overlooking by passing traffic and pedestrians. It is on this side that kitchens, parking and bin stores are placed. The inner face is relatively private. Living rooms, private gardens and balconies are placed on the inside to take advantage of this privacy. The centre of the enclosed space

▲ **A3** House-type maisonettes with small maisonettes over

▲ **A4** Access gallery to the upper maisonettes

is landscaped as a communal garden. The contrast between inside and out is emphasised by the finishing materials – brick on the 'hard' exterior and timber boarding on the 'soft' inside façades.

The hollow-square form has commonly been used for blocks of flats but the aim of this scheme was to provide for families. This is realised by concentrating most of the accommodation in forms which resemble traditional

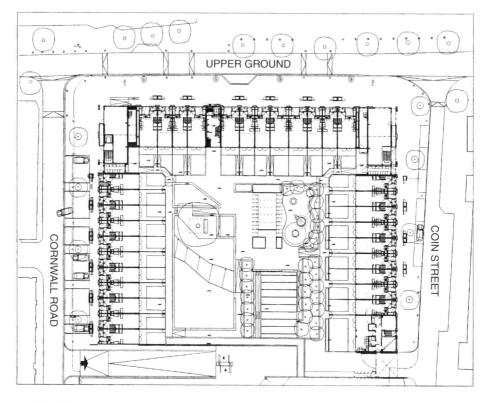

▲ **A5**   Site plan

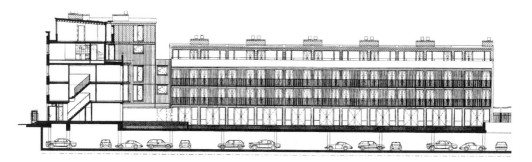

▲ **A6**   Section

houses. The two arms of the building comprise terraced housing four storeys high. These not only have private gardens but a balcony at each level and a terrace on the roof. The five-storey central section consists of three-storey house-type maisonettes with gardens. These are topped by two-storey maisonettes for smaller households reached by an external access deck. Turning the corners presents a challenge with this form of development. This is solved here by providing a shop at ground level and small flats, facing outwards on the first and second floors. The corners also contain stairs and lifts giving access to the maisonettes above.[2]

Many high-density social housing projects of the past failed because of the impact of large numbers of children in the unsupervised access systems. The Iroko scheme addresses this problem by keeping the enclosed common areas to a minimum. Seventy-five per cent of the schemes' residents are housed on the ground with their own private entrances from the street. Children have the advantage of private gardens and also direct access to the secured communal garden. There, their safety and behaviour can be supervised from the windows of the surrounding housing. Only a minority of dwellings are reached from enclosed lifts and stairs and these accommodate the smaller households. As a result, the problems created by vandalism and damage to the common areas should be minimised.

Management should be improved by the involvement of the residents themselves. The Coin Street schemes are co-operatives where tenants are responsible for managing the housing. This does not mean, though, that the residents have significant input into the design of their own homes. The brief is set by a representative group which might include some residents but not the future tenants. The design of the project is then opened to limited competition. Tenants are only allocated 6 months in advance and have little opportunity to adapt their homes to their own needs and tastes.

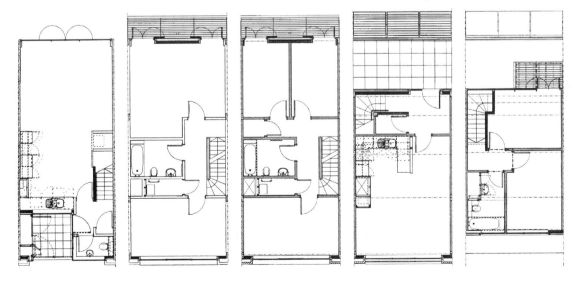

▲ **A7** Type plans – house-type maisonettes; upper maisonettes

KEY FACTS

Location	South Bank, London	
Completion date	2002	
Developer	Coin Street Community Builders	
Architect	Haworth Tomkins	
Number of dwellings	59	
Dwelling mix	8 bedroom/12 person house	1
	5 bedroom/8 person houses	22
	4 bedroom/6 person house-type maisonettes	12
	2 bedroom/4 person upper maisonettes	16
	2 bedroom/4 person flats	4
	1 bedroom/2 person flats	4
Other provision	Two retail units	
	Commercial underground car park	
	Landscaped communal garden	
Previous use of site	Temporary car park	
Density	74 dwellings per hectare	
	334 habitable rooms per hectare	
Forms of tenure	Social rented	
Key targets/issues	Providing social housing on a Central London site	
Green features	Super-insulation	
	Condensing boilers	
	Heat-recovery units	
	Roof-mounted solar hot water panels	
Transport issues	Good links to underground, rail and bus services	
	Residents' parking restricted to on-street spaces (about 35 per cent)	

High-Density Commercial Housing
Rope Works, Manchester

▲ **B1**   Overall view of the development

BACKGROUND

One of the consequences of the growth of small households has been a revival of interest in inner city living. Young singles and childless couples find no disadvantage in living in flats and every benefit in having their homes near centres of employment and recreation. By 2002 the numbers of flats completed reached its highest level since the 1970s. In the past most new inner city flats were built as social housing for families. The much smaller numbers of private flats were generally sited in prime locations such as rivers, seafronts or the boundaries of major parks. These days most flats are being built by private developers to meet the growing demand from young urban professionals. Economic changes have opened new opportunities for commercial multi-storey housing. A great deal has been built in London's dockhands. In the past few years similar residential developments have taken place in dockside or former industrial sites in the centres of Leeds, Bristol, Birmingham and other provincial English cities where previously there had been almost no tradition of living in flats.

In Manchester there has been a concentration of flat building along Whitworth Street. This is an area of large commercial Victorian buildings up to 10-storey high. Some have been converted and some redeveloped. In all some 2600 flats were developed in the areas during the 1990s.[1] Recent development include 224 flats in the 10-storey Whitworthwest building by Redrow and the 12-storey Hacienda development by Crosby Homes. What all these inner city developments have in common is that they all comprise small apartments and they are all densely crowded on their sites with little or no communal amenity provision. Despite their claims to provide 'stylish, luxury living', very few are distinguished by good design or architectural merit.

▲ **B2**   Front of the completed development

HEWITT STREET

BLOCK B

BLOCK A

LITTLE PETER STREET

APT A27
TYPE A3

APT A28
TYPE A4

APT A29
TYPE A2

APT A30
TYPE A2

APT A31
TYPE A2

APT A32
TYPE A2

APT A33
TYPE A1

APT A34
TYPE A5

APT A35
TYPE A6

APT B36
TYPE B7

APT B37
TYPE B1a

APT B38
TYPE B1a

APT B39
TYPE B3

APT B40
TYPE B10

APT B42
TYPE B8

APT B41
TYPE B9

APT B35
TYPE B11

APT B34
FLAT TYPE B3

APT B33
TYPE B1a

APT B32
TYPE B1b

APT B31
TYPE B6

▲ B3   Typical floor plan

▲ **B4** Typical kitchen

THE SCHEME

Rope Works is one of the most recently completed Manchester developments. It lies at the very end of Whitworth Street on the site of a former factory. The site is bounded by existing streets to the north and south. The development fills the site almost entirely and is divided into two blocks, one rising to five storeys and the other to eight. All the flats are either one or two bedroomed, and clearly best suited to small adult households. Most flats are similarly planned and are a little larger than Parker Morris space standards. In the south-east corner there are a few flats with more generous space standards and four penthouses with terraces at roof level. All of the flats are fully finished. Bathrooms are provided with both bath and separate shower cubicle. In the fitted kitchens a concession to customisation is the offer of a choice of door colours.

The standard of the flat interiors seems to be good and the blocks are planned with living rooms and bedrooms vertically stacked and adjoining. This is a key factor in reducing the risk of noise nuisance. The access system, however, is more questionable. Each block is served by a single lift which could cause problems in the case of breakdown. In each block, too, there is a single main entrance with a secondary staircase. This means that one main access point serves 44 flats in the smaller block and 74 flats in the larger block. These entrances are secured by electronic door entry systems with video links to every flat. Experience in social housing blocks suggests that such

▲ **B5**   Typical living room

systems break down if made to serve much more than 20 flats, causing a range of abuse to the common areas. It may be different in an owner-occupied block with a largely adult population. In many private blocks, though, security staff is employed to monitor the entrances.

The potential problems with the access system are compounded by a single central corridor in the larger block. This allows the use of a deep plan form which has advantages in design economy by reducing the ratio of external wall to floor area. But this has two disadvantages. Such corridors are oppressive, denied natural light and views out. They are not overlooked and can be prone to crime and antisocial behaviour. The second disadvantage is that, of necessity, the flats on either side of the corridor have to be single aspect. In this case it means that while many flats enjoy a southerly aspect, the remainder face north.

▲ **B6**   An elevated railway runs along the rear of the site

The development is short on amenity. About one-third of the flats have private balconies and a number have 'quasi-balconies' – inward opening glazed doors protected by a railing. A substantial number have no private outdoor space, however, and apart from a small court-yard between the blocks, the development does not provide communal recreation space. The surrounding environment is also poor. To the north there is a railway viaduct onto which many of the flats face. To the south there is a large open site which is currently used as a commercial car park. Overall, the amenity and security enjoyed by residents would have been enhanced if the site had been developed with fewer flats all facing south. At the least, more effort could have been made to provide generous private outdoor space and some shared recreation space. These short-comings are partly offset by the location of the development and the access this provides to the facilities of the city centre.

KEY FACTS

Location	Little Peter Street, Central Manchester
Completion date	2003
Developer	George Wimpey City
Architect	Carden Croft
Number of dwellings	118
Dwelling mix	2 bedroom/4 person flats 49
	1 bedroom/2 person flats 69
Other provision	One office suite
	One large three-storey commercial space
Previous use of site	Industrial
Density	Approximately 260 dwellings per hectare
	Approximately 620 habitable rooms per hectare
Forms of tenure	All flats were built for sale
Key targets/issues	Meeting demand for city-centre apartments for small households
Green features	None other than compliance with increased insulation standards of building regulations
Transport issues	Within walking distance of city centre
	Good links to bus, tram and mainline rail services
	49 residents parking spaces in under-croft (40 per cent) plus three spaces for commercial units

▲ **C1** Waterfront pavilions of private flats

BACKGROUND

Changes in international freight transport led to the gradual closure of London's docks during the 1970s. This huge area of redundant docks warehousing and industry stretched along both banks of the Thames in East London, covering 22 square kilometres. It became the biggest 'brownfield' site in Europe. Some attempts were made to improve parts of the area through community development but this would have required large-scale public investment to succeed. In 1981 the government decided that the focus should be on private investment and the London Docklands Development Corporation (LDDC) was formed with a remit to regenerate the entire area. Planning procedures were eased

and financial incentives offered to attract property developers. Over a period of 20 years much of the area has been rebuilt. The most high-profile development is the commercial complex at Canary Wharf which has the character of a new urban centre. As well as the new office blocks a great deal of new housing has been built for sale.

Over time the LDDC came in for the criticism that, while investment had been poured into new offices and private housing, almost nothing had been spent on transport, community facilities and social housing. Part of the response to this was to create a flagship project at the Royal Victoria Dock. Based on the urban village concept, the aim was to create a

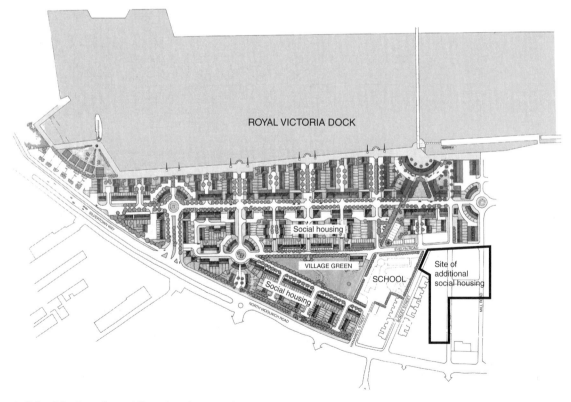

ROYAL VICTORIA DOCK

Social housing

VILLAGE GREEN

Social housing

SCHOOL

Site of additional social housing

▲ **C2**   Master plan of the development

new community which was socially and economically balanced. The project was discussed at a 'community planning weekend' in 1993 in which local residents played a major role in framing the proposals.

THE SCHEME

The new urban village occupies a site bounded on the north by the large dock and on the south side by a busy primary road. The project

▲ **C3**   Court of private housing off dock front

▲ **C4**   Social housing around the new 'village green'

was built by a consortium of social landlords working with a major property developer. The development consists of three parts. The northern part of the site is occupied mainly by private housing. A series of four-storey pavilions containing flats is set out along the dock front. Behind these are courtyards of three-storey houses. Through the centre of the site blocks of six-storey flats are set out along the main distributor road. Although some affordable housing is interspersed among the private blocks, the bulk of the social housing is located in the southern part of the development. This is lower in scale comprising two- and three-storey houses and flats grouped around a new 'village green' open space.

At the centre of the development community and social facilities are grouped around a pedestrian spine. At the base of the spine are a new primary school and a community centre with health care provision. At the top a new pedestrian bridge has been built across the dock. This leads to the new Excel Exhibition Centre and the Docklands Light Railway Station. At the centre of the spine is the 'Crescent building'. This contains shops, a pub and commercial space on the ground level with social rented flats above. The building was developed by the Peabody Trust as a demonstration project for low-technology energy-efficient design. It is constructed of dense blockwork to absorb and retain heat. There are triple-glazed windows and a low-energy passive-stack ventilation system. Phase I of the urban village is a large development which creates a coherent neighbourhood but substantial additional growth is planned. A further area of social rented housing has already been developed; two mill buildings are to be converted for commercial use and there are plans for a large-scale leisure and commercial development.[1]

There may be some criticism that the social and private housing are too clearly segregated and that the housing for sale has been allocated the more desirable dockside location. Overall, though, the scheme has a well-balanced

▲ **C5**   The Crescent building and footbridge over the dock

social mix and this has been reinforced by the fact that a proportion of the privately built flats have been taken over as student accommodation. What is particularly striking is the contrast between the housing for sale and the social housing developed by the East Thames Housing Group. Although developed and marketed by Wimpey Homes, the high-density mix of houses and flats for sale was shaped by comprehensive design codes. These not only set down the disposition and height of the buildings, but also detailed architectural regulations determined fenestration, elevations treatment and use of materials. The housing for rent was far less strictly prescribed and the social landlord has played safe. Their development is much lower density and has a character typical of most social housing built in the last 15 years.

A key objective of the urban village concept was that sufficient local employment should be developed so that there was a net balance of housing and jobs. This would reduce the need for commuting and improve the lifestyle of the residents. It cannot be said that this balance has been achieved at West Silvertown, although there are good links to employment. The light rail system links directly to the commercial centres of Docklands where there are many professional jobs. Manual work is available in the completed exhibition centre and more will be created by the new commercial development. Given this it is disappointing that such a high level of provision has been made for private car parking.

The project has achieved a high standard of urban design. The social housing around its

▲ **C6**   Six-storey blocks along the central road

village green is conventional but pleasant. The scale of the blocks along the central road gives it a genuinely urban character. The most distinctive area, though, is the dock front. The Crescent building makes a good-quality central pedestrian space. The series of apartment buildings set behind the old cranes has an unusual and striking character. It is a pity, though, that the ground floors of these pavilions have been devoted to garaging. This prevents residents having outdoor space directly onto the dockside which would have created more vitality and encouraged use of the water.

KEY FACTS

Phase 1

Location	Royal Victoria Dock, East London
Completion date	2002
Promoter	London Docklands Development Corporation
Master Planners and Architects to Peabody	Gardner Stewart (previously part of Tibbalds Monro)
Developers	Wimpey Homes Peabody Trust, East Thames Housing Group
Number of dwellings	1112
Dwelling mix	Houses and flats
Other provision	Six shops Public house 500 square metres workspace/commercial 200 square metres live/work units Community centre including health care Primary school Public green space
Previous use of site	Transport/storage/industrial
Density	78 dwellings per hectare
Forms of tenure	782 dwellings built for sale 330 dwellings social rented
Key targets/issues	Regeneration of a 'brownfield' site to create a mixed and economically viable community
Green features	Crescent building a demonstration project for low-tech, environmentally efficient design
Transport issues	Local bus services Docklands light railway station nearby High level of residents parking

Model for a Sustainable Urban Block

Homes for Change, Manchester

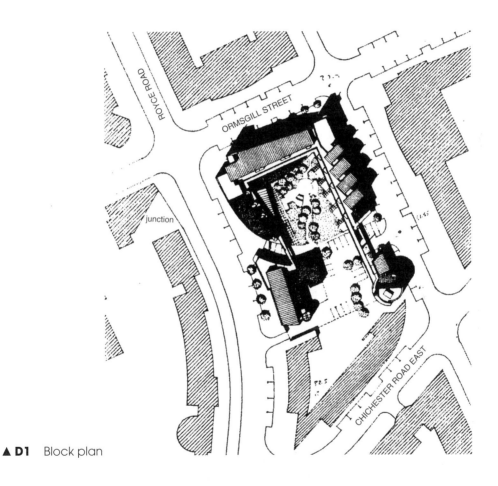

▲ **D1** Block plan

BACKGROUND

The Hulme area of Manchester was originally developed in the 1850s as low-cost housing for industrial workers. The housing was of poor quality and rapidly became overcrowded. By the turn of the century it was a notorious slum. In the 1960s the housing was cleared and replaced with 13 tower blocks and 6-deck-access blocks ranging from six- to nine- storeys high. As elsewhere, this form of housing rapidly proved unsuitable for low-income families with children. The common parts became subject to abuse and the area was notorious for poverty, crime and drug abuse. Throughout the 1980s plans were made for a second redevelopment. A concept plan was produced as the basis of a bid for government finance in 1991. This succeeded in securing funding for extensive redevelopment including the demolition of all the deck access estates.

The architects Mills Beaumont Leavey Channon (MBLC) prepared a conceptual 'master plan' supported by a Design Code. Working from the principles of the code, an urban design guide was drawn up with the contributions from the Hulme Community Architecture Project and economic development group URBED. The guide was adopted by the City Council, and MBLC was appointed to work alongside council staff to implement its principles. Hulme was to be reconstructed as a high-density mixed community with strong urban qualities. The area was divided up into parcels for re-building. Some were developed as housing for sale though the majority of sites provided new affordable housing. This was undertaken by two large housing associations sometimes working with community organisations. While a large numbers of houses and flats of modest scale had been built by 2002, a significant amount of land remained cleared and undeveloped.

THE SCHEME

The project was initiated by the Homes for Change Housing Co-operative which had been formed in Hulme several years earlier. Many co-operative (co-op) members had established work in the area and a sister co-op Work for Change was set up. Together, they planned a community-owned mixed-use building and this proposal was included in the Hulme master plan. The scheme was developed by the Guinness Trust but with co-op members involved in all decision-making. Working with architects MBLC, a complex participation process was embarked upon. Daylong design workshops took place every month for over a year. Early workshops made visits to other schemes and plundered magazines for ideas. Later rough models were made to explore building forms and spaces. At one stage full-scale models of the flat interiors were made in a local church. Finally attention was given to the selection of materials, components and colour schemes.

The completed scheme is built around a secure central courtyard containing communal gardens and limited parking mainly for business use. The west side of the site bounds a fairly busy main road. The offices, shops, workshops and communal facilities are concentrated on the ground and first floor of this frontage and on the north side of the site. On the east side of the site there is housing on the ground and first floor where it enjoys a westerly aspect and views over the communal garden. The upper levels contain flats and maisonettes. These rise to six storeys on the north and east wings. The west wing is largely restricted to four storeys. This built form optimises the orientation of the dwellings and maximises the benefits of solar gain. The upper levels are reached from a single main entrance and open access galleries run around the building at second and fourth floor levels. The galleries include high-level garden spaces. The completed scheme is managed by the co-op, and the dwellings and workspace units are rented to its members.[1]

The membership of the co-op are mostly young and largely childless, and the scheme might be a model for housing this group which is so strongly represented in household growth.

▲ **D2**   The central courtyard

▲ **D3**   The south frontage, phase 2 of the scheme in the foreground

Given this profile it might have been expected that the majority of the dwellings would be small. Instead there is a preponderance of units suitable for families. Presumably many of these units are initially shared by single people. This avoids the problem experienced by some co-ops where too many small units become unsuitable as members mature and form family units. It is questionable, though, whether this form of housing is suitable for families with children. The upper floors are served by the same sort of access decks which proved so troublesome in the old Hulme crescents. It might have been better to concentrate on more small flats on the upper levels. At least the co-op is a management form well suited to tackling problems caused by antisocial behaviour.

The block is intended as a model for future urban development. It is certainly a form which mirrors many successful urban blocks. A secure interior space is enclosed by a perimeter, which has a scale sufficient to create well-proportioned streets and other urban spaces. The considerable range of workshops and commercial space would go a long way to meeting the employment needs of a resident population of this size. Facilities such as the studios and theatre would probably serve a much wider community. Were it repeated it would be beneficial to include improved environmental design such as water recycling and passive-stack ventilation. These are features that co-op members wanted but were unable to achieve.

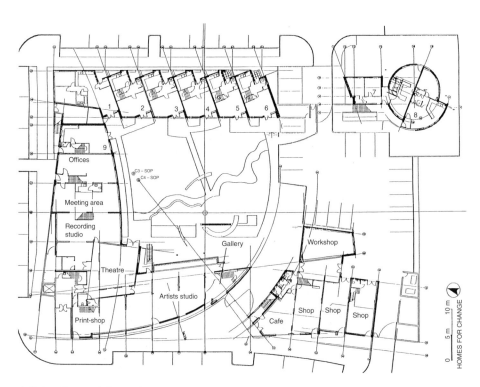

▲ **D4** Ground floor plan

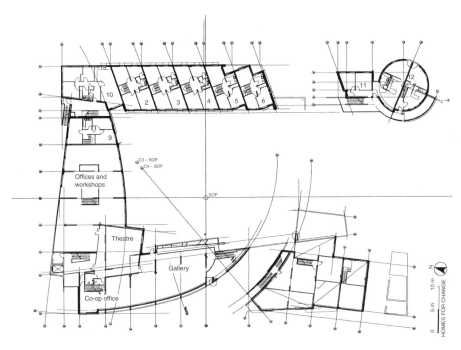

▲ **D5**   First floor plan

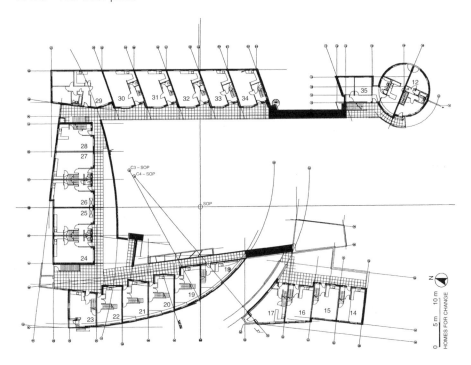

▲ **D6**   Second floor plans (upper levels similar)

KEY FACTS

Location	Hulme, Manchester	
Completion date	Phase 1	1996
	Phase 2	1999
Developer	The Guinness Trust	
	Homes for Change	
Architect	Mills Beaumont Leavey Channon	
Number of dwellings	Phase 1	51
Dwelling mix	1-bedroom flats	3
	2-bedroom flats	11
	2-bedroom maisonettes	24
	3-bedroom maisonettes	6
	4-bedroom maisonettes	7
Other provision	Three shops and a café	
	Offices studios and workshops	
	Recording studio	
	Theatre and gallery	
	Meeting room	
Previous use of site	Brewery	
Density	80 dwellings per hectare	
	190 persons per hectare	
Forms of tenure	Rented to co-op members	
Key targets/issues	To create a mixed-use building as a model for a sustainable urban block	
	Reduced carbon dioxide emissions and embodied energy	
Green features	Orientated to maximise solar gain	
	Recycled concrete ballast	
	Concrete blocks 80 per cent recycled	
	Super-insulation	
	Sustainable and non-toxic materials	
	Green roofs/'sky gardens'	
Transport issues	24 on-street parking spaces	
	16 spaces in secure courtyard	
	Located on bus route	

▲ **E1** The central 'street' and stair rising to rear entrance

BACKGROUND

Foyers are a form of housing relatively new to Britain. Essentially they are centres which provide homes and training for young people with problems. The name is imported from the French *Foyers de Jeune Travailleurs* which began during the Second World War and flourished during the 1950s. These provided basic accommodation for young single people backed up by laundry and canteen facilities, and some recreation rooms. Gradually, the *Foyers* added more support services to make them a 'home from home' and act as a bridge to independent living. The *Foyer* idea did not come to Britain until the 1990s. The first was set up in 1992 and there are now more than 100 Foyers operating in the UK. These provide high-quality accommodation in self-contained rooms or flats. Communal rooms are provided for recreation and training sessions. Most include a restaurant which is usually also open to the local community.

Their first aim is to provide a safety net for those in housing need – forced to leave home or perhaps leaving local authority care. Such young people often end up homeless and rootless. So the second aim is to provide them with the skills to support themselves by finding work and maintaining their own homes. Residents stay for a limited period, usually from 6 months to a maximum of 2 years. Each is expected to draw up their own 'Action Plan' which will set out their aims in personal development, skill training

▲ **E2**   The Retained north-east façade which marries with new structure behind

and job seeking. British Foyers are little concerned with organising training in specific work skills. They have a wide remit aimed at generating social orientation, promoting basic education and inculcating life skills such as home management, and budgeting. Encouraging residents to seek vocational training and develop a job search facility are part of this broader context.[1]

THE SCHEME

In 1994 the Gwalia Housing Society acquired the old Swansea Working Men's Club for development as a Foyer. The project was put out to limited competition with the stipulation that the scheme was to avoid creating an institutional atmosphere. The society had a strong environmental policy and was keen that the building should address the green agenda as fully as possible. Much of the old building was in poor condition but two of the façades had been listed and it was decided to incorporate a new structure within them. The new structure is lightweight based on a timber frame – using material from sustainable sources – infilled with high levels of insulation. The walls are colour washed in an echo of Welsh vernacular. Local slates cover the pitched roofs on which solar panels are mounted.

▲ **E3**   Entrances to the 'houses' which front the central 'street'

The basis of the scheme is that residents will have their own study/bedrooms but live in groups with shared kitchen/dining spaces. These groups are accommodated in five three-storey 'houses' each of which has four or five residents. The houses are grouped around an internal 'street'. To address the steep slope on the site, this is reached by stairs from the main entrance and another set of stairs sweeps up to a secondary entrance at the rear. The communal and training rooms are grouped around the front of the building which make them easily reached by visitors from outside. A lift serves the upper level galleries and this ensures that all levels are wheelchair accessible. The entire central space is enclosed in a glass atrium. This has two functions: it acts as a solar collector, and gives protection to the internal street which can be used as a meeting and recreation space.[2]

The Foyer is a new building type. It differs from general needs housing in that the residents are

Swansea Foyer

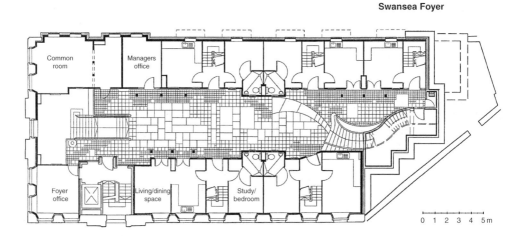

▲ **E4**   Ground floor plan

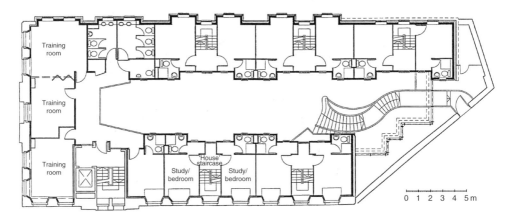

▲ **E5**   First floor plan (second floor similar)

▲ E6   The successful marrying of old and new on south-west façade

all single and their stay is short term. There is no need to make allowance for households formation or children. In terms of housing need there is a strong similarity to student accommodation. In the past such needs would be met by hostel accommodation. More recently students have been housed in small groups sharing kitchens and eating space. This type of accommodation is more like conventional family flats and is thought to be less institutionalised. It is the approach adopted here though it is enhanced by a distinguished and innovative design. The scheme is a good model but such high quality may not always be affordable. The basic approach does suggest, though, that some of the housing which has become hard to let could be successfully adapted as Foyers.

Part of the project's distinction comes from marrying old with new. Re-using old buildings helps to preserve familiar urban landmarks but it also imposes a constraint on the design of the new. Resolving these constraints often

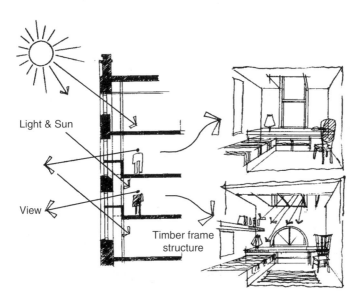

▲ E7   Marrying the old windows to new domestic storey heights

results in distinctive solutions. Generally the interaction between old and new in this building has been handled very successfully. Although a certain amount of tension was created by the need to marry new domestic storey heights to the much higher storeys of the old building. As a result, some of the tall old windows have been divided between more than one room. This may not be ideal but it certainly gives character to some of the spaces.

KEY FACTS

Location	Swansea City Centre
Completion date	1997
Developer	The Gwalia Housing Society Ltd
Architect	PCKO Architects
Residential accommodation	Five 'houses' each providing shared accommodation for four or five young people Two guest rooms
Other provision	Two offices Three training rooms Common room Restaurant Covered 'outdoor' communal space Common toilets
Previous use of site	Working men's club
Density	Not relevant
Forms of tenure	Residents stay on temporary tenancies
Key targets/issues	Re-use of redundant listed building To provide a high-quality non-institutional environment A high level of environmentally sensitive design
Green features	Super-insulation Covered space acts a solar collector Solar hot water panels Photovoltaics panels provide some electrical power Energy-saving lighting control Passive-stack ventilation Materials from sustainable sources Water-conserving fittings
Transport issues	City-centre location provides good access to facilities

▲ **F1** The canal-side frontage of the building

BACKGROUND

One of the key problems in providing good-quality homes for the growing numbers of one- and two-person households is the high cost of housing in the private market. This has led to innovations such as shared ownership and 'cost rents'. The housing charity, The Rowntree Foundation, conceived the idea of housing for young people which would be affordable but still achieve a return of 6 per cent on investment – an echo of the '5 per cent philanthropy' pioneered by nineteenth century housing reformers. The Rowntree Foundation instituted research into what sort of housing this group would like. A city-centre location was very important. There should be enough space for two people and/or occasional visitors. The apartments should be bright and clean, and should include extras not normally provided – main appliances, carpets and curtains. Personal security was an important issue for women. Men valued a secure car parking space though there was strong support for giving a discount to those without cars. A common meeting area was an appealing idea but was not considered essential.[1]

Armed with these findings Rowntree devised the City-centre Apartments for Single People at Affordable Rents (CASPAR) programme. The trust wanted to achieve high-quality design, and, before any sites were chosen a limited competition was held among five teams of architects and building professionals. Their brief was to provide schemes for high-density low-cost developments that would meet the requirements unearthed by the research. In addition, the flats were to meet the 'lifetime homes' standard which Rowntree had initiated. This requires that all housing should be suitable for wheelchair use and accommodate other forms of disability. Two sites were chosen, both near

city centres, one in Birmingham and the other in Leeds. Early in 1998 winning schemes were selected for the two developments.

THE SCHEME

The Birmingham CASPAR lies in an old district, north of the city centre, densely crammed with factories, many of which have fallen into disuse. The development was partly intended as a trigger for regeneration as a mixed-use and residential area. The site was formerly occupied by a print works and, more recently, by a temporary car park. Its south-eastern boundary is formed by one of the canals which are such a prominent feature of Birmingham's urban landscape. To avoid any possible problems with adjoining developments, it was decided to locate the building in the centre of the site leaving space either side for ground-level car parking.

The building is, essentially, two blocks of flats five-storey high at the street entrance and four-storey high at the canal end. The blocks are linked by a central space which is covered by a glazed canopy but left open at the sides and ends to allow ventilation and to act as a fire precaution. This space contains lift, stairs, and a set of walkways and bridges leading to the individual flats. All the flats are one bedroomed and, at 50 square metres, are a little more generous than Parker Morris space standards for a two-person unit. The flat plans are all very similar. The repetitive planning allows a high degree of standardisation. Full off-site construction was not pursued but many elements are prefabricated. The building has a steel frame supporting an insulated timber-framed inner skin. This is clad in brickwork externally and timber boarding in the communal space. Floors are of precast concrete planks and much of the steelwork, balconies and galleries were prefabricated. The

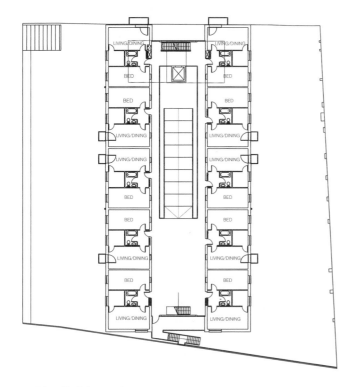

▲ **F2**   First floor plan

▲ **F3**   Typical upper-level plan

bathrooms for each flat are brought to the site as 'pods', fully fitted and finished.[2]

The most striking feature of the building is the central access space. Functionally this could have been achieved with a simple corridor but the extra space has been achieved cheaply with a lightweight glass canopy and steel bridges. Opening up the access has several advantages. First, it allows light and air to penetrate the space. Secondly, it improves security by ensuring the walkways are overlooked from several levels. This surveillance is reinforced by the small windows which overlook the central space from the flats. This high level of visual interaction will undoubtedly improve the sociability of the building.

The bridges leading to each flat can function as a partially private outdoor space – useful for

▲ **F4**   The central space, lift and stairs

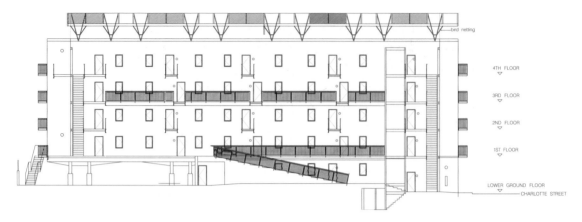

▲ **F5**   Long section

▲ **F6**   The main entrance from Charlotte Street

▲ **F7**   Bridges to the individual flats

the storage of bicycles and the setting of pot plants. The disadvantage of the access concept is that it still requires that the flats have all their main windows facing one aspect. In this case it means that a good proportion of the flats face north-east, which is far from ideal.

The building has an appropriate scale for the high-density city. However, it is questionable whether this form could be repeated as a module for the creation of successful urban blocks. It is difficult to see how a series of such buildings could enclose coherent spaces.

An outdoor recreation space would be an advantage here. Residents have small private balconies and share in the use of the central space, but they are not provided with any communal green space and it is a pity that the only outdoor space is given over to car parking. Such green spaces are an essential addition to high-density apartments, as they help deter crime, and are the most successful when enclosed and defined by buildings. A building, such as this, needs to be carefully considered and related to other built forms to make a successful urban environment.

KEY FACTS

Location	Charlotte Street, close to central Birmingham
Completion date	2000
Developer	Joseph Rowntree Foundation
Architect	Alford Hall Monaghan Morris
Number of dwellings	46
Dwelling mix	All 1 bedroom/2 person flats
Other provision	None
Previous use of site	Print works
Density	230 dwellings per hectare Approximately 460 habitable rooms per hectare
Forms of tenure	All flats are rented
Key targets/issues	Meeting demand for city-centre apartments for single people at modest rents
Green features	High degree of off-site construction Meets new higher standards of insulation
Transport issues	Within walking distance of city centre Good links to bus and mainline rail services 100 per cent residents parking at ground level

Car-Free Social Housing
Slateford Green, Edinburgh

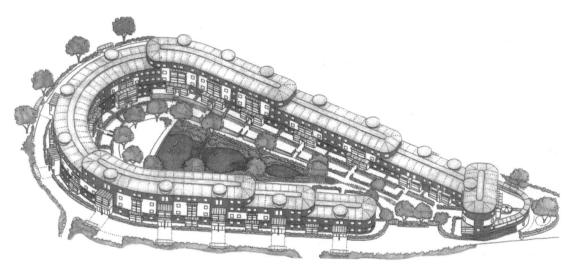

▲ **G1** Visualisation

BACKGROUND

Urban housing tradition in Scotland is different from that in most of England. While the English – even in the poorest industrial cities – preferred houses, the Scots habitually lived in flats. Tenement blocks of flats became the norm for all social classes. By the early twentieth century, however, many tenements had degenerated into slums. This was not because they were poorly built or ill serviced. It was mainly due to serious overcrowding in subdivided flats where whole families might live in one or two rooms. The response was slum clearance and, in the 1950s and 1960s, many tenement blocks were bulldozed to make way for tower blocks. These rapidly became beset with serious social and management problems. By the 1980s many of the tall blocks were, in their turn, scheduled for demolition.

The result was a reassessment of the tenement block. Traditionally these were modest in scale – four storeys was the norm. At the same time, they were high density. Generally they were built in perimeter block form enclosing courts which could be used for recreation. On the outside the blocks formed well-proportioned urban spaces. A number of recent Scottish housing schemes have recreated these advantages in modern versions of the tenement. It is not a form, though, which could accommodate high car ownership. In earlier times tenement residents would, in any case, have been dependent on walking, cycling and public transport. At the same time, transport campaigners have argued that high-density housing can work successfully without private cars, provided alternative means of transport are available. In recent years Edinburgh has been in the vanguard of transport

experiments including traffic restraint, car-sharing schemes and car-free housing.

THE SCHEME

The Slateford Green housing is built on a former railway goods yard. The scheme, which was the result of an international competition, was designed not only to be free of private cars; it was also to have high levels of sensitivity to environmental issues. In form, the new housing follows the tenement principles. All the dwellings are flats, mostly three or four storeys in height. They are built into a continuous block, the curved form of which largely follows the perimeter of the site. Inside it encloses private gardens and a communal green space. On the outside are the entrances to the flats. These are reached by a pedestrian street and cycle route which circles the block. This can also be used as access for emergency vehicles and deliveries. At the eastern end of the site the new community centre and

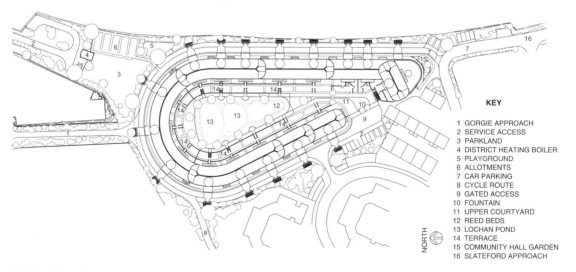

KEY

1 GORGIE APPROACH
2 SERVICE ACCESS
3 PARKLAND
4 DISTRICT HEATING BOILER
5 PLAYGROUND
6 ALLOTMENTS
7 CAR PARKING
8 CYCLE ROUTE
9 GATED ACCESS
10 FOUNTAIN
11 UPPER COURTYARD
12 REED BEDS
13 LOCHAN POND
14 TERRACE
15 COMMUNITY HALL GARDEN
16 SLATEFORD APPROACH

NORTH

▲ **G2**   Site plan

kindergarten form a 'stop end' to the block. At the western end there is parkland, a playground and allotments.

The scheme has a wealth of 'green' features. The buildings are of lightweight timber-framed construction, much of which was brought to site as prefabricated panels. All the timber is from sustainable sources and insulation is manufactured from recycled newspaper. The flats are provided with 'sun spaces' to both living rooms and main bedrooms. These are designed to collect solar gain which is maximised by placing them on both sides of the block. There is a 'passive-stack' ventilation system which uses the common stairwells. Each of these has an open turret which draws air up through the building. The flats have a district heating system which was intended to be powered by burning reject condensate from a local distillery. This is taking time to arrange and, in the meantime, the four communal boilers run on natural gas.

A key feature of the scheme is the ponds in the central communal space. These collects rainwater run-off from roofs and roads. The water is cleansed for re-use by passing it through reed beds and then through two ponds containing gravel filters. The ponds have a beneficial environmental effect by reflecting sunlight during the day and releasing heat at night stimulating air flow. They are also an opportunity for cultivating water plants. A principle of the landscaping as a whole is the planting of native species. These and the artificial wetlands encourage biodiversity. The scheme is planted with deciduous trees which allow sunlight through in winter while providing shade in summer.[1]

▲ **G4** Pedestrian/cycle/emergency vehicle 'street' which rings the scheme

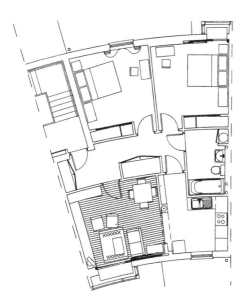

▲ **G3** Typical flat plan

▲ **G5**   'Passive-stack' vent turrets to staircases

The project aims to create a mixed community – one which contains owner-occupiers and tenants, young and old, and able-bodied and infirm. The focus, though, is on social rented housing for families with children. This type of housing has often provided the most difficult management problems. Mixing with other age and social groups is helpful. The form of the housing is also good. The building has a staircase access system traditional in tenements. Each entrance serves a small number of flats – never more than six on the upper floors. This arrangement is the easiest to secure and manage. The central courtyard space is accessible only to the residents and is secured by a fence and gates in the south-east corner.

It is the limitations on private cars which is the most notable feature of the scheme. This has major benefits in freeing a large amount of land that would otherwise have been used for storing cars. This is now available for amenity and recreational use. Lack of parking helps to reinforce the car ban but a possible weakness is the emergency vehicle route around the perimeter. Elsewhere such 'limited access' provisions have been eroded by unauthorised parking. Here, access is controlled by barriers and an on-site concierge. Management is important but so also is providing alternatives. The scheme has several bus routes nearby but the completion of the proposed light rail system would be a major advantage. Limited parking is provided and of this four spaces have been made available to a car club.

▲ **G6** The central space, ponds on the right

▲ **G7** The central space, gated access in the foreground

KEY FACTS

Location	Gorgie, Edinburgh
Completion date	2000
Developer	Canmore Housing Association
Architect	Hackland & Dore
Number of dwellings	120
Dwelling mix	Mostly 2 bedroom/4 person flats 4 flats for wheelchair users 14 flats sheltered for Edinburgh Deaf Society
Other provision	Community centre Nursery Communal open space Allotments
Previous use of site	Railway goods yard
Density	Approximately 94 dwellings per hectare
Forms of tenure	26 flats for sale 25 for shared ownership 69 social rented
Key targets/issues	A car-free residential development High level of environmentally sensitive design
Green features	Timber from sustainable sources Construction partly prefabricated Insulation made from recycled newspaper Design for passive solar gain Passive-stack ventilation Scheme of heating by industrial waste Surface water recycling Native planting for biodiversity
Transport issues	No dedicated parking for residents Sixteen parking spaces for disabled, visitors and shared use including four allocated to car club Bus route within 5 minutes walk Station on proposed light rail system next to site

<table>
<tr><td>

**Case
Study
H**

</td><td>

A Prototype for Sustainable Urban
Housing

Bedzed, Sutton

</td></tr>
</table>

▲ **H1**   South façade of housing shown in typical plans

BACKGROUND

By the late 1990s many of the issues affecting urban housing design were clearly identified. The demographic and social needs were understood. The need to reduce greenhouse gases was agreed and the policy implications were established. The technology of environmentally sensitive design had been developed by small-scale applications in a number of projects. The need to cut waste and pollution was also recognised. But nowhere had all these issues been brought together. The Zero Energy Development (ZED) concept was devised by a team led by architect, Bill Dunster, to do just that. It would aim to be neutral in its impact on the environment.

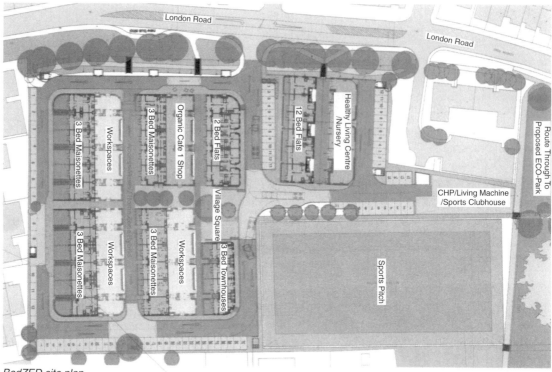

BedZED site plan

▲ **H2** Site plan

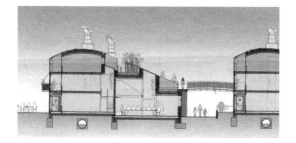

▲ **H3** Typical section

This would be achieved in three ways:

- *Efficient land-use planning.* Housing would be high density but maintain a high level of amenities. A variety of tenures and dwelling sizes would be included to create a mixed community. A large number of workspaces

would be integrated into the development to reduce commuting. This would be reinforced by a green transport plan.

- *High levels of energy efficiency.* The development would aim to be 'carbon neutral'. Consumption and waste of energy would be kept to a minimum. Energy would be generated from renewable sources. Generation would be supplemented by garnering as much solar energy as possible.

- *Concern for environmental conservation.* Building would be done with non-toxic materials obtained from sustainable sources, preferably local. Waste would be reduced by recycling as far as possible. This would

▲ **H4**   The power plant and bioworks

include water management and the recycling of both black and grey water.

The ZED team aimed to create a large-scale demonstration project. Support and funding was obtained and a site was found in outer London which became the Beddington ZED (BedZED).

THE SCHEME

The basis of the scheme is a series of blocks which combine housing and workspace. The blocks are aligned strictly on an east–west axis so that the flats and maisonettes face south while the workspaces behind face north. All the homes have gardens, either at ground level or on the roofs of the workspace units. This interlocking form of built space occupies the southern half of the site. To the north of the access road is a separate block of rented flats. Behind them is the healthy living centre and nursery building. At the north end of the site

is a mixed-use building containing the power plant and green-water treatment plant, together with office space and a clubhouse for the football pitch alongside. There is also a communal allotment where residents grow food. Extensive parking is located around the edge of the site but some is reserved for a car club which may reduce car use.

Energy efficiency is achieved partly by super-insulation. A heavy concrete block inner skin and party walls act as heat stores. These are protected by 300 millimetres rockwool cavity insulation. The design maximises solar gain by placing 900 millimetres deep sun spaces on the whole of the south-facing façades. These are double glazed and windows on the north and east façades have triple glazing. These arrangements ensure that most of the heat gained from the sun and from domestic activity is stored and only slowly released. This system is so efficient that no conventional central heating is required. Electricity and hot water are provided by the combined heat and power

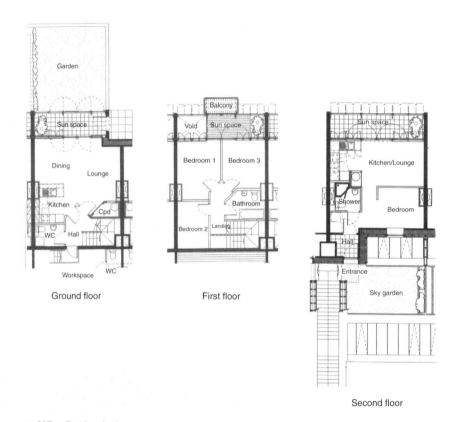

Ground floor   First floor

Second floor

▲ **H5**   Typical plans

(CHP) plant which runs on forestry waste. This is supplemented by photovoltaic (PV) panels which provide power to some units. Energy use is reduced by a passive ventilation system which uses roof cowls to expel exhaust air and draw in fresh.

Rainwater is collected and stored in tanks under the football pitch. All drainage effluents are piped to the treatment plant where it is processed in a 'bioworks' – tanks containing plants which purify the waste by biological action. The 'green' water produced is mixed with stored rainwater and used for flushing toilets, watering plants and the like. Rainwater run-off is slowed by 'green' roofs of sedum matting. Excess stored rainwater is discharged

into a ditch on the western edge of the site. The sedum roofs and the wetland, together with the private gardens, add significant biodiversity.

The BedZED project is undoubtedly a remarkable achievement and has gained widespread attention. It has also attracted to it a resident population committed to the 'green' lifestyle with a fervour reminiscent of that generated by the first Garden City at Letchworth a century ago. They help to ensure its success – but there are weaknesses. The complexity of the interlocking is fraught with potential problems particularly noise nuisance. Locating the private gardens on top of other people's premises, particularly those reached by bridges, also

▲ **H6**   Gardens on top of workspaces reached by bridges over access road

▲ **H7**   Typical sun space

creates potential for conflict. There has been difficulty letting the workspaces and some have been converted to live/work units.[1]

This problem may be due to the suburban location and it is this which begs the biggest question. Is BedZED a viable model for urban housing? Its layout is determined by the strict adherence to maximising solar gain. This creates relatively narrow service-cum-access roads between the blocks. Off these are the maisonette entrances and access to the flats above which is via narrow external stairs enclosed by walls. This access arrangement is poorly secured and little overlooked. It might well be subject to all sorts of abuse in an urban location. Most importantly, this form of development does not define and enclose space. The creation of coherent spaces both within and between urban blocks is a critical feature of successful urban housing.

KEY FACTS

Location	London Road, London Borough of Sutton	
Completion date	2002	
Developer	Bio-Regional/Zed Factory with Peabody Trust	
Architect	Bill Dunster Architects	
Number of dwellings	82	
Dwelling mix	1 bedroom flats	31
	2 bedroom flats	22
	3 bedroom maisonettes	25
	4 bedroom maisonettes	4
Other provision	1600 square metres workspace (23 units) Shop and café, sports pitch Healthy living centre with childcare facilities	
Previous use of site	Sewage works	
Density	128 dwellings per hectare net (excluding sports pitch) 352 habitable rooms per hectare Working population – 203 per hectare	
Form(s) of tenure	34 owner occupied 23 shared ownership 10 cost rent for key workers 15 social rented	
Key targets/issues	A demonstration project for urban living which is environmentally and socially sustainable	
Green features	High levels of insulation, minimal heating Recycled materials (steel, timber, some doors) Toxin-free paints and finishes Materials from local and sustainable sources Design for passive solar gain Passive ventilation with heat recovery CHP unit fuelled by tree surgery waste Energy supplemented by PV panels Rainwater and grey water recycling Domestic waste recycling Green roofs	
Transport issues	81 parking spaces but plan to reduce car use Close to suburban railway stations, on bus route	

A Project Using Modular Construction
Sixth Avenue, York

▲ I1   General view

BACKGROUND

With a large number of new homes needed in some parts of Britain, housing output is currently falling well short of that needed to meet demand. Considerable faith is being placed in the potential of off-site construction to boost supply. Government has decreed that a significant proportion of new housing should include some prefabrication. Ten per cent of new homes built in 2003 were prefabricated and there were expectations that this could be progressively increased.[1] Most of these, however, were individual houses built using tried and tested panel systems. There were still doubts over whether prefabrication could be successfully applied to high-density multi-storey

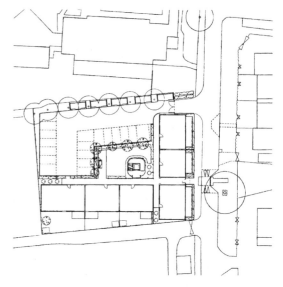

▲ 12   Site plan

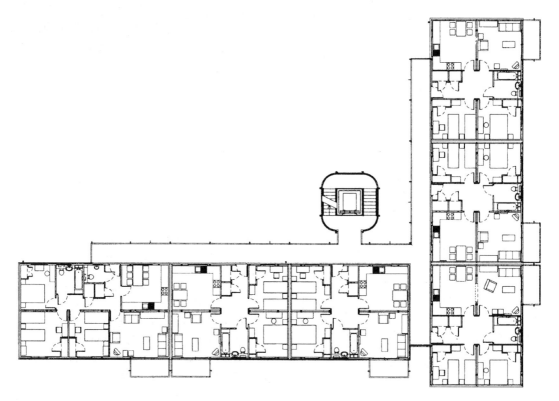

▲ 13   Upper floor plan

housing. These doubts were rooted in the relatively high costs of heavy panel systems extensively used in the 1960s and 1970s, and particularly in the extensive defects subsequently found in them.

A great deal of interest was aroused by the Murray Grove Scheme completed in London in 2000 (see Chapter 5, p. 111). This five-storey block of flats was the first collaboration between architect Cartwright Pickard and Yorkon, manufacturers of 'Portacabins' widely used as temporary buildings. In that scheme each flat was built in the factory and brought to site as two large 'boxes'. This modular system seemed to offer advantages both in speed of construction and a low risk of defects. There was concern, however, at the relatively high cost. This was partly due to a significant number of elements being non-standardised and requiring a high degree of on-site labour. Sixth Avenue is a follow-up collaboration between the same designers and producers, this time based in the manufacturer's home city.

▲ 14   York Minster viewed alongside lift/stair enclosure

THE SCHEME

Where Murray Grove neatly closed the corner of an urban block, the location of the Sixth Avenue scheme is quite different. Although not far from the city centre the Tang Hall estate is a 1920s municipal development designed on 'Garden City' principles and distinctly low density. The new block of social housing is only four storeys high but it dwarfs its neighbours. It is, thus, not only a demonstration project for prefabrication but also an illustration of the way densities can be raised by intensification of suburban areas.

The three upper floors of the L-shaped block are identical, each containing five two-bedroom flats and one three-bedroom flat. The ground floor differs only because of the need to create an entrance passage reducing one of the flats to one bedroom. The upper floors are reached by a single lift and stair, and an external access balcony at each level. The project was to be extensively prefabricated, but before production commenced, a prototype was constructed in the factory. This enabled tests to be made on manufacturing techniques and on performance including thermal and acoustic qualities. The flats were factory built including all interior finishes, fittings, services, doors and windows. They were then brought to site as box modules and craned into place on prepared foundations. Each flat comprised two modules running parallel to the façade.

Lift, stairs, balconies and roof had to be constructed on-site as, somewhat surprisingly, does the external cladding.

The modules are larger than at Murray Grove where the prefabricated boxes were placed at right angles to the façade. This has resulted in a cost saving. Economies were also made by simplifying the access system and by cladding the building, mostly in cedar boarding rather than the more expensive terracotta tiles. At Sixth Avenue these are used only on the ground level of the street façade – the location thought most vulnerable to vandalism. The project was completed within Housing Corporation standards and financial constraints, making its construction cost comparable to conventional social housing. However, the building was completed more quickly – 14 months from commission to completion. This is about half the time a conventional building would take and results in considerable savings in land and finance costs.[2]

This form of construction gives a very high standard of finish and construction precision. The building is also very attractive in appearance. Its form, though, is questionable. Bitter experience of serious management problems in social housing suggests it is best to keep most family accommodation on the ground and restrict the number of people having access to the upper floors. The most successful forms have large family maisonettes at ground level with their own gardens and separate entrances. The upper floors are then

▲ 15   The street façade and block entrance

▲ **16** Generous balconies protected by roof but private gardens are poorly defined

reserved for smaller households (see Chapter 6, p. 133). At Sixth Avenue all dwellings are family flats and each floor contains one large six person flat. The simplification of the access system routes all residents and visitors through a single main entrance. The access balcony is also a less than desirable form since it routes all residents past other people's windows. This is just acceptable where these are kitchen or bathroom windows but, in this case, bedrooms are also overlooked. The treatment of external space is also disappointing. Private gardens are poorly defined and the bulk of the communal space is given over to car parking.

Not all these shortcomings are due to prefabricated construction. But some of them are. Modular construction is only cost effective if there is a high degree of standardisation and repetition. This has led to the adoption of two basic

▲ **17** Access balcony passes kitchens and some bedrooms

flat types and their repetition at each floor level. The less than satisfactory access system is also a result of economy measures. All this is not inevitable. Prefabricated housing could be built in different forms with more variation in plan types. But this could only be achieved on larger schemes where economies could be realised over longer production runs. As is often argued, higher production volumes may be necessary to get the best out of modular construction.

KEY FACTS

Location	Tang Hall, York	
Completion date	2002	
Developer	Yorkshire Housing	
Architect	Cartwright Pickard	
Number of dwellings	24	
Dwelling mix	1 bedroom/2 person flat	1
	2 bedroom/4 person flats	19
	3 bedroom/6 person flats	4
Other provision	Small communal open space	
Previous use of site	Derelict land	
Density	Approximately 140 dwellings per hectare	
	600 habitable rooms per hectare	
Forms of tenure	All flats social rented	
Key targets/issues	To maximise prefabrication within Housing Corporation cost limits	
Green features	High level of off-site construction	
	Reduced waste	
	Low level of defects	
	Extensive use of timber	
Transport issues	16 parking spaces on site	
	Low-density location suggests poor public transport	

Case Study J

Regenerating Social Housing: I
Marquess Estate, London

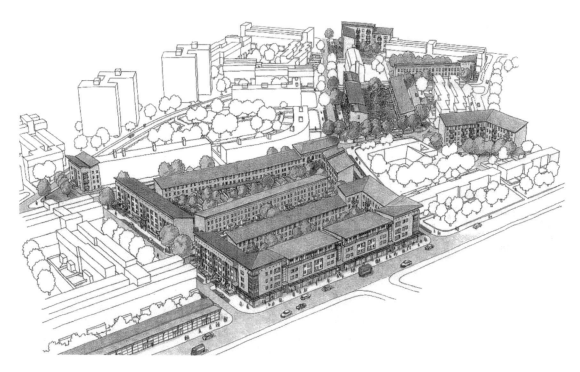

▲ **J1**   Isometric of new housing

BACKGROUND

Marquess Estate is in inner London some 2 to 3 miles from the central business and commercial areas. It was designed by influential housing architects Darbourne and Dark, and built over a period of several years completing in 1975. At the time it was built, the design was celebrated as a break from the discredited tower and slab blocks that characterised high-density social housing in the 1960s. By contrast the Marquess Estate concentrated family housing on the ground with each maisonette entered through its own garden. The upper floors contained only small dwellings. However, the organisation of the estate was complex and owed much to the concerns of the time. Separation of vehicles and pedestrians was a key issue. One hundred per cent parking was mandatory and this was provided in extensive underground

▲ **J2**   The original estate design

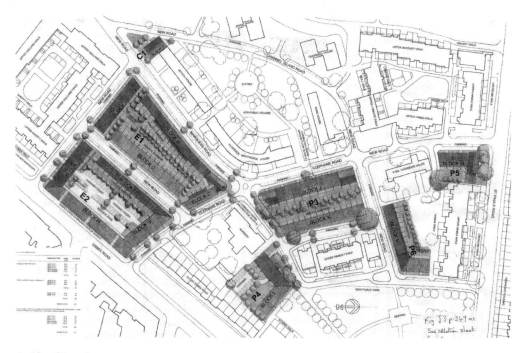

▲ **J3**   Site plan

car parks. The original street pattern was obliterated and ground-level circulation was through narrow carriageways designed for pedestrians and emergency vehicles only. At the upper level all the blocks were linked together by an elevated pedestrian deck.

From the start, the garages became a focus for vandalism and soon had to be closed. The buildings were affected by widespread leaks, both from rainwater and the plumbing system, and the resolution of these was hindered by the complex planning and construction. As the problems mounted parts of the estate became hard to let. As elsewhere the access system became degraded by a range of abuse and crime. In the mid-1990s Islington Council carried out a major study to consider radical solutions to the estate's social and technical problems. This concluded that the most complex and problematic part of the estate should be demolished with the aim of creating an environment which was more manageable and buildings which were easier to maintain. A master plan was prepared and government funding was secured. A competition was held in 1997 to find an architect and developer for the redevelopment.

THE SCHEME

Under the master plan parts of the original estate were to be retained. These were blocks which were more popular and manageable, mainly on the periphery of the estate. These blocks were to be comprehensively refurbished. At the centre of the estate the existing buildings were cleared and the original street pattern was re-established. Six sites for redevelopment were defined and inter-related to existing buildings to define traditional streets. New housing

▲ **J4** New terraced housing

has been built on these sites comprising a mix of three-storey family houses and blocks of flats mainly of four storeys. The density of the new development is high – twice as dense as the original scheme in terms of the number of dwellings. However, there is a much higher proportion of small dwellings, so the new scheme is only slightly denser in terms of the numbers of people housed. Car parking provision is low but this is consistent with the traditionally low car ownership levels on social estates in the area.

The project addresses the issue of manageability in a number of ways. First, the new housing forms urban blocks with semi-private space on the inside and streets on the outside. This improves surveillance of public areas and

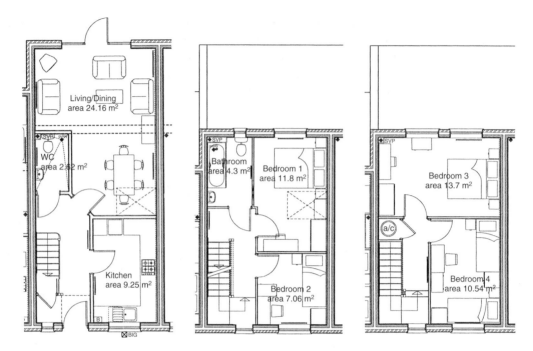

▲ **J5** Typical house plans

▲ **J6** Typical flat plan

discourages antisocial behaviour. Secondly, the access systems are kept simple – a contrast with the warren of stairs and decks in the original scheme. In the new blocks of flats staircase access has been provided – the system which has been shown to present fewest problems. The bulk of the family accommodation is in houses which have no common areas other than the public street. Thirdly, there is a much lower proportion of family housing which means the child density is reduced. In many estates large numbers of children had been a major cause of vandalism and petty crime. Finally, the social mix has been improved with almost half the new homes provided for owner-occupation or shared ownership. It may be significant, though, that the bulk of the private housing is on the edges of the estate.

These changes to the physical layout, and the composition of age groups and tenures have been supplemented by initiatives to address social problems in the parts of the estate left standing. The community development arm of the new social landlord has consulted the remaining tenants throughout the development process both on the form of the buildings and the facilities provided. Funding was also secured from the government 'breaking barriers' programme. This was used to develop employment and training schemes, and to tackle low attainment in literacy and life skills.

In many urban estates with social problems the solution has been sought in wholesale clearance. The scheme for the Marquess Estate – now re-branded New River Green – deals with the problems selectively. A significant proportion of the existing buildings has been retained and this keeps much of the urban fabric intact. It also preserves much of the existing community, enabling many tenants to stay in an area familiar

▲ **J7** Flats for shared ownership

▲ **J8** New housing for owner-occupation

to them. The new buildings are shaped by the urban design guide that formed part of the competition brief. Their design is straightforward but they do create coherent spaces and introduce a degree of visual variety to the area. At the same time they are in harmony both in form and materials with the surrounding environment.

KEY FACTS

Location	Islington, London	
Completion date	2002–2004 in phases	
Developer	Southern Housing Group (affordable homes)	
	Copthorn Homes (owner-occupied flats)	
Architect	PRP Architects	
Number of dwellings	324	
Dwelling mix	3 bedroom/5 person houses	54
	4 bedroom/7 person houses	21
	1 bedroom/2 person flats	67
	2 bedroom/3 person flats	122
	2 bedroom/4 person flats	60
Other provision	800 square metres retail space on main road frontage	
	Existing open space retained and improved	
Previous use of site	Social housing estate	
Density	170 dwellings per hectare	
	620 habitable rooms per hectare	
Forms of tenure	Social rented – 75 houses, 107 flats (56 per cent of homes)	
	Shared ownership – 79 flats (24 per cent of homes)	
	Owner-occupied – 63 1- and 2-bedroom flats (20 per cent of homes)	
Key targets/issues	Creating more manageable urban environment	
	Diversifying social mix	
Green features	Self-finished gypsum blocks and metal doorsets have been used to reduce on-site labour and waste	
	Partnership project in line with 'Egan' agenda	
Transport issues	Good links to underground, rail and bus services	
	Parking generally restricted to on-street spaces (i.e. 20 to 30 per cent)	

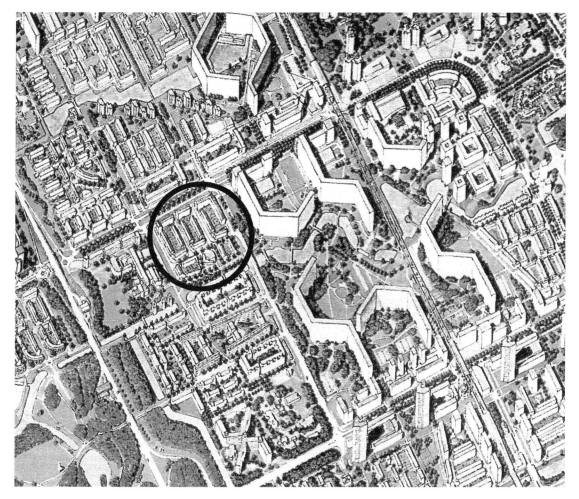

▲ **K1** Axonomietric showing location of Gulden Kruis in Bijlmemeer

BACKGROUND

Most twentieth century social housing estates built in Europe differed from those in Britain in two key respects. First, they were located on the urban periphery rather than the inner city. Second, they were much larger. Bijlmemeer is fairly typical. It was built on reclaimed land on the outskirts of Amsterdam in the 1960s and 1970s to allow 40 000 people to move from the congested inner city. True to the spirit of the time, they were housed in high-rise apartments set in parkland. The scheme was a series of multi-storey slab blocks laid out in a hexagonal pattern. The project benefited from the provision of a new metro station. Despite that, its remote location combined with high rent levels made the flats hard to let. The blocks were also difficult to manage. Each contained 400 flats with multiple lifts, stairs and entrances. As elsewhere, these common areas were subject to a wide range of abuse. The estate entered a spiral of decline.

Bijlmemeer came to public prominence when, in October 1993, a cargo plane crashed into one of the blocks causing many deaths and much destruction. In the pubic spotlight the estate was revealed to have a population of low-income tenants, 60 per cent of whom were migrants from other countries. A major renewal programme was put in place, aimed at creating a more stable and mixed community. Some of the multi-storey blocks have been scheduled for demolition. Others have been improved. This has included changes to the access system with new, more spacious entrances and more security. It has also involved filling in the troublesome unused space beneath the blocks, a major focus of antisocial behaviour. Some of this has been used to make new family maisonettes. Elsewhere, the space has

▲ **K2**   New maisonettes and entrances built into lower levels of multi-storey block

been converted into shops and small business units. These improvements have been supplemented by an extensive programme of new development aimed at creating a better mix of both housing form and tenure.[1]

THE SCHEME

Although Bijlmemeer is a high rise estate it is not particularly high density. The slab blocks are surrounded by large open spaces. One of these formed the site for the Gulden Kruis development. This was the first of a series of new housing areas. It was built to provide new homes for many of the slab block residents so that a rolling programme of demolition and reconstruction could be started. The new housing is in strong contrast to the old. Where the existing blocks are 11 storeys the new housing is restricted to a maximum of four. Where the old flats were reached by a complex series of lifts, stairs and walkways, the new homes are, almost entirely, entered directly from the ground.

The scheme is a mixture of two-storey houses and four-storey maisonettes. There are also three small blocks of flats. The houses are basically very conventional in form though some unusual geometry has been introduced into the planning to create more distinctive internal spaces. The maisonettes are of an uncommon form known as 'up and over', which has been used elsewhere in Amsterdam. Each maisonette has a separate entrance with the staircase to the upper unit passing through the lower one. The lower maisonette has a garden and is planned as a house with day rooms on the ground and bedrooms upstairs. The upper maisonettes have the bedrooms on the lower level with living room and kitchen above giving

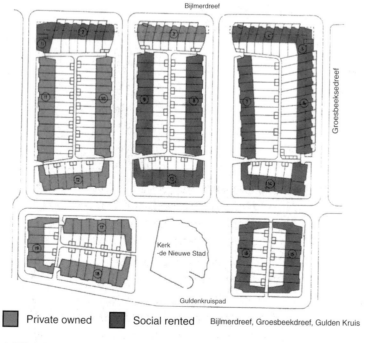

Bijlmerdreef

Groesbeeksedreef

Kerk -de Nieuwe Stad

Guldenkruispad

██ Private owned   ██ Social rented   Bijlmerdreef, Groesbeekdreef, Gulden Kruis

▲ **K3**   Site layout

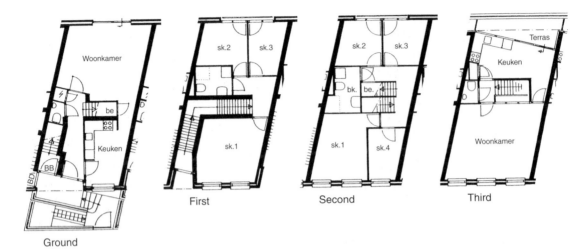

Ground   **First**   **Second**   **Third**

▲ **K4**   Maisonette type plans

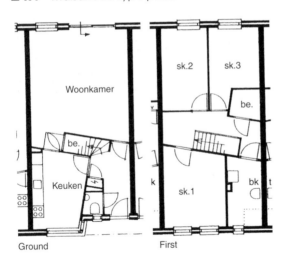

Ground   **First**

▲ **K5**   House type plans

▲ **K6**   New houses on Gulden Kruis

onto a generous terrace. This arrangement minimises noise transference with bedrooms zoned together in the middle floors. The maisonette blocks have a semi-basement which provides shared storage.[2]

The elimination of communal access removes the most serious management problem of multi-storey housing and makes the new homes inherently secure. This security is reinforced by the layout which re-creates a traditional street pattern. The housing forms five urban blocks. On the inside of the blocks are

▲ **K7**   Entrances to upper and lower
maisonette and access to basement storage

▲ **K8**   Central paved area. Houses and
maisonettes behind

the private gardens. These are reached by a central alley giving access to sheds for cycle storage. These alleys have been gated to maintain security. On the outside the blocks enclose street spaces which are used for parking. The central street also includes a wide paved area with some play equipment. The appearance of the bullrings may be unexciting but, on the whole, the scheme provides good-quality housing which should be relatively free from management problems. One criticism might be the size of the upper maisonettes. Each of these have four bedrooms housing five to six people. With walk-up access, these units might have been better devoted to smaller households.

In resolving the problems of Bijlmemeer, several issues had to be addressed. Creating manageable forms of housing is one; the greater social diversity needed on the estate is another. Given the location and the endemic poverty it is also important to stimulate the local economy. Gulden Kruis creates a better social mix with a substantial proportion of private ownership both of houses and maisonettes. It also makes a contribution to increasing local employment with a number of live–work units. These help to supplement the employment generated by conversion of parts of the multi-storey blocks. The impact of new building and development will intensify the density of the estate and increase economic activity.

KEY FACTS

Location	Bijlmemeer, Amsterdam	
Completion date	1997	
Developer	Patrimomium Housing Company	
Architect	Lafour en Wijk	
Number of dwellings	226	
Dwelling mix	3- and 4-bedroom houses	132
	2-, 3- and 4-bedroom maisonettes	70
	1- and 2-bedroom flats	24
Other provision	Six maisonettes have office/workshop space Church, school and other community facilities nearby	
Previous use of site	Vacant land within social housing estate	
Density	62 dwellings per hectare Approx 234 habitable rooms per hectare	
Forms of tenure	Social rented – 154 homes (68 per cent) Owner occupied – 72 homes (32 per cent)	
Key targets/issues	Creating more manageable urban environment Diversifying social mix Generating local employment	
Green features	Not known	
Transport issues	Metro station and bus services nearby 165 on-street parking spaces (73 per cent)	

▲ **L1**   Harbour-front blocks in phase 1

BACKGROUND

There is a long tradition of living in flats in Sweden. During the 1930s innovative designs for slab and point blocks were built which were widely admired and provided models for developments elsewhere. In the post-war period there was extensive housing development in Sweden culminating in the 'Million Dwellings Programme' of 1965–1974 which effectively eliminated housing shortage. Some of this housing suffered the same pattern of degeneration as multi-storey estates elsewhere. A 10-year Housing Improvement Programme was inaugurated in 1983 which successfully addressed these problems.[1] All this gave Sweden a reputation for successful urban housing.

Like other industrialised countries, Sweden has had to deal with economic change. Lake Hammarby Sjo is about 5 kilometres from the centre of Stockholm. During the twentieth century the area had been developed for industry. The focus was a dock, in the south-east of the lake, linked to the sea by a canal. Around this there was a complex of factories and warehouses. By the end of the 1980s this had become redundant along with much of the industrial land. Stockholm City Council decided to develop the area as a new fully serviced residential district with a high level of employment. A special project organisation was set up to oversee the economics, design and implementation of the development. It also had responsibility for transport infrastructure, utilities and parks. The aim was to create, within a 10–15-year period, a district housing 20 000 people and supporting 10 000 jobs. There were high environmental aspirations for the project with the aim of making as little demand as possible on natural resources.

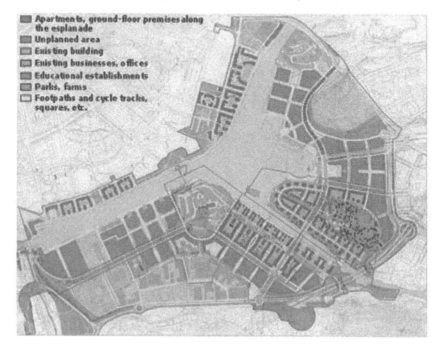

▲ **L2**   Development plan

THE SCHEME

The development is based around a new spine road running through the south-east of the area and bridging over the dock. The residential areas are being developed in phases as a series of new neighbourhoods. Two of these were complete by 2004 and two more at detailed planning stage. The first phase was completed in 1999, with 1250 new flats were built along the dockside. The north-east orientation of the dock frontage prevented a linear development. Instead the new flats are built in a series of slab blocks six to eight storeys high. These are placed at right angles to the dock so that flats have a southern or westerly aspect. The blocks are of varied design but the layout allows the flats to be provided with large balconies enjoying oblique views of the water. The lower floors are devoted to business and commercial uses. These front on to a new pedestrian broadwalk along the waterside.

The second phase is Sickla Udde set on a headland on the north-east side of the dock. At its heart is an oak wood which is conserved as an amenity area. This neighbourhood contains 1200 new flats and these are laid out in a traditional urban pattern. The main spine road runs though the centre and this gives on to a network of streets. These are formed by a series of urban blocks of irregular shape. Inside, there are green spaces and communal gardens but the blocks are not closed. Gaps are left in the buildings allowing views in and out. The headland is lined with a series of individual blocks of flats spaced out to allow access to waterfront footpaths and recreation areas. The flats are generally five-storey high but rise to six on the main road frontages where commercial uses are built in at ground floor level. All the flats have large windows and generous terraces or balconies.

The aim is to ensure that the whole district has an environmental impact which is half that of

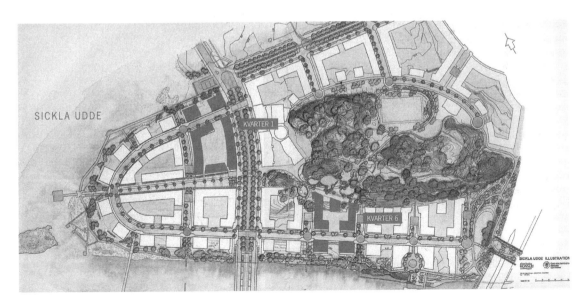

▲ **L3**   Overall plan of Sickla Udde

▲ **L4**   Street frontage in Sickla Udde

other modern developments. To achieve this an 'ecocycle model' has been developed. This includes a local sewage treatment plant where heat is recovered and the nutrients recycled. Surface water is collected and cleansed for re-use. Energy is generated in a district heating plant which primarily uses renewable fuels. 'Smart' controls are used to reduce energy use in the home. As much domestic waste as possible is recycled and the remainder is pumped pneumatically to a central location where it is incinerated in the heating plant.

There is an environmentally sensitive transport system. Ferries use the waterways to link the new district with the city centre. There is a network of buses which connect with a main line station. The metro is to be extended through to Sickla Udde. To reduce car use a car pool system is being developed and there is a network of walking and cycle routes.[2]

▲ **L5**   Green inner space and communal garden to an urban block

▲ **L6**   Individual flat blocks along the waterfront

▲ **L7**   Waterside recreation area

Hammarby Sjöstad is good model for the development of large 'brownfield' sites. Public investment was required to initiate and organise the development and to make sure the infrastructure was provided at the same time as the new homes. The development makes efficient use of land through being relatively high density. At the same time, the form and layout of the buildings creates good urban qualities related to human scale. The housing is entirely in the form of multi-storey flats. This might not meet urban housing demands in other countries. But there is no reason why similar design principles should not be followed to provide a mix of terraced houses and flats of a modest scale.

KEY FACTS

Location	Hammarby Sjo, Stockholm	
Completion date	Phase 1 – Norra Hammarbyhamnen	1999
	Phase 2 – Sickla Udde	2003
	Full completion	2009–2014
Developer	Project Hammarby Sjöstad – a quasi-autonomous organisation formed by Stockholm City Real Estate, Streets and Traffic administrations	
Architect	Blocks allocated to different architects/developers	
Number of dwellings	Phase 1 – 1250	
	Phase 2 – 1200	
	Full development – 8000	
Dwelling mix	All dwellings are flats	
	Typical mix 16 per cent	Studios
	28 per cent	1 bedroom
	50 per cent	2 bedroom
	6 per cent	3/4 bedroom
Other provision	Phase 1 has new school	
	Phase 2 has public park	
Previous use of site	Docks and industrial	
Density	Comparable to European urban norm	
Forms of tenure	Mixed	
Key targets/issues	To regenerate redundant industrial area	
	To be as near environmentally neutral as possible	
Green features	Own sewage treatment with heat and waste recycled	
	Water collection and recycling	
	District heating by sustainable fuels	
	Domestic waste recycling	
	High-tech energy monitoring	
Transport issues	Bus, metro, train and boat links to city centre	
	Car pooling arrangements	
	Network of walking/cycle routes	

Renewal of an Old Urban Area
Ferencváros, Budapest

▲ **M1** Renovated tenement

BACKGROUND

Budapest grew rapidly in the last decades of the nineteenth century. The city's expansion was governed by a municipal master plan of 1870. This set down the main urban features, including the radial-concentric street pattern. Its regulations set out the size of blocks, the height of buildings and the main facing materials. The Ferencváros neighbourhood was part of that expansion – a mixture of small-scale industry and tenement blocks. The quality of its housing was always poor and nothing had been done to improve it by the time the communist regime took power after the Second World War. The great majority of existing urban housing was nationalised but the new regime focused on meeting housing needs by new development. A very large number of new two-roomed flats were built around the edges of the city. These were developed on the Soviet model – huge estates of uniform multi-storey blocks built with pre-cast concrete panels.[1]

Meanwhile, housing stress in the inner city deepened. The population of Ferecváros was low income and ageing. Its tenements had low space standards, high levels of overcrowding and lacked separate sanitary facilities. Their physical state was poor and deteriorating. In 1985 the city government started a renovation programme for several of the inner districts, among them the middle part of Ferencváros. Little progress has been made by the collapse of communism in 1990. Under the new economic system most state-owned housing was progressively privatised. The local authority in Ferencváros, however, retained its ownership of the housing in the area scheduled for improvement. It set up a new public–private partnership, based on the French SEM model to revitalise and accelerate the renewal.

THE SCHEME

The aim of the renewal scheme was to regenerate the area physically – through redevelopment or rehabilitation; to create a community more socially mixed; and to improve the environment and the local economy. A key task was to identify the buildings to be retained. Many were in an advanced state of decay having had little or no maintenance in their lifetime of 100 years or more. Those that were in relatively good repair, or capable of successful adaptation were scheduled for rehabilitation. This work fell to the local authority who organised the construction

▲ **M2**   New and old housing

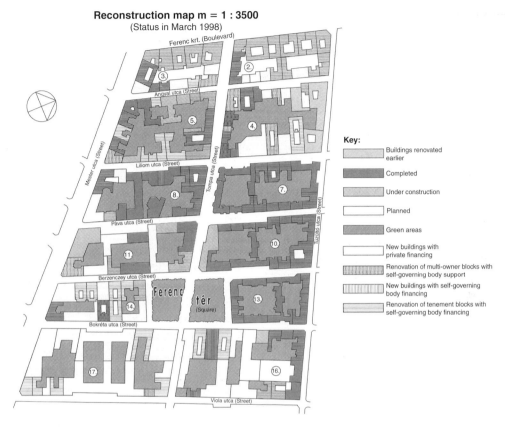

Reconstruction map m = 1 : 3500
(Status in March 1998)

Key:

Buildings renovated earlier

Completed

Under construction

Planned

Green areas

New buildings with private financing

Renovation of multi-owner blocks with self-governing body support

New buildings with self-governing body financing

Renovation of tenement blocks with self-governing body financing

▲ **M3**   Development plan of the initial renovation area

programme and funded it from their own resources. The aim of rehabilitation has been to renovate the buildings and convert them to modern standards of self-containment, space and facilities.

It has been the role of the partnership company to organise demolition and the sale of the cleared sites to private developers. A substantial number of buildings were scheduled for demolition, and the scale of new building has been very significant. In some parts entire blocks have been rebuilt. Mostly, it has been a more mixed approach with new building 'infilling' against the old. The rebuilding has

been subject to a firm design code. This has required new housing to follow the street frontages and match the scale of the existing buildings. In some places, new façades have been set back a little to allow in more sun and daylight. In the centres of the blocks new secure green spaces and communal gardens have been created.

It has also been the role of the partnership company to develop the infrastructure of the area and to stimulate employment-generating activity. The existing green square has been renovated and environmental improvements have been carried out to the local shopping

▲ **M4**   Tenement courtyard

▲ **M5**   Typical new housing

street, which runs through the centre of the area. This has made it more attractive to businesses and visitors. Commercial developers have been encouraged and this has led to the building of two new hotels and the construction of small office blocks. All this has generated new employment and brought more spending power to the area.[2]

Alongside extensive physical changes there has been significant social change. Where the buildings are rehabilitated by the municipality, residents are temporarily rehoused and given the right to return. The improved flats may be social rented or they may be offered for sale to the residents at a substantial discount of the market price. Where buildings are demo-

lished, the residents are rehoused elsewhere but there is little prospect that they will be able to return. The new buildings are all flats for sale and have brought an influx of middle-income households. It is estimated that as much as 50 per cent of the original residents have left the area. This degree of change has generated some criticism. Experience has shown, though, that an influx of middle-class residents has helped to boost the economy of run-down areas and to stimulate improvements in local services, facilities and urban management. It is only questionable whether this process has gone too far in Ferencváros.

It is unfortunate that intervention to regenerate the area was left so late – as a consequence,

▲ **M6**   Setback in building line to improve sun and daylight

▲ **M8**   Environmental improvements to central shopping street

▲ **M7**   Communal open space inside street block

a large number of the original buildings have been lost. Nevertheless, the renovation scheme has very successfully preserved the essential character of this established urban area. So much so that the regeneration programme has subsequently been extended to cover a much larger area. Success has been achieved through public intervention to manage private investment. This makes it a potent model for other Eastern European countries, many of which have placed excessive reliance on the private market to achieve housing renewal.

KEY FACTS

Location	Middle-Ferencváros, Budapest	
Completion date	About 50 per cent complete	2003
	Full completion	2010–2015
Developer	SEM IX Joint Stock Company – partnership between Local authority (51 per cent) and banks (49 per cent)	
Architect	Blocks allocated to different architects/developers	
Number of dwellings	Whole area has approximately 4000 flats Approximately 1200 partially or fully renovated More than 1200 new build	
Dwelling mix	All dwellings are flats	
Other provision	Nursery with swimming pool Two hotels Two office blocks	
Previous use of site	Residential and industrial	
Density	Reduced through improvement process but remains comparable to European urban norm	
Forms of tenure	Renovated flats are subsidised New build flats are owner occupied	
Key targets/issues	Improving housing and creating more green space Creating a better social mix Improving the environment Increasing employment	
Green features	Environmental awareness post-dated the development of this project	
Transport issues	Bus, metro, and tram links to city centre Parking mainly on-street but a multi-storey car park was constructed as part of the project	

REFERENCES

INTRODUCTION

1 Department of the Environment, Transport and the Regions (DETR) (1999) *Towards and Urban Renaissance – Final Report of the Urban Task Force Chaired by Lord Rogers of Riverside*. London: HMSO/E & F Spon, p. 29.
2 John Burnett (1986) *A Social History of Housing 1815–1985*, 2nd edition. London: Routledge, pp. 4, 7.
3 Ibid., p. 141.
4 Freidrich Engels (1958) *The Condition of the Working Class in England in 1844* (translated and edited by W.D. Henderson and W.H. Chaloner). Oxford: Basil Blackwell.
5 Edwin Chadwick (1965) *Report on the Sanitary Condition of the Labouring Population of Great Britain (1842)*. Edinburgh: Edinburgh University Press.
6 Karl Marx and Freidrich Engels (1848) *Manifesto of the Communist Party*.
7 Alice Mary Hadfield (1970) *The Chartist Land Company*. Newton Abbot, David & Charles.
8 Colin and Rose Bell (1972) *City Fathers – The Early History of Town Planning in Britain*. Penguin.
9 Peter Davey (1980) *Architecture of the Arts and Crafts Movement – The Search for Earthly Paradise*. London: Architectural Press.
10 Ebenezer Howard (1898) *Tomorrow – A Peaceful Path to Social Reform*. London: Swan Sonnenschein.
11 Local Government Board for England and Wales and Scotland (1918) *Report of the Committee Appointed by the President of the Local Government Board* (The Tudor Walters Report). London: HMSO, Cd 9191.
12 J.B. Cullingworth (1964) *Town and Country Planning in Britain*. London: George Allen & Unwin, pp. 196ff.
13 Office of the Deputy Prime Minister (2002) *Housing Statistics Postcard*, June 2002.
14 Scottish Parliament Development Department (2002) *Housing Trends in Scotland*, June 2002.
15 Anne Power (1993) *Hovels to High Rise: State Housing in Europe Since 1850*. London: Routledge, p. 190.

16 Miles Glendinning and Stefan Muthesius (1994) *Tower Block – Modern Public Housing in England, Scotland, Wales and Northern Ireland*. New Haven and London: Yale University Press, pp. 1ff; Patrick Dunleavy (1981) *The Politics of Mass Housing in Britain 1945–1975 – A Study of Corporate Power and Professional Influence in the Welfare State*. Oxford: Clarendon Press, p. 41.

17 Department of the Environment (1977) *Inner Area Studies – Liverpool, Birmingham and Lambeth*. London: HMSO.

18 *The Brixton Disorders 10–13 April 1981* (1981). Report of an inquiry by the Rt. Hon. Lord Scarman O.B.E. London: HMSO, Cmnd, 8427.

19 Report, *The Guardian* (6 December 1996): 7.

20 Report, *Regeneration and Renewal* (4 October 2002): 3.

21 Report on figures from the Office of National Statistics, *The Observer* (7 December 2003): 12.

CHAPTER I

1 Maf Smith, John Whitelegg and Nick Williams (1998) *Greening the Built Environment*. London: Earthscan Publications Ltd, pp. 17–23, 36; David Rudlin and Nicholas Falk (1999) *Building the Twenty-first Century Home –The Sustainable Urban Neighbourhood*. Oxford: Architectural Press, p. 79; Speech at public meeting by Michael Meacher, Minister for the Environment, 6 November 2002; Report, *The Observer* (5 January 2003): 17; Report, *The Guardian* (6 August 2003): 5; DTI (2004) *Its Only Natural Planning* Supplement (April 2004).

2 Council for the Protection of Rural England (2001) *Compact Sustainable Communities*. London: CPRE, p. 4.

3 Reports, *The Guardian* (6 June 1996 and 9 May 1997).

4 National Statistics Online, December 2002.

5 Department of the Environment, Transport and the Regions (1999) *Towards an Urban Renaissance – Final Report of the Urban Task Force Chaired by Lord Rogers of Riverside*. London: HMSO/E & F Spon.

6 National Statistics Online, December 2002; Report, *The Guardian* (27 August 1999): 3.

7 Joseph Rowntree Foundation (1999) *The Problems of Low Demand in Inner City Areas*. Housing Research Findings No. 519. York: JRF.

8 See Ref. [1]

9 Report, *Planning* (9 November 2002): 4.

10 Ben Jupp (1999) Love thy neighbour. *The Guardian Society* (27 October 1999): 2; Report, *Building Design* (30 October 1998): 6; Anna Minton (2002) Utopia Street. *Guardian Society* (27 March 2002): 10.

11 Town and Country Planning Act (1990) Section 106, Agreement, The Stationery Office Ltd.

12 Reports, *Regeneration and Renewal* (25 July 2003): 3 and (13 February 2004): 5.

13 Graham Towers (2000) *Shelter Is Not Enough*. Bristol: The Policy Press, pp. 190ff.

14 Ben Willis (2004) Housing market renewal. *Regeneration and Renewal* (30 January 2004): 20–23.

15 Report, *Planning* (4 June 2004): 5; Report, *Regeneration and Renewal* (4 June 2004): 8.

16 Department of the Environment, Transport and the Regions (1999), *op. cit.* pp. 180ff.

17 Greater London Authority (2000) *London's Housing Capacity – Report of Study*. London: GLA.

18 Report, *Planning* (20 September 2002): 8.

CHAPTER 2

1 Tudor Walters Report (1918) *Report of the Committee on Questions of Building Construction in Connection with the Provision of Dwellings for the Working Class*. London: HMSO.

2 John Burnett (1986) *A Social History of Housing 1815–1985*, 2nd edition. London: Routledge, pp. 222–226.

3 Ministry of Health (1944) *Design of Dwellings* (The Dudley Report). London: HMSO; Ministry of Health, Ministry of Works (1944) *Housing Manual 1944*. London: HMSO; Ministry of Health (1949) *Housing Manual 1949*. London: HMSO.

4 Ministry of Housing and Local Government (1961) *Homes for Today and Tomorrow* (The Parker Morris Report). London: HMSO.

5 Ministry of Housing and Local Government (1963) *Design Bulletin 6: Space in the Home*. London: HMSO.

6 Department of the Environment (1972) *Design Bulletin 24; Spaces in the Home – Part 1: Bathrooms and WCs; Part 2: Kitchens and Laundering Spaces*. London: HMSO.

7 Ministry of Health (1949) *Housing Manual 1949*. London: HMSO, pp. 82–93.

8 Graham Towers (2000) *Shelter Is Not Enough – Transforming Multi-storey Housing*. Bristol: The Policy Press, pp. 52–62.

9 Report, *The Observer Cash* (13 January 2002): 10.

10 DETR (1998) *The Use of Density in Urban Planning*. London: DETR.

11 Helen Cope with Avebury International (2002) *Capital Gains – Making High Density Housing Work in London*. London: London Housing Federation.

12 David Rudlin and Nicholas Falk (1999) *Building the Twenty-first Century Home – The Sustainable Urban Neighbourhood*. Oxford: Architectural Press, p. 219.

13 Helen Cope with Avebury International, op. cit., p. 108.

14 Sheena Wilson (1978) Vandalism and 'defensible space' on London housing estates. In R.V.G. Clarke (Ed), *Tackling Vandalism*, Home Office Research Study No. 47. London: HMSO.

15 Helen Cope with Avebury International, op. cit., p. 135.

16 Ibid., p. 109.

17 Leslie Martin and Lionel March (1972) *The Structure of Urban Space* (Figure 2.3). London: Cambridge University Press.

18 Harley Sherlock (1991) *Cities Are Good for Us*. London: Paladin, p. 219.

19 Llewelyn Davies (2000) *Sustainable Residential Quality – Exploring the Housing Potential of Large Sites*. London: London Planning Advisory Committee.

20 Patrick Dunleavy (1981) *The Politics of Mass Housing in Britain 1945–1975 – A Study of Corporate Power and Professional Influence in the Welfare State*. Oxford: Clarendon Press, p. 73.

21 Maf Smith, John Whitelegg and Nick Williams (1998) *Greening the Built Environment*. London: Earthscan Publications Ltd, Chapter 5.

22 David Rudlin and Nicholas Falk, op. cit., p. 158.

23 Ibid., p. 220.

CHAPTER 3

1 DTLR/CABE (2001) *Better Places to Live – By Design*. London: Thomas Telford Publishing, p. 16.

2 Ibid., p. 26.

3 Mike Biddulph (2000) Villages don't make a city. *Journal of Urban Design* 5(1): 65–82.

4 Ian Colquhoun and Peter Fauset (1991) *Housing Design in Practice*. Harlow Essex: Longman Scientific and Technical.

5 Michael Young and Peter Wilmot (1957) *Family and Kinship in East London*. London: Routledge and Kegan Paul.

6 Ministry of Housing and Local Government Design Bulletin 19 (1970) *Living in a Slum – A Study of St. Mary's, Oldham*. London: HMSO.

7 *Report of the Royal Commission on Local Government in England and Wales* Chairman Lord Redcliffe-Maud. London: HMSO, 1969.

8 William Hampton and Jeffrey Chapman (1971) Towards neighbourhood councils. *The Political Quarterly* 42(3): 249; Ibid., 42(4): 414.

9 Nick Wates and Charles Knevitt (1987) *Community Architecture*. London: Penguin, p. 38; Pamela Buxton (2004) Hampton Court: 20 years on – The Carbuncle Effect. *Building Design* (28 May): 16.

10 HRH The Prince of Wales (1989) *A Vision of Britain – A Personal View of Architecture*. London: Doubleday.

11 *Urban Villages* (London: The Urban Villages Forum, 1997) first published 1992, pp. 30–32, 38ff.

12 Mike Biddulph, Bridget Franklin and Malsolm Tair (2002) *The Urban Village: A Real or Imagined Contribution to Sustainable Development*. London: ESRC, July.

13 *Urban Villages*, op. cit., p. 92; DTLR/CABE, op. cit., p. 86.

14 Jeff Torrington (1992) *Swing Hammer Swing*. London: Secker and Warburg.

15 *Urban Villages*, op. cit., pp. 13, 86–88.

16 Ibid., pp. 89–91; Biddulth, Franklin and Tait, op. cit.
17 Report, *Building Design* (20 February 1998): 1.
18 Report, *Regeneration and Renewal* (20 September 2002): 8.
19 Report, *Building Design* (20 February 1998): 1, 2, 8.
20 Report, *The Guardian* (10 June 1999): 3.
21 Office of the Deputy Prime Minister (2000) *Millennium Villages and Sustainable Communities.* London: ODPM.
22 David Rudlin and Nicholas Falk (1999) *Building the 21st Century Home – the Sustainable Urban Neighbourhood.* Oxford: Architectural Press, p. 215.
23 DTLR/CABE, op. cit.
24 Michael Gwilliam, Caroline Bourcie, Caroline Swain and Anna Prat (1998) *Sustainable Renewal of Suburban Areas.* York: Joseph Rowntree Foundation.
25 *Urban Villages*, op. cit., p. 98.

CHAPTER 4

1 Peter Hall (1975) *Urban and Regional Planning.* Harmondsworth: Penguin Books Ltd, Chapter 2.
2 Ibid.
3 Graham Towers (2000) *Shelter Is Not Enough – Transforming Multi-Storey Housing.* Bristol: The Policy Press, Chapter 2.
4 Further details of all the named schemes can be found in Iain Colquhoun (1999) *RIBA book of 20th Century Housing.* Oxford: Butterworth-Heinemann.
5 Graham Towers, op. cit., Chapter 4.
6 Barry Goodchild (1997) *Housing and the Urban Environment: A Guide to Housing Design, Renewal and Urban Planning.* Oxford: Blackwell Sciences Ltd, pp. 27–30.
7 Peter Hall, op. cit., p. 30; see also Chapter 2.
8 Graham Towers, op. cit., pp. 52–59, 113–116, 180–182.
9 Report, *Architecture Today* (No. 107 April 2000): 50–59.
10 Report, *Building Design* (6 September 2002): 5.
11 Report, *Regeneration and Renewal* (18 October 2002): 10.
12 Report, *Building Design* (25 May 2002): 5.
13 Report, *The Observer Cash* (1 December 2002): 19.
14 Report, *The Guardian* (14 December 2001): 11; Report, *Building Design* (30 May 2003): 3.
15 Caitriona Carroll, Julie Cowans and David Darton (Eds) (1999) *Meeting Part M and Designing Lifetime Homes.* York: Joseph Rowntree Foundation.
16 Selwyn Goldsmith (1984) *Designing for the Disabled.* London: RIBA Publications; Stelios Voutsadakis (1989) *Housing for People with Disabilities – A Design Guide.* London: Islington Council.
17 Centre for Accessible Environments (1998) *The Design of Residential Car and Nursing Homes for Older People.* Leeds: NHS Estates.

18 Colin Ward (1997) *Havens and Springboards – the Foyer Movement in Context.* London: Calouste Gulbenkian Foundation; Housing Research Findings (1995) 142. York: Joseph Rowntree Foundation.

19 Report, *Architecture Today* (No. 107 April 2000): 22–32; Core Values. *The Architects Journal* (3/10 August 2000); 28–37.

20 Live-work in Hackney. *Architecture Today* (No. 123, 2001): 22–27.

21 Gordon Cullen (1961) *Townscape.* London: Architectural Press.

22 *A Design Guide for Residential Areas.* Essex County Council, 1973.

23 Llewelyn Davies (2000) *Urban Design Compendium.* London: English Partnerships/The Housing Corporation, pp. 64–66.

24 DTLR/CABE (2001) *Better Places to Live – By Design.* London: Thomas Telford Publishing, p. 49.

25 Ibid., p. 44.

26 Ian Colquhoun and Peter Fauset (1991) *Housing Design in Practice.* Harlow Essex: Longman Scientific and Technical, pp. 192ff.

27 Department for Transport *Traffic Advisory Leaflet 10/01 Home Zones – Planning and Design* (January 2002).

28 Report, *Regeneration and Renewal* (6 December 2002): 9.

CHAPTER 5

1 Brian Edwards and David Turrent (Eds) (2000) *Sustainable Housing – Principles and Practice.* London: E & F. N Spon, pp. 51, 120.

2 Feature, *Architecture Today* 54 (January 1995): 28.

3 Feature, *Architecture Today* 60 (July 1995): 23.

4 Feature, *Architecture Today* 96 (March 1999): 44; Case Study on www.ecoconstruction.org

5 Brian Edwards and David Turrent (Eds), op. cit., p. 131.

6 Randall Thomas (Ed) (2001) *Photovoltaics and Architecture.* London: Spon Press, p. 61.

7 Maf Smith, John Whitelegg and Nick Williams (1998) *Greening the Built Environment.* London: Earthscan Publications Ltd, p. 41.

8 Brian Edwards and David Turrent (Eds), op. cit., p. 20.

9 Edward Harland (1999) *Eco-Renovation – The Ecological Home Improvement Guide.* Vermont: Chelsea Green Publishing Company, p. 105.

10 Brian Edwards and David Turrent (Eds), op. cit., p. 129.

11 Ibid., pp. 139–141.

12 Brenda and Robert Vale (1991) *Green Architecture.* London: Thames & Hydson, p. 148.

13 Battle McCarthy (1999) *Wind Towers.* Chichester: Academy Editions, pp. 17ff; Brian Edwards and David Turrent (Eds), op. cit., p. 157; Edward Harland, op. cit., pp. 48ff.

14 Edward Harland, op. cit., p. 103.

15 DTI (2004) Its only natural. *Planning* (Supplement, April): 7.

16 Derek Taylor Renewable Energy in Housing. In Brian Edwards and David Turrent (Eds), op. cit., p. 57.

17 Ibid., Randall Thomas (Ed), op. cit., p. 14.

18 Report, *Regeneration and Renewal* (27 February 2004): p. 10.

19 Report, *Building Design* (30 November 2001): 16; DTI, op. cit., 4.

20 Derek Taylor, op. cit., 57.

21 Brian Edwards and David Turrent (Eds), op. cit., p. 22.

22 Edward Harland, op. cit., p. 138.

23 Ibid., p. 135.

24 Caroline Mackley (2001) Embodied energy and recycling. In Craig A. Langston and Grace K.C. Ding (Eds), *Sustainable Practices in the Built Environment*. Oxford: Butterworth-Heinemann; Nigel Howard and David Shiers (1998) *The Green Guide to Specification*. Garston: Building Research Establishment.

25 Feature, *Architecture Today* 133 (November 2002): 32–40.

26 Rock Garden (2000) *The Architectural Review* (May 2000): 59–61.

27 Brian Edwards and David Turrent (Eds), op. cit., p. 20.

28 DETR (1998) *Rethinking Construction – The Report of the Construction Task Force*. London: DETR, p. 18.

29 Report, *Building Design* (11 April 2003): 1.

30 Jon Broome and Brian Richardson (1991) *The Self-build Book*. Green Books.

31 Geoffrey Pitts (1989) *Energy Efficient Housing – A Timber Framed Approach* (TRADA).

32 Austin Williams (2002) Absolutely prefabulous. *The Architects' Journal* (6 June 2002): 39–39.

33 Ibid.

34 Report, *Building Design* (23 May 2003): p. 6.

35 'Offsite 03' exhibition and seminar at the Building Research Establishment, Watford. May 2003.

36 *Defects in Housing Part 2; Industrialised and System Built Dwellings of the 1960s and 1970s*. London: Association of Metropolitan Authorities, 1984.

37 Report, *Building Design* (3 June 2003): 1; Report, *Regeneration and Renewal* (20 February 2004): 1.

CHAPTER 6

1 Peter F. Smith (2000) Transforming the existing housing stock. In Brian Edwards and David Turrent (Eds), *Sustainable Housing – Principles and Practice*. London: E. & F. N. Spon.

2 Report, *Daily Express* (3 September 2003): 8.

3 *Empty Homes: Temporary Management, Lasting Solutions*. London: ODPM, 2003.

4 *Unpopular Housing – National Strategy for Neighbourhood Renewal, Report of Policy Action Team 7*. London: DETR, 1999; Ben Willis (2004) Housing market renewal. *Regeneration and Renewal* (30 January 2004): 20.

5 Huw Morris (2004) Criteria to improve building standards. *Planning* (28 May): 14.

6 Edward Harland (1999) *Eco-Renovation – The Ecological Home Improvement Guide.* Vermont: Chelsea Green Publishing Company, pp. 52–61.

7 Ibid., pp. 86–89.

8 Graham Towers (1995) *Building Democracy – Community Architecture in the Inner Cities.* London: UCL Press, pp. 104–106.

9 Ibid., pp. 151–156.

10 Graham Towers (2000) *Shelter Is Not Enough – Transforming Multi-storey Housing.* Bristol: The Policy Press, pp. 87, 67.

11 Ibid., Chapter 6.

12 Kieran Long (2001) Wooden heart. *Building Design* (18 May): 18–19.

13 *Living Over the Shop – A Guide to the Provision of Housing Above Shops in Town Centres.* National Housing and Town Planning Council/Joseph Rowntree Foundation, 1990.

14 Report, *Building Design* (10 October 2003): 4.

15 Report, *Regeneration and Renewal* (16 November 2002): 10.

CHAPTER 7

1 Report, *Building Design* (13 December 2002): 3.

2 Ben Page (2002) Local liveability tops the agenda. *Regeneration and Renewal* (2 August): 12.

3 Ibid.

4 Report, *Planning* (28 September 2001); Report, *Building Design* (25 June 2004): 1.

5 John Allen (2002) *Berthold Lubetkin.* London: Merrell Publishers Ltd, p. 123.

6 Ian Colquhoun and Peter Fauset (1991) *Housing Design in Practice.* Harlow Essex: Longman Scientific and Technical, pp. 118–121.

7 Parker Morris Report, *Homes for today and tomorrow*, Ministry of Housing and Local Government and the Central Housing Advisory Committee, 1961.

8 Rob Winkley (2003) Developing a design for life. *Planning* (3 October): 8.

9 *A Design Guide for Residential Areas.* County Council of Essex, December 1973.

10 DETR/CABE (2000) *By Design.* London: Thomas Telford, p. 45.

11 Susan Nelson (2001) *The Changing Process of Urban Renewal in Paris and London.* PhD Thesis. University of Sheffield.

12 Charles Jencks (1975) *Le Corbusier and the Tragic View of Architecture.* London: Penguin Books Ltd, pp. 122–123.

13 N.J. Habraken (1961) *Supports – and Alternative to Mass Housing.* Scheltema & Holkema NV (English edition, London: Architectural Press, 1972), p. 60.

14 Graham Towers (1995) *Building Democracy – Community Architecture in the Inner Cities.* London: UCL Press Ltd, pp. 131–132.

15 Arnulf Lüchinger (1987) *Herman Hertzberger – Buildings and Projects 1959–1986.* Den Haag: Arch-Edition, pp. 72–85.

16 Borneo Street Life. *Habitat Magazine* (November 2002): 10–15; Oosterlijk Havengebeid Amsterdam (Development Report).

17 Ralph Erskine (1984) Designing between client and users. In Richard Hatch (Ed), *The Scope of Social Architecture*. New York and London: Van Norstrand Reinhold.

18 Graham Towers (2000) *Shelter Is Not Enough – Transforming Multi-storey Housing*. Bristol: The Policy Press, pp. 140–142.

19 Graham Towers, *Building Democracy*, op. cit., pp. 89–94.

20 Nick Wates (1982) The Liverpool breakthrough. *The Architects' Journal* (8 September 1982): 51–58.

CHAPTER 8

1 Peter Newman and Jeffrey Kenworthy (1999) *Sustainability and Cities – Overcoming Automobile Dependence*. Washington, DC: Island Press, pp. 94–103.

2 Ibid.

3 John F.C. Turner (1976) *Housing by People – Towards Autonomy in Built Environments*. London: Marion Boyars.

4 Peter Newman and Jeffrey Kenworthy, op. cit., pp. 94–103.

5 Elizabeth Denby (1938) *Europe Rehoused*. London: George Allen & Unwin, p. 23.

6 Ibid., p. 26.

7 Graham Towers (2000) *Shelter Is Not Enough – Transforming Multi-Storey Housing*. Bristol: The Policy Press, pp. 32–39.

8 Anne Power (1993) *Hovels to High Rise: State housing in Europe Since 1850*. London: Routledge, p. 108.

9 Ibid., p. 41.

10 Hans Skifter Andersen and Philip Leather (1999) *Housing Renewal in Europe*. Bristol: The Policy Press.

11 STERN information brochure (1987) *Internationale Bauausstellung Berlin*, Berlin.

12 Madeleine Bunting (1990) Rebirth of Block 102. *Environment Guardian* (31 August): 1.

13 K. Zhukov and V. Fyodorov (1974) *Housing Construction in the Soviet Union*. Moscow: Progress Publishers.

14 *A Future for Large Housing Estates – European Strategies for Prefabricated Housing Estates in Central and Eastern Europe*. Berlin: European Academy of the Urban Environment, 1998.

15 Peter Newman and Jeffrey Kenworthy, op. cit., pp. 94–103.

16 Peter Newman and Jeffrey Kenworthy (1989) *Cities and Automobile Dependence: A Sourcebook*. Aldershot, Hants and Brookfield. Vermont: Gower Publishing Company Ltd, pp. 127ff.

17 Anne Power (1997) *Estates on the Edge – The Social Consequences of Mass Housing in Northern Europe*. Basingstoke: Macmillan Press Ltd, pp. 147–184.

18 *Sustainable Communities: Building for the Future*. London: Office of the Deputy Prime Minister, 2003.

19 Report, *Society Guardian* (7 January 2004): 3; Colin Marrs (2004) The house that Kate built. *Regeneration and Renewal* (16 January 2004): 20–21; Report, *The Guardian* (18 March 2004): 22.

20 Barry Munday (2002) Designs on high density. *Regeneration and Renewal* (16 August 2002): 18.

21 Report, *Planning* (13 June 2003): 3.

22 Report, *Planning* (6 June 2003): 5.

23 Jamie Doward (2003) Jam tomorrow. *The Observer* (13 July 2003): 12.

24 Report, *The Guardian* (3 December 2004): 22.

CASE STUDY A

1 Graham Towers (1995) *Building Democracy – Community Architecture in the Inner Cities*. London: UCL Press Ltd, pp. 135–138.

2 *Architecture Today* (April 2002): 22–23.

CASE STUDY B

1 David Rudlin and Nicholas Falk (1999) *Building the 21st Century Home – The Sustainable Urban Neighbourhood*. Oxford: Architectural Press, p. 90.

CASE STUDY C

1 *Urban Villages* (London, The Urban Villages Forum, 1997) first published 1992, pp. 89–91.

CASE STUDY D

1 George Mills (1998) Sustainable housing in Manchester: a case study of Hulme. In Brian Edwards (Ed), *Sustainable Architecture. European Directives and Building Design*. Oxford: Architectural Press, pp. 96ff; David Rudlin and Nicholas Falk (1999) *Building the 21st Century Home – The Sustainable Urban Neighbourhood*. Oxford: Architectural Press, pp. 207–230.

CASE STUDY E

1 Colin Ward (1997) *Havens and Springboards – The Foyer Movement in Context*. London: Calouste Gulbenkian Foundation; Report, *Building Design* (20 February 2004): 15.

2 Building Study, *The Architects' Journal* (19 June 1997): 33–38.

CASE STUDY F

1 "CASPAR developments" from www.jrf.org.uk
2 Review, *Architecture Today 107* (April 2000): 22–31.

CASE STUDY G

1 Report, *Architecture Today 96* (March 1999): 57.

CASE STUDY H

1 Report, *Building Design* (9 February 200): 12–13; Report, *Building Design* (5 October 2001): 14–17; Report, *Building Design* (4 October 2002): 14–15.

CASE STUDY I

1 Report, *Regeneration and Renewal* (13 February 2004): 10.
2 *Architecture Today 131* (September 2002): 32–41.

CASE STUDY K

1 Supplementary Case Study 1 In PRP Architects *High density Housing in Europe: lessons for London.* London: East Thames Housing Group, 2002; Thomas Blair (1992) Bijlmemeer: designing the future of urban renewal. *The Architects' Journal* (2 December 1992): 17–19.
2 Case Study 6. In PRP Architects, op. cit.

CASE STUDY L

1 Ingemar Elander (1999) National strategies for urban renewal and housing rehabilitation: the case of Sweden. In Andersen and Leather (Eds), *Housing Renewal in Europe.* Bristol: The Policy Press.
2 Supplementary Case Study 2. In PRP Architects *High density Housing in Europe: lessons for London.* London: East Thames Housing Group, 2002; material from www.hammarbysjostad.stockholm.se

CASE STUDY M

1 Zoltán Kovács (1994) A city at the crossroads; social and economic transformation in Budapest. *Urban Studies* 31(7): 1081–1096.
2 *Budapest Ferecváros Reconstruction.* Budapest: Ferecváros Self-Governing Body, 1998; case study from NEHOM www.nhh.no/geo/NEHOM/

FURTHER READING

Full sources of information and corroboration are given in the 'References' section. The following are recommended as particularly valuable or interesting further reading for those wishing to explore the issues further.

HISTORICAL AND CULTURAL BACKGROUND

John Burnett *A Social History of Housing 1815–1985* Second edition (London, Routledge, 1986)

Colin and Rose Bell *City Fathers – the early history of Town Planning in Britain* (Penguin, 1972)

URBAN SUSTAINABILITY

Harley Sherlock *Cities are good for us* (London, Paladin, 1991)

Department of the Environment, Transport and the Regions *Towards and Urban Renaissance – Final report of the Urban Task Force chaired by Lord Rogers of Riverside* (London, HMSO/E & F Spon, 1999)

David Rudlin and Nicholas Falk *Building the 21st Century Home – the sustainable urban neighbourhood* (Oxford, Architectural Press, 1999)

'GREEN' DESIGN AND CONSTRUCTION

Brenda and Robert Vale *Green Architecture* (London, Thames & Hydson, 1991)

Maf Smith, John Whitelegg, and Nick Williams *Greening the Built Environment* (London, Earthscan Publications Ltd, 1998).

Brian Edwards and David Turrent (Eds) *Sustainable Housing – principles and practice* (London, E & FN Spon, 2000)

Edward Harland *Eco-Renovation – the ecological home improvement guide* (Vermont, Chelsea Green Publishing Company, 1999)

HOUSING FORM

Stefan Muthesius *The English Terraced House* (New Haven and London, Yale University Press, 1982)

Miles Glendinning and Stefan Muthesius *Tower Block – Modern public housing in England, Scotland, Wales and Northern Ireland* (New Haven and London, Yale University Press, 1994)

Graham Towers *Shelter is Not Enough – transforming multi-storey housing* (Bristol, The Policy Press, 2000)

URBAN DESIGN

Gordon Cullen *Townscape* (London, Architectural Press, 1961)

Llewelyn Davies *Urban Design Compendium* (London, English Partnerships/The Housing Corporation, 2000)

DTLR/CABE *Better Places to Live – by design* (London, Thomas Telford Publishing, 2001)

ARCHITECTURAL DESIGN

Peter Davey *Architecture of the arts and crafts movement – the search for Earthly Paradise* (London, Architectural Press, 1980)

Charles Jencks *Le Corbusier and the Tragic View of Architecture* (London, Penguin Books Ltd, 1975)

John Allen *Berthold Lubetkin* (London, Merrell Publishers Ltd, 2002)

Iain Colquhoun *RIBA Book of 20th Century Housing* (Oxford, Butterworth-Heinemann, 1999)

PARTICIPATION IN DESIGN

Richard Hatch (Ed) *The Scope of Social Architecture* (New York and London, Van Norstrand Reinhold, 1984)

Nick Wates and Charles Knevitt *Community Architecture* (London, Penguin, 1987)

Graham Towers *Building Democracy – community architecture in the inner cites* (London, UCL Press, 1995)

HOUSING IN EUROPE

Elizabeth Denby *Europe Rehoused* (London, George Allen & Unwin, 1938)

Anne Power *Hovels to High Rise: State housing in Europe since 1850* (London, Routledge, 1993)

Hans Skifter Andersen and Philip Leather *Housing Renewal in Europe* (Bristol, The Policy Press, 1999)

INDEX

Architectural Press

An imprint of Elsevier
www.architecturalpress.com

Visit www.architecturalpress.com

Our regularly updated website includes:

- News on our latest books
- Special offers, discounts and freebies
- Free downloadable sample chapters from our newest titles
- Links to companion websites giving you extra information on our books
- Author biographies and information
- Links to useful websites and extensive directories of relevant organisations and publications
- A search engine and a secure online ordering system for the entire catalogue of **Architectural Press** books

You can also get **free membership** of our **eNews** service by visiting our website to register. Once you are a member, you will receive a monthly email bulletin which gives you:

- Exclusive author articles
- The chance to enter prize draws for free books
- Access to offers and discounts exclusive to **eNews** members
- News of our latest books sent direct to your desktop

If you would like any other information about **www.architecturalpress.com** or our **eNews** service please contact:

Neil Boon, Marketing Manager
Email: n.boon@elsevier.com
Tel: +44 (0) 1865 314594
Fax: +44 (0)1865 314572
Address: Architectural Press, Linacre House, Jordan Hill, Oxford, OX2 8DP, UK